From Independence Towards Freedom

GENDER STUDIES

from Oxford University Press, India

The Gender Studies series presents a diverse range of books, for academic as well as general readers, foregrounding the concerns, issues and experiences of South Asian women.

Aparna Basu, *Mridula Sarabhai: Rebel with a Cause*
Prem Chowdhury, *The Veiled Women: Shifting Gender Equations in Rural Haryana, 1880–1990*
Monica Dasgupta, Lincoln C. Chen & T.N. Krishnan (eds), *Women's Health in India: Risk and Vulnerability**
Mary E. John, *Discrepant Dislocations: Feminism, Theory and Postcolonial Histories*
J. Krishnamurty (ed.), *Women in Colonial India: Essays on Survival, Work and the State**
Gail Minault, *Secluded Scholars: Women's Education and Muslim Social Reform in Colonial India*
Parita Mukta, *Upholding the Common Life: The Community of Mirabai**
Yuko Nishimura, *Gender, Kinship and Property Rights: Nagarattar Womanhood in South India*
Tulsi Patel, *Fertility Behaviour: Population and Society in a Rajasthan Village*
Gloria Godwin Raheja & Ann Grodzins Gold, *Listen to the Heron's Words: Reimagining Gender and Kinship in North India*
Vijaya Ramaswamy, *Divinity and Deviance: Women in Virasaivism*
Bharati Ray (ed.), *From the Seams of History: Essays on Indian Women**
Bharati Ray and Aparna Basu (eds.), *From Independence Towards Freedom: Essays on Indian Women Since 1947*
Aparna Rayaprol, *Negotiating Identities: Women in the Indian Diaspora*
Meenakshi Thapan (ed.), *Embodiment: Essays on Gender and Identity*
Kamala Visweswaran, *Fictions of Feminist Ethnography*

* *available as Oxford India Paperbacks*

From Independence Towards Freedom

Indian Women since 1947

edited by

BHARATI RAY

APARNA BASU

OXFORD
UNIVERSITY PRESS

OXFORD
UNIVERSITY PRESS

YMCA Library Building, Jai Singh Road, New Delhi 110001

Oxford University Press is a department of the University of Oxford. It furthers the University's objective of excellence in research, scholarship, and education by publishing worldwide in

Oxford New York
Athens Auckland Bangkok Bogota Buenos Aires Calcutta
Cape Town Chennai Dar es Salaam Delhi Florence Hong Kong Istanbul
Karachi Kuala Lumpur Madrid Melbourne Mexico City Mumbai
Nairobi Paris Sao Paolo Singapore Taipei Tokyo Toronto Warsaw

with associated companies in

Berlin Ibadan

ISBN 0 19 564575 8

Dedicated to Sukhendu and Prahlad

Printed in India at Pauls Press, New Delhi
and published by Manzar Khan, Oxford University Press
YMCA Library Building, Jai Singh Road, New Delhi 110 001

Contents

Tables

Notes on Contributors

Indu Agnihotri is Senior Fellow at the Centre for Women's Development Studies in Delhi. She teaches history at Vivekananda College, University of Delhi and is well-known as an activist in the field of women's development issues.

Aparna Basu is Vice-President, All India Women's Conference and was former Head of the History Department, Delhi University. Her books include *Women and Struggle: History of the All India Women's Conference*, jointly authored with Bharati Ray, and *Mridula Sarabhai: Rebel with a Cause* (Oxford University Press).

Ela R. Bhatt is the Founder-Mahamantri of SEWA (Self-Employed Women's Association), and she also founded the SEWA Bank and Milk Co-operative in the Gujarat area. She was a member of Parliament (Rajya Sabha), and has been a member of the governing body of the Indian Institute of Management, Ahmedabad since 1995. Amongst the many honours she has received are the prestigious Ramon Magsaysay Award for Community Leadership in 1977, the National Citizen's Award, India in 1993 and the CARE Humanitarian Award, Washington DC, 1994.

Nabaneeta Dev Sen is Professor of Comparative Literature at Jadavpur University, Calcutta. She is a well-known Bengali poetess, short story writer and novelist.

Tapati Guha-Thakurta is a Fellow in History at the Centre for

Studies in Social Sciences, Calcutta. She has a DPhil from the University of Oxford and is the author of *The Making of a New Indian Art: Artists, Aesthetics and Nationalism in Bengal* (Cambridge University Press, 1992). She is currently working on the disciplines of archaeology and art history in colonial India.

Zoya Hasan is a Professor at the Centre for Political Studies, School of Social Sciences, Jawaharlal Nehru University, New Delhi and the author of, amongst other publications, *Quest for Power: Oppositional Movements and Post-Congress Politics in Uttar Pradesh* (Oxford University Press, 1998).

Vina Mazumdar is currently Chairperson of the Indian Association of Women's Studies and the Centre for Women's Development Studies, New Delhi, of which she was the founder Director. She has received various international awards for innovative leadership in the field of women and development, and was formerly Director of Women's Studies at the Indian Council of Social Science Research.

Bidyut Mohanty is an economist, currently heading the Women's Studies cell at the Institute of Social Sciences, New Delhi. She has worked on famines and women for her doctoral dissertation at the Delhi School of Economics and her current research is on women's development in Orissa, and on women's participation in Panchayats.

Mukul Mukerjee did her PhD from Delhi School of Economics. She is now attached to the Women's Studies Research Centre at the University of Calcutta, after a long teaching career in Delhi University. She has a published a number of papers on economic history, women and development, and women and work. She is currently working on formulating a district level gender development index in West Bengal, and on women's status in North East India.

Mrinal Pande has a long and distinguished career in the media. She worked on the Status Report on Women in the unorganized sector *(Shramashakti)*, edited a monthly magazine in Hindi for women for the Times of India group and the weekly news magazine *Saptahik Hindustan* for the Hindustan Times group, and has also worked with NDTV as Senior Editorial Adviser, Hindi. She is currently working as a free-lance journalist and writer.

Bharati Ray served as Professor of History and then as Pro-

Vice Chancellor (Academic Affairs) at the University of Calcutta where she is also the Founder Director of the Women's Studies Research Centre. Her publications include *Hyderabad and British Paramountcy* and *From the Seams of History: Essays on Indian Women* (both Oxford University Press, 1988 and 1995 respectively). She is also co-author, with Aparna Basu, of *Women's Struggle: A History of the All India Women's Conference* (1991), and author of *Women and Politics: France, India and Russia* (forthcoming). She is a member of Parliament (Rajya Sabha).

Lotika Sarkar has been a teacher and activist in law throughout her professional career. She served as a Member on the Committee on the Status of Women in India (1971–74) and was a Founder Member of the Centre for Women's Development Studies in New Delhi, where she has been a Distinguished Fellow since 1996. She has written widely on law and gender justice.

Leela Visaria received her PhD in sociology from the University of Princeton, and has been a Professor at the Gujarat Institute of Development Research in Ahmedabad since 1987. She has undertaken field-based research on a wide range of issues, including health, family planning, education and demographic transition. She is co-author of *Contraceptive Use and Fertility in India* (Sage Publications, 1995) and co-editor of *Maternal Education and Child Survival: Pathways and Evidence* (Vikas Publishing House, 1997).

Introduction

The twelve essays in this volume address the relationship between the Indian nation and its women. They explore the presence and participation of women in national life in post-independence India. Judging by the sudden visibility of a number of women—mostly elite and middle class—the overall progress of women looks impressive. Several indicators of social change, such as maternal mortality and infant mortality rates, point to their general improved status. However, in comparative terms women still remain behind men in all objective and material measures of well-being: economic self-sufficiency, education, nutrition, life expectancy and mortality. Further, the daily experiences of most women still unfold against the backdrop of resiliently patriarchal social structures and cultural ideas.

Nevertheless, a massive shift has taken place in the awareness of many women and some men about what women's specific problems are and what constitutes gender justice—in that sense women are indeed making themselves visible through their demands and challenges to the prevailing order. The issues that have surfaced as of particular concern include violence against women, the economic and educational hegemony of men, the patriarchal bases of law that claim to protect women against discrimination or oppression, the almost monopolistic control of men over political power and the State, as well as the gendered premises of traditional myths and prescriptive codes of conduct. Concepts that in many ways underpin the nation—family, household, work, marriage and motherhood—have, in the last fifteen years, been questioned and redefined. The essays in this anthology examine some of these issues in the context of the lives of ordinary women in contemporary India. It is a book to be read not by specialists but by all readers interested in the unfinished story of Indian women.

No picture of women's lives in India can be complete without a consideration of both material and ideological factors. In other words the effects of cultural representations of women are no less important than the constraints of the economy. In this book, women and men are treated not as biological groups who naturally embody feminine and/or masculine traits, but rather as groups created culturally and bounded socially. In other words, we treat masculinity and femininity as socially constituted and argue that it is the cultural construction of a woman's biology that matters, not the fact of biology itself. It is this cultural construction that limits for her the socially permissible range of experiences and also conditions the nature of her response to experiences. The oppression that results from unequal gender practices is inscribed on both the minds and bodies of women. Yet, this book does not treat the categories of men and women as two unmediated opposites either. Ideologies of masculinity and femininity are always created in interaction with ideologies of caste, class, nation and religion. Gender, then, is a complex phenomenon, not amenable to simple analysis. It is socially defined in a variety of ways through cultural practices, symbolic representations, legal frameworks and prescriptive work divisions. Gender oppression occurs in a plurality of sites—the home, work place and educational institutions—and yet gender relations never work alone, but are interwoven with the other prevailing hierarchies of Indian society.

The understanding that relationships of gender are multi-dimensional and complex has led us to present the contributions in this volume without any editorial interference. In contrast to the tendency to universalize patriarchy or women's experience, we seek to posit their differential operation among different social groups and in different areas. It has obviously not been possible to examine all important issues in this rather brief collection. For instance, arguably two of the most burning problems for women today, namely, the violence of communalism-casteism and violence against women in various forms, have not really been touched upon here. A number of seminars have recently taken place on women and violence, and women activists have done some extremely important work in this area—indeed they have been instrumental in the passage of new rape laws in India. A recent volume, *Women and the Hindu Right*, edited by Tanika Sarkar and Urvashi Butalia, is an excellent source on the threat communalism poses for women. Since poverty, a critical issue for both men and women in India, most severely affects women-headed households and single parent households, it has been addressed in several of the essays rather than in isolation. We have tried to present some of our gains, some of our constraints and limitations and something of our struggle to give a better life to women in post-independence India—our journey towards real and substantive *freedom*.

Political independence from colonial rule was accompanied by the trauma of Partition. The bloodshed, violence and displacement of people that it generated constitutes the most shameful and tragic chapter in the history of both the newly constituted and fragmented countries—India and Pakistan. As in other territorial partitions, women were especially victimized in the process—apart from being homeless and deported, many were widowed or lost their children, while others were raped and abducted, and some later 'recovered'. The written history of Partition has been mostly based on data from official documents that concentrate on the differences between political parties, the Congress and the Muslim League, and on the British policy of 'divide and rule'. The physical and psychological scars left by the Partition on women remain almost totally ignored. Many of the victims were illiterate, and for those who could write the memories were much too harrowing to recall or record. Creative writers such as Kartar Singh Duggal, Sadat Hasan Manto, Krishna Sobti and Rajinder Singh Bedi provide us with some clues, and recently some researchers, such as Urvashi Butalia and Gyanendra Pandey, are exploring the issue. Bharati Ray's article is based on the story *Sei Chheleta* (That Boy) written by Jyotirmoyee Devi (1894–1989) against the backdrop of Partition. The story reflects the painful emotions of two women, a mother and a daughter, separated during the catastrophe and meeting once again under totally different circumstances. It raises certain questions, especially relating to the gendered construction of womanhood and the dicta of our traditional prescriptions, the exploration of which gives us an insight into the ways in which gender is implicated in the creation of the Indian State and the price women have to pay because they are regarded as the upholders of the family (and also the State) honour. If they are invested with such responsibility, what rights and powers do they command within the family and the State? Do they have decision-making authority at the household level and, more importantly, political power at the national level?

Some political power has been granted to women by the 73rd Constitutional Amendment reserving 33% of the total seats for women at all the three tiers of panchayati (local government) administration. The aim was to facilitate women's participation in active politics and women's political empowerment at the local level. Bidyut Mohanty queries whether this participation will actually empower them. In her view, it may be too early to evaluate the impact, but the presence of one million women in the political arena, some of whom are political activists, will undoubtedly usher in a new era in Indian polity and society. However, in order to ensure this, certain social and economic measures have to be adopted and full-fledged training for women elected in the local bodies is absolutely essential. It needs to be mentioned in this connection that a Bill is pending before Parliament for reserving 33% seats for women both in Parliament and in the state legislatures. If passed, this will be a momentous step towards empowerment of Indian women.

Economic self-sufficiency is as important for women as political power. The Self Employed Women's Association (SEWA), initiated in Gujarat, works towards economic empowerment of women, that is towards 'second freedom' as distinguished from mere political independence from the British. Ela Bhatt, the founder of SEWA, says in her article, 'SEWA's story is the story of poor women heading towards the Second Freedom.' Bhatt traces the inception and growth of this unique movement, the many challenges it faced and the emergence of some success at the end of a long and still continuing battle. Was there a blueprint for SEWA to read or copy, or any defined methodology for building a trade union of poor self-employed women workers—the migrant female cart pullers or vendors or head-load carriers? As late as 1971, even according to one labour association, a *bidi* maker—and a female one at that—was not a 'worker', since she was working in her home. Labourers in the informal sector were outside the labour movement. And yet in this country the formal sector accounts for only 5% of our work force and 60% of the huge informal work force is women. SEWA struggled for their rights since 1971, and in 1996 the ILO convention gave international official recognition to home-based workers as 'workers'. With the help of innovative strategies such as the publication of *Shramashakti*, the building of SEWA Bank and the organization of a landless agricultural women's co-operative, SEWA today has become a trade union with a membership of 2,18,799 spread over seven states. Its struggle continues for better life situations—health care, housing, employment, fair wages, protection against unscrupulous moneylenders, higher status in the family—for female workers still toiling in the informal sector.

Mukul Mukherjee's research on India's five-decade journey towards economic emancipation of women confirms Ela Bhatt's activist experiences. Through an analysis of statistical data, Mukherjee shows how women's work is undervalued in economic terms and how a much smaller proportion of women vis-à-vis men participate in gainful employment. A very large proportion of women are occupied as unpaid family helpers in agriculture or household production rather than as 'workers' with a tangible income commensurate with their labour. This 'hidden legion' of women, performing a host of resource-generating activities, stand as a buffer against economic deprivation, particularly in low-income households. Another disturbing fact, Mukherjee points out, is that in the last five decades there has been a continuous displacement of women from older industries uncompensated by their entry into modern industries and services. As a result, there has been growing deployment of women as wage labour and casual labour rather than as self-employed cultivator. Looking at women's livelihood outside agriculture one finds that even though women account for 15% of the total employees in the organized sector, they represent only 4%

of total women workers, indicating the functioning of vast multitudes of women within the shadowy ambit of the informal sector. A silver lining in this dismal situation is the emerging State intervention in favour of women offering them more economic opportunities and scope for development of skill. It is, however, necessary to generate public awareness, if the continuing cultural prejudices against women and the disadvantaged work situation for women are to be radically changed.

Another crucial issue demanding public awareness and public action is the adverse sex ratio of women vis-à-vis men. The census of 1991 shows roughly 32 million less women than men in India, whereas in most countries of the world women outnumber men by as much as 3 to 5%. Reminding us of Amartya Sen's reference to the missing millions of women in this country, Leela Visaria analyses the magnitude and implications of the deficit of women, the regional variations and the implicit threats for women in such a situation. She indicates how the 'masculinity ratio' has increased at a faster rate than that of the population and observes that the major factor explaining the deficit of women is their excess mortality. This notwithstanding the fact that life expectancy at birth has increased at a faster rate for females than for males, implying that women have gained somewhat from health care facilities. But then, what is being done about the human intervention which is altering the sex ratio at birth itself, thanks to amniocentesis? And why is the masculinity ratio higher in the 7+ age population than in the all-ages ratio at the all-India level? A variety of complex factors operate for the neglect of the girl child and devaluation of women right from birth, through education and employment, if any, up to the last days of existence. In the next century, government and non-government organizations must work hand in hand to solve this deep-rooted problem with a view to improving women's life situations.

What remedies or protection does the legal structure offer to women against injustice and bias? In the pre-independence era, when women fought along with men to put an end to colonial rule, women's organizations backed by liberal men had lobbied for the codification of Hindu laws in order to prohibit bigamy, give the wife and daughters property rights, and allow women the right to divorce and to maintenance. After a prolonged struggle, the Hindu Code Bill was enacted piecemeal in 1955–6. Lotika Sarkar pinpoints the lacunae in these Acts and the biased attitudes of the law-making and law-interpreting bodies. To what extent have the restricted provisions in the Acts and the viewpoint of the judiciary hindered the attainment of full justice for women, and conversely, how far have the legal reforms helped to bring social justice to women?

Zoya Hasan's paper explores the official discourse of the State on reforms of personal laws in order to unravel the relationship between State and religious communities. Focusing on State policy towards Muslim personal law, she argues that the popular perception of Muslim personal law as rigid and inflexible is not correct. Until the introduction of the Shariat Act in 1937, legal and social codes observed by Muslims varied in different parts of the country. No attempt has been made after independence to reform Muslim personal law, and successive governments in India have been hesitant to interfere for fear of hurting the religious sensibilities of Muslims. Hasan argues that the reform of Muslim law should be based on a reconceptualization of democratic citizenship that provides space for both national and minority identity and ensures women's equality and rights.

For any reform movement to be successful the willing co-operation of the people is an all-important requirement. Education is an awareness-builder. What is the educational scenario of Indian women, be they Hindu or Muslim? Aparna Basu examines the historical and contemporary reasons for the fact that in the human development index India ranks 138th among 175 countries and that 40% of Indian women are still illiterate. She traces government policy since 1947, as enunciated in various Education Commission Reports and Five Year Plans as well as the National Policy on Education (1986) and the Plan of Action (1992), until the present. Why has India failed to achieve the objective of education for all? Why is girls' drop-out rate so high even while enrolment at the primary level has gone up? The plain truth is that at every stage girls lag behind boys, the gap increasing as they go up the educational ladder.

Interestingly, some of the educated women are entering the media as a profession. Mrinal Pande, one of the distinguished figures in the media, describes in an introspective essay the impact of women's entry upon the world of electronic media. She writes of the new women who have emerged as producers and anchors and of their successes and failures in producing films and programmes.

Tapati Guha-Thakurta notes women's 'triumphant arrival on the Indian art scene'. In 1987, and in 1997, the National Gallery of Modern Art in New Delhi staged exhibitions of contemporary women artists of India. The world of art today is dominated by Baroda, Bombay and Delhi; consequently the creative enterprises in other areas do not always receive the attention they deserve. However, the point to note is that the constraints which impede women's development or progress in other professions exist in the domain of art as well. The author, while discussing women artists, raises the question of the ways in which the biological or gendered self resides within the artistic self.

Poet and writer Nabaneeta Dev Sen dwells not on the literature produced by women and the representation of women in women's writings, a task impressively performed by Susie Tharu and K. Lalita when they edited *Women's Writing in India*, but on Sita, still regarded as the ideal embodiment of traditional virtues. In a deeply analytical interpretation of Sita in the Indian psyche, Dev Sen investigates the songs that village women in Bengal, Maharashtra and Andhra Pradesh sing. Through these songs Sita offers a voice to the silenced women of the subcontinent. She is just any other hard-working woman, ill-treated by her in-laws, neglected by her husband and punished harshly for no fault of hers. In a country where the maternal mortality rate is still high and 88% of the pregnant women have anaemia, while 67% of women give birth without the help of any doctor or nurse, it is not surprising that rural women sing about the pain and fear of Sita's lonely childbirth in the forest. While singing of Sita, they sing of their own lives, in which justice and equality are but dreams and suffering under a patriarchal order an everyday reality.

How to change the situation for these millions of women? Vina Mazumdar and Indu Agnihotri urge women's involvement in the process of amendment. In sketching a history of the women's movement in India, they show how though women had fought along with men in the war of independence, in the two decades after independence, their specific problems and issues faded from the public arena. The 1970s saw a resurgence of the women's movement with the worsening of their situation, highlighted by the publication of the Report on the Status of Women in 1974–5. The essay highlights the current phase of the movement—its new issues, and shifts in priorities and strategies. India has a rich and articulate women's movement, but it is not homogeneous or monolithic; it is multi-level and multi-class and comprises a large number of organizations, national and local, with divergent objectives and ideologies. The critical task for our journey towards real freedom, the authors maintain, is to create new opportunities and fora that provide space for interaction between people—both men and women—from different backgrounds to promote and fight for equitable gender relations.

New Delhi
15 August 1998

Bharati Ray
Aparna Basu

1

Bharati Ray

Women and Partition
Some Questions

I

It was the early 1950s. Three young women were waiting at a bus stop near Queen's Park in New Delhi, merrily munching peanuts. All freshers in a college, these three friends had gone there to submit applications for a modest teacher's job in a teaching centre. A beggar woman with a small boy clinging to her knees approached them and asked for money. Two of the young women, Sujata and Baruna, opened their hand-bags to dole out some small coins, while the third, Raj, asked the boy, 'Would you like some peanuts?' The beggar woman looked at her and asked, 'Bibi, where is your home?' 'Karol Bagh,' Raj replied tersely. 'No, Bibi, I am asking where is your native home? Where from have you come to Delhi?' 'Lahore, Anarkali Bagh. Why?' asked Raj. Sujata and Baruna laughed and joked, 'Raj, she wants to go there to get some money, and a nice *chunni* from you.' The beggar woman said softly, 'Your name is Raj! Lahore Anarkali Bagh was your home!' She stepped back and mumbled, 'Ah, my Raj,' and disappeared behind a nearby bush. The bus had arrived. 'Where are you, woman? Come, take some money,' shouted Sujata. The woman did not come; apparently she had melted away. And the three friends boarded the bus. Sujata asked, 'Does she know you, Raj? We heard her calling you by your name.' Raj quietly answered, 'No. You called my name. That is how she knew.'

Research for this article was funded by the Ford Foundation, India.

Raj reached home and started doing her daily chores. They were a large joint family, and had arrived in Delhi as refugees from Lahore, and were trying to make both ends meet. 'Who was the beggar woman?' Raj asked herself, 'Who called me "my Raj"?' Yes she knew her. She had recognized her as soon as the woman had uttered her name. Her mother! Raj clearly recalled the terrible night when they were evacuating Lahore in trucks—hundreds of them—afraid for their lives. Her mother, so youthful and beautiful, healthy and happy, had gone upstairs to fetch her box of jewellery. The truck had left without her, and since then there was no news of her. The family assumed that she was dead. That was what they told everybody. But she was alive! Why did she not try to find them? Or contact her natal family, a distinguished family of Ludhiana? How many days of begging had reduced her beautiful mother into such a typical beggar? And if she was her mother, what did she have to do with that little boy? Who was he? Raj could not think any more, nor could she share her secret with anyone. She started going back to the spot near Queen's Park every day, but there was no trace of the woman or the boy. Each night the face of the beggar woman with the beggar boy appeared before her: the woman who was her mother, with the little boy, who was not her brother.

This is, in a nutshell, the story of *Chheleta* (That Boy), written by Jyotirmoyee Devi (1894–1989), set against the backdrop of the Partition of Punjab in 1947. The locale might easily have been Calcutta instead of Delhi and one could read Partition of Bengal, or for that matter, Partition of India instead of Partition of Punjab. There are a number of creative writings on the Partition of India, a human tragedy of almost unimaginable proportions. I have chosen this particular story—first, because Jyotirmoyee Devi was, in my view, a feminist writer possessing an empathy and sensitivity towards women rare for an author of her times, and second, because the story reflects the painful emotions of two women, a mother and a daughter, who constitute one of the most intimate of human relationships. This story also gives us a window into the world of pain and suffering that women experience during times of war, external or civil, because of their gender. The story under discussion raises two important questions:

1. Why did the mother not acknowledge her daughter?
2. Why did the daughter not recognize the mother publicly and why did she refuse to accept the brother even privately, when she was just alone with herself?

The exploration of these questions gives us an insight into the ways in which gender is implicated in the creation of the Indian State and into the price women have had to pay precisely because they are the upholders of the spiritual private life of 'traditional' India.

I answer these questions by situating the story in its historical context, that is the Indian Partition in 1947.

II

For those of us who, whether as children or adults, lived during that period, the word *Partition* brings to our mind the streams of refugees entering India, the squatting colonies and pavement shanties, the inflation, the rationing and black-marketing, the nightmare that was Sealdah Station, the political agitation and the extreme agony of the refugees. However, the most distressing aspect of Partition was the communal holocaust that accompanied and followed it. The history of this violence has scarcely begun to be addressed. Partition riots have left indelible marks on the body and soul of an entire generation, but very few victims have kept written records or diaries, perhaps because personal experiences were too harrowing to document. The exact scale and intensity of the actual tragedy—of plunder and rape, murder and abduction, migration and dislocation—will probably never be known. Here was the compulsive destruction of Hindus, Sikhs and Muslims by one another, the violence of the people as distinguished from the violence of the State, and the 'convergence of elite and popular communalism'. This grim episode in India's history made a mockery of the principle of non-violence and the too-loudly proclaimed (even today) strain of unity in diversity of Indian culture. Too many in the Punjabi as well as the Bengali communities, Hindu, Muslim or Sikh, became temporarily bereft of all decency, morality and sense of human values. Apart from a handful of serious studies on this 'epic tragedy', we only have a mass of literature on separatist politics, on the negotiations between the Congress, the Muslim League and the colonial power, or on the policy, activity and contribution of leaders.

While historians and political scientists have, until recently, focussed little on the impact of the Partition on private and family life, a number of creative writings—like the story by Jyotirmoyee Devi that is under discussion—have ably and sensitively reflected the inner anguish and traumatic experiences of a generation caught in the crossfire of religious sectarianism. Mushirul Hasan, in creating a space for these voices, quotes from Mehr Nigar Masroor's *Shadow of Time* (Lahore, 1995):

> ...today having seen the lacerated bodies of Muslims, Sikhs and Hindus, I feel that this city (Delhi) has become a vestibule of hate. History, it appears, is an invitation to revenge. Religion, it seems, is a licence to kill.

The trail of migration that followed or accompanied the violence had begun even before 1947 and continued, especially in Bengal, for four decades. Particularly during 1946–50, nearly 80 lakh people crossed the newly created boundaries of Bengal and Punjab. According to the 1951 Census, 26.9% of Calcutta's population came from the former East Bengal. In Punjab, within a week of independence, about 11 lakh Hindus and Sikhs had crossed over from west to east, and in the week following, another 25 lakh had collected in the refugee camps in East Punjab. The ordeal was by no means one-sided. On the other side of the border, in the then East Bengal and in West Punjab, people were suffering similar experiences of migration, desolation and uprooting from homes, families, friends and environment and the trauma of communal holocaust.

Of course, all classes and castes on both sides of the border were victims of murder and forcible evacuation, but women were the worst affected. Through rape and abduction, women became central to the whole act of violence. Official statistics—and nowhere are statistics probably less accurate than here—have tried to chart the number of cases of rape and abduction during and following the Partition of 1947. There is something deeply troubling about the way in which the emotions and responses of women affected by those traumatic experiences have been ignored in official records. Official documents fail to clarify, not to mention analyse, the plight of total desolation and helplessness, of the pain and suffering, of the loss of self-respect and humiliation of these women.

How was rape or abduction or its haunting memory constituted in women's minds? How did they see themselves and their lives after going through the horrifying experience? To what extent could they cope with the bewildering loss of home, property, relationships and their own identities? Once the raped or abducted women crossed the border with or without State help, what sort of reception did they receive from their families? How did the State and their communities view them? Did their communities change their codes of honour to accommodate the 'lost' women within their fold? Did the State make any attempt to reconstitute understandings of 'the legitimate family' or 'community honour'? Apart from a handful of scholars such as Urvashi Butalia, Ritu Menon, Veena Das and Gyan Pandey, researchers have not yet begun to address these issues. This paper, too, does not claim to *answer* any of these as yet unexplored questions. It only attempts to read these events through one story, written by a woman in 1960. Our focus is only on one raped woman with her 'illegitimate' son and only on the moment of wilful non-recognition of each other by a mother and her daughter.

The fear of rape or abduction or falling into the enemies' hands had driven hundreds of women to take their own lives—to jump into wells, take or carry poison in case it was needed, beg their male kinsmen to help them die rather than face dishonour, or commit suicide after suffering rape or abduction. *Our protagonist chose to live, and hence gave rise to the two questions we are going to examine.* Interestingly, Jyotirmoyee Devi did not give her a name. In the story she refers to her as Raj's mother, perhaps because in most Indian families a married woman's identity was tied up with her husband or her children. We are thus compelled to refer to her as Raj's mother during our discussion of the two questions.

III

We take the first question first. Why did Raj's mother not reveal her identity to her daughter? We must pause here a little and recall that the earliest Hindu religious texts in India had prescribed strict rules governing women's behaviour patterns and her physical purity. Concern for paternity and caste purity had led to a tightening of control over women's sexuality. And the concept of *pativratya* (physical and mental chastity) had been gradually evolved and made into the principal ideology for women. In fact, virginity before marriage and *pativratya* after marriage were not obligations for just the woman, they were obligations for the men of her family as well. On the chastity of the women depended the honour of the menfolk. In other words, women's bodies were the repositories of men's honour. Men had obligations to one another to hand over their women chaste while giving them away through marriage. It was as if a sort of contract existed between men to keep the women 'pure'. That was why a woman had to be guarded consecutively by her father, husband and son throughout her life.

With time, the introduction of *purdah* ensured women's withdrawal even from the male gaze. The public/private dichotomy restricted women's movements within the home, while the model of the *pativratya* was extolled as the ultimate paradigm of good womanhood. Ran the Bengali proverb, '*Urle meye purle chhai, tabe meyer gun gai*' (only when a woman is dead, we can sing her praise). That is to say that as long as a woman is alive, she is a suspect and has the possibility of going astray or being disloyal to her husband. One can say good things about her with some certainty when all fears and suspicions are put to rest by her death.

When the nineteenth century social reform movement prioritized the 'woman question' in its agenda, it abolished the rite of *sati* (the practice of immolation on the husband's pyre), legalized widow marriage, and introduced women's education, but did not interfere in the least with the concepts of pre-nuptial virginity and post-nuptial *pativratya*. Nor did it interfere with the traditional ideology of gender or patriarchal relationships. In the new construction of womanhood, it was the conventional image of women as wife and mother, simply garnished by education and some Victorian womanly ideals borrowed from the West, that was projected as 'ideal' for the 'good' Indian woman. Even *Bamabodhini Patrika*, the journal for women's enlightenment, published in Bengal by the 'enlightened' and educated Brahmos, propagated such a model. The emphasis on traditional ideology by a 'progressive' journal is striking but typical. Consider this, from *Bamabodhini Patrika* in 1311 B.S. or 1904 A.D.

> The wife, who like Goddess Lakshmi worships her husband as if he is God Hari, will go to heaven after her death and will

> taste every happiness along with her husband just as God and Goddess, Hari and Lakshmi, enjoy eternal happiness.

It has to be clearly understood that during the debate over the 'woman question', the *bhadralok* reconceptualized the home and the woman under the twin pressure of colonization and emerging nationalist sentiments. There was a confrontation between the culture of the colonial rulers and that of the colonized, in which the condition of Indian women was the principal target of colonial attack, indicating ideological hegemony along with political ascendancy over the colonized people. Precisely because this necessitated an 'improvement' of women's condition and a programme of social reform, there developed an assertion of Indian national identity, leading to the glorification of an ancient past when women held a high position in society along with an emphasis on women's *traditional* qualities. Hard work, discipline, routine, orderliness, punctuality and education were some of the qualities that were believed to have been the key to European prosperity and political power. On the one hand, books on domestic science exhorted Indian women to emulate these qualities that Western women had. On the other hand, the 'quintessential nationalist claim of being different but modern' ensured that Indian tradition was not forgotten. In their resolution of the 'woman question', as Partha Chatterjee has shown, the nationalist males projected the home as a spiritualized inner space where women preserved the age-old Indian *dharma*. The material world might have been lost to the colonial rulers, but the home remained the site of nationalist victory. That is why the idea of the modern, educated housewife was always tied to the older patriarchal imagination of the mythical divine figure of Lakshmi. Lakshmi was a model Hindu wife united in complete harmony with her husband in a spirit that combined submission with loyalty. A truly good wife, it was said, would be so auspicious as to mark the eternal return of the cosmic principle embodied in the Goddess Lakshmi, the Goddess of domestic well-being, by whose grace the family, the extended family and the whole clan would live and prosper. As Dipesh Chakravarty so aptly describes: Lakhsmi had an antithesis—Alakshmi. Lakshmi symbolised *dharma* (right conduct), Alakshmi *adharma*. Lakshmi was an ideal housewife, Alakshmi either a *bibi* (Westernized woman) or a *veshya* (prostitute). Lakshmi ushered in peace, happiness, prosperity and honour for the family, Alakshmi brought decline, humiliation and dishonour in her trail.

Seen in this light, Raj's mother was Alakshmi. It is possible that, socialized by Hindu beliefs like other women of her class and community, she herself might have believed that she had sinned and had failed in her moral responsibility of upholding the honour of the family. Perhaps she, too, asked herself as a woman in A. J. Major's paper 'The Chief Sufferers' asked herself, 'What is left in me now, religion or chastity?' Bereft of both, she was ashamed to greet her daughter with the fruit of her 'shame', to admit to her that she had betrayed the family and borne another man's son. She, therefore, deliberately gave up her only chance—however slender—of reunion with her family and rehabilitation in a middle class home. Continuing the life of a beggar woman seemed to her to be the only option.

The alteration in her appearance and apparel made it doubly difficult for her to disclose her identity to her daughter. The violence she had experienced and the poverty she was living in had destroyed her former radiant personality. It was only natural for Raj to think, as she did think for a while and argued with herself sitting at home:

> Perhaps she was not her mother.... So thin and dark, not pretty at all.... In that old house in Lahore, mother used to serve food and milk and pickles to everybody in the family. And while doing so, she used to laugh and talk, and she often used to wear a lovely white salwar and a colourful *kurta*, with a light blue *chunni*.

All that was changed now, and she was begging for a second-hand *chunni*. Beyond the separation of time and space, there had been created a chasm of unequal circumstances. What was there to say? And how to say it? She had endured ordeals that were totally outside the normal experiences of a married woman. Exceptional trauma or a holocaust, it has been argued by scholars like Lyotard and Elaine Scarry, reduces the victims to silence. Perhaps for Raj's mother, the memory of the violence and pain destroyed her capacity to communicate.

In any case, the mother had no place in her husband's family. Her husband and her in-laws had declared her dead. How were they to explain to society her sudden return? That would mean an admission that a woman married into the family had been molested by Muslims, had diluted the purity of the family and was nevertheless alive! And the little boy was a living and breathing evidence of that violation.

Raj's mother did not try to go back to her natal family either, although she knew the residential address at Ludhiana. She was apprehensive of rejection. Her natal family would have considered that she had brought humiliation to them, and indeed to the *kul* (clan), by being raped and not having had the courage to take her own life. The family might well have asked her to leave rather than have admitted a sullied woman back into its fold. Had she abandoned that boy, if none came to know about his existence, there might have been *some* chance of her finding a shelter at the natal home, although there, too, she would not have been able to live with honour. With the son whom she obviously had no intention of relinquishing, she would be summarily rejected.

'That boy', as Jyotirmoyee Devi called Raj's mother's son, was the crux of the problem, or, more strictly speaking, complicated the problem. An illegitimate child born of a Hindu mother and a Muslim father could at best be accommodated in a camp or in an orphanage, unless, of course, disposed of in a more convenient way, which was possible in the case of a foetus. Be that as it may, illegitimate children born of Muslim fathers had to be disowned as 'impure' and ineligible for membership of the family and community.

That Raj's mother's fear was not ill-founded, or a figment of the author's own imagination, becomes clear when we look at the real-life fate of Hindu women who had been abducted during the Partition riots and were 'recovered' in independent India. In an insightful essay, Ritu Menon and Kamla Bhasin have shown how the Government of India tried to 'recover' *its* women, often against the wishes of the victims, and 'rehabilitate' them, most often in camps, since the families were unwilling to accept women 'defiled' by the Muslims. Menon and Bhasin quote the public appeals, one made by no less a person than Mahatma Gandhi and the other made by Jawaharlal Nehru, the then Prime Minister of India. Gandhi said:

> I hear...that the Hindus are not willing to accept the recovered women because they say that they have become impure. I feel that this is a matter of great shame. That woman is as pure as the girls who are sitting by my side. And if anyone of those 'recovered' women should come to me, then I will give them as much respect and honour as I accord to these young maidens.

Gandhi's call, charged with emotion, made little impact on Hindu society. The belief system was too deeply ingrained and time-honoured to be discarded because of the exhortations of one man, even though he might be the father of the modern Indian nation. Nehru's speech, too, fell flat. In January 1948, he made a particularly strong public appeal.

> I am told that there is unwillingness on the part of their relatives to accept those girls and women [who had been abducted] back in their homes. This is a most objectionable and wrong attitude to take, and any social custom that supports this attitude must be condemned. These girls and women require our tender and loving care and their relatives should be proud to take them back.

Needless to say, Nehru misjudged the Hindu sentiment. Nothing in their socialization in Hindu culture could have made the relatives of the abducted women proud. The repeated appeals of Gandhi and Nehru merely indicate that the number of families refusing to give up their beliefs was significantly large. Here, as Urvashi Butalia succinctly comments, 'For the community, it was women's sexual purity that became important. For the state... their religious identity was paramount.' The State was trying to establish its own legitimacy and authority; on the communities their ideological inheritance had a powerful bearing. Even the handful of families 'broadminded' enough to take back these women, in the vast majority of cases, merely allowed them to live in the household, but did not rehabilitate them in the *home* in the manner in which they had earlier been a part. It was an act of kindness, generosity and sacrifice on the part of those who accepted the 'recovered' women.

Let me elaborate a little further on this discussion by referring to another text also written by Jyotirmoyee Devi, a book entitled *The River Churning*. Here a young girl, having spent a few days with a Muslim family in East Bengal, manages to cross the border and come over to West Bengal. Her relatives accommodate her and let her grow up in the household, but never really accept her. She can never be a part of the family and is destined to remain in the periphery. And yet she has not come back burdened with a child.

One point of omission in Jyotirmoyee Devi's story must not be ignored. The boy's father is never mentioned. One does not know whether he had offered protection to Raj's mother—as indeed many a Muslim men had done to Hindu women either through marriage or by providing a position in the household. It is reasonable to assume for lack of contrary evidence that he had not done so, and that Raj's mother had no alternative but to leave what was now a foreign land after the Partition and seek shelter in the land of her birth. But then, why did she not get rid of the boy, who could only create complications for her? Desertion of unwanted babies was a common enough occurrence in India. Was it only natural maternal affection that prompted her to protect the baby boy? Or, was it a pragmatic consideration that made her cling to the son as the sole source of security in an uncertain and unenviable future?

IV

We now turn to Raj.

Let us first highlight the nature of the opposition between her two sentiments: compassion for her mother and hatred for the little boy. Raj had recognized her mother but did not acknowledge her before her friends. How could she? The social construction of motherhood in India had idolized it. A mother was a symbol of self-sacrifice and love and she was supposed to live her life for the children. The mother's image projected before Indian children has been articulated in a typically sentimental Bengali poem, '*Sneha bihval karuna chhalchhal shiore jage kar ankhi re, mitechhe sab kshuda, sanjiban sudha enechhe anasan lagi re*' (My mother's eyes laden with love and compassion are awake by my bedside. I feel fully fulfilled and happy, as if nectar has been offered to me to satisfy my hunger). Not that motherhood had not been idolized in the West. One recalls Oscar Wilde's reputed play *Lady Windermere's Fan*:

Mrs. Erlynee	:	You are devoted to your mother's memory.
Lady Windermere	:	We all have ideals in life.... Mine is my mother.
Mrs. Erlynne	:	Ideals are dangerous things. Realities are better. They wound, but they're better.
Lady Windermere	:	If I lost my ideals, I should lose everything.

Mothers almost all over the world under patriarchy have been put up on a high pedestal. It has been an almost binding compulsion for the mother as well as the children to abide by the mother-image. But in few places has motherhood been deified to the extent it has been in India. Since the dawn of our civilization, Sanskrit hymns have been sung in praise of motherhood. '*Janani janmabhumischa swargadapi gariosi*' (The mother and the motherland stand higher than the heaven). A Hindu mother is, according to tradition, like a goddess, endowed with goddess-like qualities. Whatever the actual traits of a mother, whatever the real relationship between the mother and her children, the normative codes are clear and emphatic.

Raj, too, was brought up like ordinary middle class Indian children. She, too, had cherished in her mind the traditional image of a mother, heightened now with the belief that she was dead. Could the beggar woman with a beggar boy, her illegitimate son, be her idol? How could she reconcile herself to this reality, or reveal the truth, so cruelly humiliating, before her friends?

Indeed, the Partition of India had transformed the socio-economic situation in India as a whole, and in Bengal and Punjab in particular. However, the social and familial ideologies continued to survive the shock. Karuna Chanana, on the basis of a survey of Punjabi refugee women in New Delhi, argues that despite many changes, and despite the expanded social space and opportunities for education and employment for women, the ideological underpinnings of feminine roles were barely touched. 'The family ideology ensures that radical departures and shifts do not take place in the perceptions and actions of women.' And families tend to remember women who took their own lives to save the family honour and forget those who decided to live despite 'dishonour' or who left their families. To put it bluntly, in their view, the latter group had no right to live. Raj, in our story, was shocked to realize that her mother was alive. She asked herself, 'Could she not then escape from her enemies? Could she also not die?' These were her first thoughts. Later, she felt pity and sympathy for her mother, even remorse that she had not acknowledged her and talked to her. Nevertheless, she knew that a family reunion was out of the question. That is why she did not mention the encounter to anyone in the family.

> What could she say about the little boy? Whose son was he? Mother's? Could mother have come back to us? Then, why did she hide herself so?

The chief fault, in Raj's perception, was the boy's. Had the boy been a legitimate stepson of her father, he might have been accommodated in the family. To accept as a brother a mother's illegitimate son, conceived through *lutera* (rapist), born of a wrong father, was just not possible. It defied every sensibility, every tradition held so dear, since it defiled the image of the mother—that is to say, motherhood.

Let us for a brief moment indulge in a fanciful digression. What would have happened if Raj had met her father, in similar circumstances, a victim of Partition, reduced to penury, holding the hand of a boy who was not Raj's mother's son? It does not require much imagination to be able to assert that there would have been a tearful embrace between the long-lost father and his daughter, followed by a joyous reunion with other members of the family, and an acceptance by the family of the illegitimate boy, even if with a frown and some amount of restraint. Double standards of morality for men and women were decreed by Hindu prescriptive texts in India and perpetuated by custom. For instance, a widow was not culturally allowed to marry (in middle class families), while a widower was encouraged, even often persuaded, to marry. A wife had to be physically and mentally chaste to her *one* husband, but polygamy was permitted for men. In short, what befell Raj's mother could not have occurred in the case of her father. The honour of the men of the clan is not constructed on their bodies.

There is another significant angle in the Raj–mother encounter: that of class. In a woman's life (and for that matter in a man's life as well) caste, class and gender are inseparably connected. Raj was the daughter of an once rich family in Punjab that had lost their fortune during Partition riots. They had struggled and were still struggling to go up the ladder once again. In any case, they had reached the middle class level. Raj was looking for a teaching job, and indeed she managed to get one. But her mother had been reduced to penury. Her whole presence was that of a poor woman, saddled with a child, and poverty depriving her of self-respect as well as of any form of grace. The social contrast between Raj and her mother at that point of time was too sharp and the gap unbridgeable. All the middle class instincts of Raj must have been, even if sub-consciously, repelled at the thought of an umbilical link with a woman from the lowest social rung, dressed in filthy and tattered clothes. To acknowledge the beggar woman would be demeaning for Raj in front of her social equals who belonged to the middle class.

V

Jyotirmoyee Devi's story is but one example to drive home the point that in times of external war or civil war, it is women who are inevitably singled out for particularly humiliating treatment—molestation, rape, abduction or forcible marriage—and it is they who have to suffer for the imposed ignominy. Women's bodies are considered by Indian men, Hindu, Muslim or Sikh, as the repository of men's honour. 'Power rape', the raping of women to demonstrate and defeat rival men in patriarchal societies, is quite common in many parts of India, as indeed in many other areas of the world. The rape of a woman is akin to the rape of the community to which she belongs.

Veena Das, in an excellent article, argues that the sexual violence to which women are subjected in times of war or any form of aggression cannot be understood as belonging only to the discourse of family. It has to be comprehended in terms of a double belief system in the domains of kinship and politics. A woman falls into the position of becoming a debtor whenever the normal order of society or family is disturbed, and whenever politics and hostilities are set in motion.

> There is a relation between the normal position of women as signs in the matrimonial dialogue of men—to use the evocative phrase of Levi Strauss—and their becoming signs through which men create memories for each other by heaping indignities and tortures upon them.

Since the Hindus and the Muslims at that point of time perceived one another as harmful enemies, they sought to take revenge by inflicting insults on the womenfolk so that memories of the injury would persist. To plunder women's bodies, perceived as men's property, was to indicate that the enemy had occupied the most intimate possessions of the men to whom the women belonged. On women's bodies, thus, the 'political programmes' of the mutual enemies were 'inscribed'.

VI

It is usual to draw together the different threads of a discussion in a concluding paragraph. However, reading and re-reading Jyotirmoyee Devi's story today, in this fiftieth year of Indian independence, gives rise to certain fresh and compelling kind of questioning. For instance, has the situation changed for women in the half century of glorious freedom? If at all, to what extent? If not, why not? One may also ask, who was really responsible for the 'partitioned' women's sufferings? In more general terms, the question is, apart from a couple of high profile women, such as Mridula Sarabhai and Rameswari Nehru, were ordinary women, or their representatives, consulted regarding Partition? How many women representatives were there in the Assembly? To what extent were women's organizations taken into confidence? Were women in India or Pakistan connected with the political decision that unleashed so much violence? It is well known from history that while violence is made by men, women are the worst sufferers. What preventive measures were taken or planned by the then decision-making authorities in India to check the inevitable rape or molestation or abduction of women, Hindu, Muslim or Sikh, during the communal riots that preceded and accompanied the Partition? Even after Partition, as we have already seen, the Indian State, while carrying on the task of 'restoration' of abducted women, proclaimed its concern for 'our honour' and 'our women', which meant the 'honour' of its men and the women who belonged to the men. No official space was provided to hear from women their experiences or to ascertain their views and to act accordingly. Women did not come forward to relate their stories, which would be perceived by society as stories of shame. The civil community was unsympathetic, and the State machinery indifferent. The term 'democracy' appeared to be a synonym for a male-dominated political system, and the new Indian State, sovereign and republic, a medium in the translation, communication and enforcement of patriarchal ideology.

Fifty long years after the constitutional guarantee of equality, a serious issue needs to be resolved. Almost every community, indeed every family, in India entrusts women with the extremely difficult task of maintaining its honour, its tradition and its norms. Given that women's bodies, more than anything else, are regarded as the single key factor of upholding this honour, the question is, why should these bodies not play the key role in the decision-making processes of the community—the decisions that affect its honour, its tradition and its norms? In India, where decision-making is organized through 'democratically' elected institutions, the views of the elected representatives are assumed to be the views of the population irrespective of class, caste or gender differences. Given this definition and the massive under-representation of women, it can easily be seen that their views on security and peace, if and when a separate view exists, are unlikely to be articulated, much less heard. We may extend the argument. In India, as in most countries of South Asia, where society is structured in terms of male domination and female subordination, the awareness of women of themselves as having different priorities on issues of peace and security, war and partition, has been either stifled or tailored to fit conventional male views. Peace and security are concerns of both men and women, but women's colossal problems, their particular sufferings, are hardly taken into account by the male-dominated body that we call the State.

The tediously old and glaringly biased patriarchal ideology and practices still continue. And the State is deeply implicated in their perpetuation. Plans and proposals for the alleviation of poverty and the empowerment of women continue to be churned out. But how real have been the changes in our cultural notions? It is perhaps only when women in good numbers get access to political power and decision-making positions that women's disadvantaged situations will be focused upon, and there will be some change in the dual system of social ethics. Perhaps not in a day or in a year, but slowly and gradually. Perhaps not inevitably, but hopefully.

REFERENCES

1. Agarwal, Purushottam, 'Surat, Savarkar and Draupadi: Legitimising Rape as a Political Weapon', in Tanika Sarkar and Urvashi Butalia (eds), *Women and the Hindu Right*, Kali for Women, New Delhi, 1995.
2. Butalia, Urvashi, 'Community, State and Gender: On Women's Agency during Partition', *EPW* 28 (17), April 1993.
3. Butalia, Urvashi, 'Muslims and Hindus, Men and Women: Communal Stereotypes and the Partition of India', in Tanika Sarkar and Urvashi Butalia (eds), *Women and the Hindu Right*, Kali for Women, New Delhi, 1995.
4. Chakravarty, Dipesh, 'The Difference—Deferral of a Colonial Modernity: Public Debates on Domesticity in British Bengal', in David Arnold and David Hardiman (eds), *Subaltern Studies VIII*, Oxford University Press, Delhi, 1994.
5. Chakravarty, Uma, 'What Happened to the Vedic Dasi?', in Kumkum Sangari and Sudesh Vaid (eds), *Recasting Women*, Kali for Women, Delhi, 1989.
6. Chanana, Karuna, 'Partition and Family Strategies: Gender-Education Linkages among Punjabi Women in Delhi', *EPW* 28(17), April 1993.
7. Chatterjee, Partha, 'The Nationalist Resolution of the Women's Question', in Kumkum Sangari and Sudesh Vaid (eds), *Recasting Women*, Kali for Women, Delhi, 1989.
8. Das, Suranjan, *Communal Riots in Bengal, 1905–47*, Oxford University Press, Delhi, 1991.
9. Das, Veena, *Critical Events*, Oxford University Press, Delhi, 1995.
10. Desai, Neera and Maithreyi Krishnaraj, *Women and Society in India*, Ajanta Publications, New Delhi, 1998.
11. Devi, Jyortirmoyee, '*Chheleta*'. Translated from Bengali by Sukhender Ray, 'The Little Beggar Boy' in *The Impermanence of Lies*, Stree, Calcutta, 1998

12. Devi, Jyotirmoyee, '*Epar Ganga Opar Ganga*'. Translated from Bengali by Enakshi Chattopadhyaya, *The River Churning*, Kali for Women, New Delhi, 1995.
13. Hasan, Mushirul, *Legacy of a Divided Nation: India's Muslims Since Independence*, Oxford University Press, Delhi, 1997.
14. Kasturi, Leela and Vina Mazumdar, *Women and Indian Nationalism*, Vikas Publishing House, Delhi, 1994.
15. Khosla, G. D., *Stern Reckoning: A Survey of Events Before and Following Partition of India*, Oxford University Press, Delhi, 1952.
16. Major, A. J., 'The Chief Sufferers: A Preliminary Look at the Abduction, Recovery and Rehabilitation of Women in the Punjab, 1947–48', Paper presented at Seminar on Northern India and Indian Independence at Nehru Memorial Museum and Library, 6–9 Dec., 1993.
17. Menon, Ritu and Kamla Bhasin, 'Recovery, Rupture, Resistance: Indian State and Abduction of Women during Partition, *EPW* 28(17), April 1993.
18. Pandey, Gyanendra, 'The Prose of Otherness', in David Arnold and David Hardiman (eds), *Subaltern Studies VIII*, Oxford University Press, Delhi, 1994.
19. Ray, Bharati (ed.), *Sekaler Narisiksha: Bamabodhini Patrika* (Women's Education of Yester Years: Bamabodhini Patrika), Calcutta University Press, Calcutta, 1994.
20. Ray, Bharati (ed.), *From the Seams of History: Essays on Indian Women*, Oxford University Press, Delhi, 1995.
21. Scarry, Elaine, *The Body in Pain: The Making and Unmaking of the World*, Oxford University Press, New York, 1985.

2

Bidyut Mohanty

Panchayat Raj Institutions and Women

The 73rd Constitution Amendment Act 1993 was a form of affirmative action to reserve 33% of the total seats for all three tiers of panchayats and functionaries for women. The idea was to facilitate women's participation in grassroots politics, thereby empowering them to become partners in the decision-making process. This paper tries to answer the question as to how far participation in panchayats has empowered women so far and what strategies should be adopted.

The first section discusses panchayats in the historical perspective and the salient features of the Constitution (Seventy-third Amendment) Act 1993 and the need for such affirmative action. The next section takes up the state experiences in terms of magnitude, characteristics of the women elected representatives and quality of participation. This is followed by the lessons learnt from other similar movements such as the Total Literacy Campaign and then a summing up.

Panchayats in the Historical Perspective and Participation of Women

Even though it is widely believed that panchayat institutions (self-governing village communities) existed in the Vedic period in a rudimentary form, participation of women did not take place till the Balwantrai Mehta Committee Report was published in 1959. The committee recommended the co-optation of two women in the panchayat bodies who were interested in working for the welfare of women and children. The co-optation, however, was invariably done on the basis of familial relationships of the rural elites. Uttar Pradesh and some other states did adopt the recommendations of the committee but did not co-opt any woman. The panchayats invariably got superseded and the co-opted women were effectively kept out of political power.

In 1974 a committee (Towards Equality) was set up to study the status of women comprehensively and it suggested the setting up of statutory women's panchayats at the village level to look after development and welfare programmes meant for women and children. It was felt that if women panchayats were constituted, the social and other cultural barriers preventing them from coming to the public field would be eliminated. The committee (1974) recommended their election and not nomination. And they in turn would depute women to the block and district level. After submission of the report only two states, Maharashtra and Andhra Pradesh, constituted all-women panchayats. The most common argument against reserving seats for women was that it would exclude them rather than integrate them into the political process (Santha, 1995).

In 1978, the Ashok Mehta Committee Report was released. Unlike the previous committees, it recommended a fundamental change in the concept of panchayati raj. It sought to make the panchayats an integral part of the decision-making process instead of treating them as implementing agencies (Mathew, 1995).

In order to implement this recommendation, the need for a constitutional amendment was felt. It took more than a decade for the first steps in this direction to be taken in the form of the 64th Constitution Amendment Bill, which was defeated in the Rajya Sabha. In 1992, the 73rd Amendment Bill was introduced in Parliament, which adopted it in the same year. It became an Act in the following year. The important features of this Act are: (1) Panchayats will be considered political institutions in a truly decentralized structure. (2) The gram sabha shall be recognized as the life line of the panchayats. The voters of the village or villages will constitute its members. The panchayat shall be accountable to the gram sabha. (3) There will be direct election in all the three tiers of governance: gram panchayat at the village level, taluka or block panchayat at the intermediate level and zilla panchayat or parishad at the district level. (4) In so far as the empowerment of women is concerned the Act has provided that *at least* one-third of the total seats at all levels shall be reserved for women of whom one-third shall be from the Scheduled Castes and Scheduled Tribes. In this context it is important to note that at least one-third of the total posts of the office bearers at all levels will also be reserved for women. The Orissa government has made it mandatory that wherever the chairperson is a man, the vice-chairperson's post would be reserved for a woman. (5) Each panchayat will have a tenure of five years and in case it is dissolved by the state government fresh election will be held within a period of six months. (6) The election to local bodies has to be conducted regularly. (7) There will be a separate Election Commission and also a Finance Commission for panchayats in every state. (8) It is obligatory on the part of the centre as well as the state to provide adequate funds for the panchayats to enable them to function properly. In addition, the panchayats will have their own fund-raising capacity on the basis of local resources. (9) Rajasthan, Haryana and Orissa have debarred candidates having more than two children from contesting the election with a view to controlling population growth. However, given the low average age of marriage of girls—19—they would have crossed the two-child norm by the time they contested the elections. Hence, it will be difficult for the states to get suitable women candidates for the panchayat election. The sole purpose of empowering women may get defeated by this clause. (10) Some state Acts, like those of Bihar, Himachal Pradesh, Uttar Pradesh, Haryana and the earlier Act of Karnataka, have the provision of nyaya panchayat to settle local disputes at all the three levels.

The new central Act does not make it obligatory for states to provide for nyaya panchayats to solve local disputes. Secondly, although the objective of the Act is to build the panchayat as an effective decentralized political institution at the grassroots level, the division of functions in its 11th Schedule makes it, in reality, essentially an implementing agency for developmental activities. In other words, the resource-raising capacity of the panchayats is limited. For example, the 'sarpanches' and chairpersons of the panchayats are supposed to implement the schemes under Jawahar Rozgar Yojana (JRY) and Indira Awas Yojana, which may not reflect the local conditions adequately. For example, Himachal Pradesh, having a labour-scarce economy, is unable to implement JRY, which is labour-intensive. In Kerala, the panchayats have to supervise tutorial colleges. Nonetheless, the act has ushered in a new era in which the villagers can at least try to decide their own destiny.

Need for Affirmative Action

That Indian women are discriminated against at all levels requires no further proof. In politics the participation of women is minimal not only at the all-India level but also at the state level (Shantha, 1995). Even Kerala, with 86% female literacy, has few women in politics.

Since the beginning of planned development, women have been viewed as a deprived section requiring welfare measures. In 1975, the publication of the Report on the Status of Women and the UN Declaration of that year as women's year compelled the national government to shift the emphasis of its women's programmes from welfare to development. More attention was given to health, education and employment. In 1985, after the Women's World Congress at Nairobi, the National Perspective Plan was prepared laying down forward-looking strategies for women's development. In this document the question of their political participation was highlighted and it was recommended that 33% of the total seats should be reserved for women.

The National Perspective Plan also recommended that some posts should be reserved for women at the block and village level bureaucracy. On the economic front a number of income-generating schemes were introduced for women, such as Development of Woman and Child in Rural Areas (DWCRA). In addition, provisions were made to keep a certain proportion of women as beneficiaries in IRDP, JRY, NRY, TRYSEM and other developmental schemes. Thus, we find a host of national and international events coupled with complex social and economic factors influencing the decisions that culminated in the reservation of 33.3% of the total seats for women at the panchayat level.

EXPERIENCES FROM THE STATES

Table 2.1 reveals the percentage of women elected in different layers of panchayats at the state level. Table 2.2, on the other hand, compares these participation rates with other variables such as female work

Table 2.1: Women elected members in different tiers of panchayats as on 1.1.96

	GP	PS	ZP	Total percentage
Gujarat	21,351 (64,052) (33.30)	1,275 (3,765) (33.90)	254 (764) (33.20)	33.36
Haryana	17,928 (54,159) (33.10)	807 (2,418) (33.40)	101 (303) (33.30)	33.12
Himachal Pradesh	NA	NA	NA	37.80
Karnataka	37,689 (80,627) (46.70)	1,343 (3,340) (40.20)	335 (919) (36.50)	43.38
Kerala	3,954 (10,685) (37.00)	564 (1,543) (36.55)	105 (300) (35.00)	36.90
Madhya Pradesh	184,000 (484,394) (38.00)	2,991 (9,097) (32.90)	315 (942) (33.40)	37.88
Punjab	23,832 (78,983) (30.17)	326 (2,441) (13.36)	89 (274) (32.60)	29.68
Rajasthan	33,566 (103,712) (32.36)	1,740 (5,257) (33.00)	331 (997) (33.10)	32.41
Tripura	1,809 (5,427) (33.30)	67 (196) (34.20)	24 (70) (34.30)	33.37
Uttar Pradesh	120,591 (406,895) (29.60)	18,880 (52,417) (36.00)	793 (2,127) (37.40)	30.4
West Bengal	22,014 (62,139) (35.43)	3,202 (9,516) (33.65)	227 (664) (34.10)	35.18

Note: Figures within parentheses are total membership and percentages respectively.
Source: Directors of panchayats of different states.

Table 2.2: Female participation rate in local government level (rural) and other variables in different states

Name of the State	FWPR (1991)	RFLR (1991)	PCY (1991)	FPLBR (1993)
Gujarat	36.46	38.65	5687	33.36
Haryana	13.21	32.51	7502	33.12
Himachal Pradesh	36.57	49.79	NA	37.80
Karnatala	36.33	34.76	4696	43.38
Kerala	17.94	85.12	4207	36.90
Madhya Pradesh	39.07	19.73	4149	37.88
Punjab	7.02	43.85	8373	29.68
Rajasthan	32.77	11.59	4113	32.41
Uttar Pradesh	14.72	19.02	3516	30.40
West Bengal	13.54	38.12	4753	35.18

Source: (1) Census of India, 1991 Paper 3 of 1991 provisional population totals: workers and their distribution.
(2) P.V. Rajiv (1995) 'Development Key Lies on Economy', *The Economic Times*, New Delhi edition November 10.
(3) From the respective state panchayat directors compiled by Institute of Social Sciences, 1995.
FWPR—Female Work Participation Rate Rural.
RFLR—Rural Female Literacy Rate.
PCY—Percapita Income.
FPLBR—Female Participation in Local Bodies (Rural).

participation rates, female literacy rates and per capita income at the current prices as a proxy for economic prosperity of different states. It is important to note here that the highest percentage of women has been elected in Karnataka and the lowest in Punjab, the second and third lowest being Uttar Pradesh and Rajasthan respectively. In Punjab, the reservation of seats for women has been done in a much more complicated way. Secondly, the election of functionaries at the level of samiti and zilla parishad is yet to be held. Punjab, Uttar Pradesh and Rajasthan have not been able to fulfil the mandatory requirement of the Constitution. At the same time it is interesting to find that Madhya Pradesh has elected 38%

of women at the panchayat level followed by 33% in each of the other two layers. This is the second highest in India. Similarly, in Himachal Pradesh, 38% of the total elected members are women. On the other hand, the industrialized Gujarat and agriculturally prosperous Haryana have allotted only 33% of the total seats to women. Orissa has given 35% of the total seats to women in the recent panchayat election. Again, given the female literacy rate (86%) in Kerala one would have expected to find a very high proportion of women coming to politics but it is only 37%, lower than that of Karnataka and Madhya Pradesh. Similarly, the progressive state of West Bengal has given 35% of the total seats to women even after two decades of experience in panchayat rule.

It can be inferred from the table that political will, coupled with a liberal interpretation of the provision of reserving seats for women, status of women and economic prosperity (Karnataka) in that order would determine the percentage share of elected women in local self-government. But the question still remains as to how they would perform once they are elected. The economic, demographic and social characteristics of these elected women would shed some light on this aspect. In addition, there are some success stories to suggest that a new beginning has been made towards empowering women in the effective decision-making process.

Demographic and Other Characteristics of the Elected Women

Four years have passed since the Constitutional Amendment came into force. Both Karnataka (1987) and Maharashtra (1990) held elections even before the Act's enforcement and mandatory reservation of seats for women under it. Some micro studies indicating the demographic and other social and economic characteristics of the elected women representatives are already available. It will be worthwhile to discuss these characteristics to find out their economic and social background.

According to Mathew (1994), women from the dominant castes, Lingayats and Vokkaligas, formed 60% of the elected women members at the level of zilla parishad in Karnataka. A similar picture emerged from a primary survey conducted in Orissa in the coastal belt as well as in the tribal area (B. Mohanty, 1995). Around 66% of the women elected members in the state are Karans (Kayasthas) and Khandaits (cultivating castes). In yet another study relating to Orissa, it is revealed that the percentage of non-Scheduled Castes (57.1) in the posts of upa-sarpanches is higher than that of Scheduled Castes (28.6) and Scheduled Tribes (14.3). But in the ward membership, the lower caste dominated. For example, Scheduled Tribes constituted 45.9% and Scheduled Castes 27%. In contrast, women from general castes formed 27%.

With regard to the marital status, it is noticed that almost all women elected representatives are married. It is also important to note that at least 16% of the total women representatives in Orissa are widows. The West Bengal study by Development Alternative (1995) showed that around 84% of the women panchayat members are married. Parida's (1997) survey in the coastal district of Orissa confirmed the same trend. But he did not find any widow in his study.

It is interesting to note the literacy level of the women who have been elected to the third tier of governance. The Orissa study shows that the percentage of literate women at the sarpanch level is 86% whereas at the ward membership level it is only 68%. Incidentally, according to the Orissa Panchayat Act 1994, the candidates have to be literate. A recent pre-poll survey also confirmed the above trend. Most of the total women candidates interviewed (48%) have passed at least Secondary examination (Parida, 1997). In the case of Karnataka, surprisingly, we find that only 20% of the women representatives are literate. Of course, Bijapur, to which the figure relates, is a relatively backward district. Again, women representatives lagged behind their male counterparts in literacy. For instance, 20% of the men are either professionals or post-graduates. In contrast, only 5% of the total women elected at the zilla parishad level are so (Mathew, 1994).

In contrast to the Karnataka experience, the West Bengal study suggested that all the women elected members were literate. But most of them had not gone beyond the middle school stage.

The above micro studies, which are based on small samples, are, no doubt, not an adequate mirror of the educational status of women panchayat members. But they make one point clear: that a majority of the women elected in the eastern and southern parts of India are not illiterate, except in the backward districts.

With regard to the age composition of the women members, it is to be remembered that Karnataka was the first state that had lowered the voting age to 18 years. According to Mathew (1994), the political parties there found it extremely difficult to get candidates in the higher age groups, i.e., above 45. They could persuade only the younger women to contest the election. As a result, more of them were less experienced in politics than men.

Both the studies of Orissa (1995, 1997) and those of West Bengal and Kerala confirmed the above trend. In Orissa, for example, 80% of the women interviewed were in the age group of 20 to 40. The experience of Maharashtra, which had conducted the panchayat elections earlier, revealed similar features in one of the micro studies of the state. However, studies from Haryana show that women belong to the post-reproductive age group.

Thus, on the basis of the above studies, it can be said that most of the women representatives are younger, less exposed to public life and less educated than their male counterparts particularly from the southern and eastern states in contrast to the northern states. High caste members predominate at the high posts of Sarpanches, Block chairpersons and zilla parishad president. However, the elected women representatives from the south and east are likely to be more receptive than those of the northern belt, being educated and young.

Quality of Participation

Given the above background it is difficult to expect that the women elected representatives would work effectively in the initial stage. Reports are in abundance from Rajasthan, Madhya Pradesh, Orissa, to some extent Bengal and even Kerala, that women are treated with indifference by their male colleagues in the meetings. The bureaucracy also does not treat them with dignity. In many cases they are used as proxy women and their male family members conduct meetings in panchayats. In addition, the women elected members face violence and rape if they dare to come out alone to attend meetings. The working conditions in the panchayats are not congenial. Besides these handicaps the general atmosphere of the politics has been vitiated with corruption, violence and petty mindedness. It also takes a great deal of money to contest elections. All these factors affect the choice of good candidates among women and also their efficiency.

However, not all the women elected representatives are proxy women. In many cases, they have been assertive. The members of the all-women Kultikri panchayat in West Bengal, for example, have set their agenda for overall development of the panchayat. This panchayat has been declared the best in the state (Mukhopadhyay, 1995). Similarly, the all-women panchayat in Vitner, Maharashtra, is engaged in providing clean drinking water, pucca road and electricity to its own constituency.

In Karnataka, the women elected representatives refused to blindly follow their family members once they are exposed to the meetings. The experience of Madhya Pradesh is no different. After undergoing training organized by the UNICEF, women no longer stay behind the veil. Many women have been instrumental in bringing together disparate programmes. For example, many women panchayat members started popularizing the sale and consumption of iodized salt after they become convinced of the ill-effects of iodine deficiency. Similarly, they are asking for protected sanitary facilities such as pit toilets and washing and bathing facilities (Kulkarni, 1997). Likewise in the case of Rajasthan, where women are even not allowed to enter the 'chaupal', which is reserved for men and in which all the important matters including politics are discussed. A detailed survey of several low caste women sarpanches revealed that they are more accessible to people and take more care to get things done for the villagers in terms of drinking water, health and income-generating schemes meant for women than the previous sarpanches (Mayaram and Pal, 1996).

Orissa experience in this context is worth noting, particularly in the districts of Jagatsinghpur in the coastal belt, Nuapada in the most backward region and Rayagada in the tribal belt, in which we have been monitoring and evaluating the performances of 210 women elected representatives through various activities, on behalf of the Institute of Social Sciences, New Delhi.

We noticed that after one year, the women elected representatives including ward members are well aware of the importance of palli sabha and gram sabha, the life lines of the panchayats. In terms of quality of participation, women from the coastal belt stood first and those of the tribal belt last.

The women elected representatives of Jagatsinghpur know by now that Indira Awas, widow pension and other schemes are part of the Integrated Rural Development Programmes (IRDP) so they are finalizing the list of people living below the poverty line from which beneficiaries can be recruited. The women elected representatives of Nuapada know about the Indira Awas scheme and other welfare schemes but do not know about the IRDP. In Rayagada, on the other hand, some of them are very articulate and try to finalize the list of beneficiaries through gram sabha; they also do not know about IRDP. Besides, the women elected representatives of all the three districts can identify sources such as fishery or wasteland development to augment panchayats' income in addition to grants from the Jawahar Rozgar Yojana (JRY), which forms the substantial portion of the panchayats' revenue. It is interesting to note that almost all the women elected representatives now freely talk of corruption at the bureaucracy level. They also feel that they get by-passed by the BDO (Block Development Officer) and by the personnel of other lines or departments.

In Haryana, Madhya Pradesh and other states women elected representatives have worked effectively in so far as liquor issue is concerned.

Whenever these women are organized or are assisted by Mahila Samakhya, like-minded NGOs or political groups, they have started functioning well in the panchayat institutions.

Lessons from Other Movements

In this context it is important to find out the impact of literacy campaign and anti-arrack movements on the women. The National Literacy Mission (NLM) was started on May 5, 1988, in different parts of the country. The objective was to address the problems of illiteracy in the age group of 15–35. Since more women than men in this age groups are illiterate, more women took part in this campaign. According to Saldanha (1995), about 41,000 females were enrolled in the literacy campaign in contrast to 19,000 males in different districts of Maharashtra and Goa. The same phenomenon was observed in other states.

Saldanha noticed that around 68% of the total learners belonged to the weaker section and 6% to the Muslim communities. It is important to note that the campaign was conducted in a decentralized manner by involving voluntary sectors, for example, the Gyan Vigyan Samities, and later on it got the support of the administrators, academicians and political parties. It caught the imagination of the rural masses because the trainers used different cultural expressions and folklore to teach the lessons. In Andhra Pradesh, the lessons taught contained daily problems which they face at home, such as alcholism.

As a result, according to Saldanha (1996), the women and girl children have been able to break out of the 'historically structured constraint' and have come out in large number to the training camps.

While delivering the J.P. Naik Memorial Lecture in Delhi on February 26, 1996, Saldanha further elaborated on the above point. He stressed that in many places the self-perception has undergone a radical change because of the literacy campaign. He cited three examples to support his contention.

In Sindhdurg, Maharashtra, after attending the training, the women decided to ride bicycles *en masse*. In Dumka, Bihar, women decided to lift their veils and started working outside the households. The women of Nellore district in Andhra Pradesh learned about the problem of alcoholism and how it was contributing to poverty. Then they started the anti-arrack movement, which forced the then Chief Minister N.T. Rama Rao to cancel licences to liquor vendors though excise duty was the most lucrative source of revenue. The emergence of local leaders, such as Mayawati, has shaken up the conciousness of the low caste women.

In a similar manner, the reservation of seats for women in panchayats would break age-old constraints and they would be able to participate in the decision-making process in a more meaningful way.

Participatory planning adopted to formulate the Ninth Five Year Plan at the grassroots level in Kerala has motivated elected women representatives to attend gram sabha meetings and also to contribute to the preparation of the developmental plan for the panchayats. A group of NGOs, academicians and bureaucrats have played an active role in this. In other words, the conditions have been created for elected women representatives to get empowered in the most literate state. This example may trigger similar effects on elected women representatives of other states.

Summing Up

During the decades of planned development, women were treated as beneficiaries till 1974, when the (Towards Equality) Committee suggested that representation be given to women in the panchayat bodies. In the meantime, the concept of panchayati raj institutions underwent a change from being an implementing agency to being part of the democratic polity. The Perspective Planning (1988) recommended thirty three percent of the total seats in the panchayats for women and the dream was fulfilled when the 73rd Constitution Amendment Act was passed.

The fact that about one million women came into the public arena for the first time is expected to create a ripple in tradition-bound Indian society. But their quality of participation in the panchayat bodies may not be that effective in the beginning. Nonetheless, there are success stories. Even low caste women sarpanches, zilla parishad members, samiti members as well as members from all women panchayats are asserting their viewpoints and getting things done for the benefit of villagers. The Orissa experience shows that the women elected representatives are realizing the importance of palli sabha and gram sabhas, the IRDP and accompanying corruption in the system.

Experiences from movements such as the Total Literacy Campaign show that once women become aware of the issues they try to execute programmes successfully and in the process their self-perceptions undergo change. This has a multiplier impact on the children, the family, the neighbourhood and the village. An elected woman is no longer perceived (even if she is a proxy woman) as an unpaid domestic worker; she has a constructive role to play in society.

Thus, the feedback so far shows that one-third reservation of seats for women in the panchayats is likely to lead to the empowerment of women in India. In many places this opportunity has led these women elected representatives to be effective partners in implementing government schemes. In addition, they organize the palli sabhas and gram sabhas to finalize the list of people below the poverty line entitled to get loans and ration through the public distribution system. However, a concerted effort is required by the NGOs, governments and other concerned institutions to make the opportunity into a reality. If we suppress 50% of the population from participating in political and thereby economic and social activities, India's growth process will remain lopsided. The development of 'women agency' through empowerment influences family planning and population control, primary health care, education and many other measures of development. Besides, emancipation of women is an integral part of social process and not just a 'women's issue' (Drèze and Sen, 1995).

REFERENCES

Ashok Mehta Committee, *Report of the Committee on Panchayati Raj Institutions*, New Delhi, 1977.

Balwantrai Mehta Committee, Report of the Team for the Study of Community projects and National Extension Service 1959.

Bhaskar, Manu, 'Women Panchayat Member in Kerala, A Profile', *EPW*, April 26, 1997.

Drèze, J. and A. Sen, *India: Economic Development and Social Opportunity*, Oxford University Press, Delhi, 1995.

Kaushik, Sushila, *Panchayati Raj in Action: Challenges to Women's Role*, FES, New Delhi, 1995.

Kulkarni, Manu, 'Women and the Panchayats', *The Eye* 4 (3), March 1997.

Mathew, George, *Panchayati Raj: From Legislation to Movement*, Concept, New Delhi, 1994.

Mathew, George (ed.), *Status of Panchayati Raj in the States of India, 1994*, Concept, New Delhi, 1995.

Mayaram, Shail and Pritam Pal, 'Politics of Women's Reservation: Women Panchayat Representatives in Rajasthan Performance, Problems and Potential', working paper No. 074 (1996), IDS, Jaipur, Rajasthan.

Mohanty, Bidyut, 'Panchayati Raj, 73rd Constitutional Amendment and Women', *EPW*, 30 December 1995.

Mohanty, Bidyut (ed.), *Women and Political Empowerment: Proceedings of the Women's Political Empowerment Day Celebrations 23–24 April 95*, ISS, New Delhi, 1996.

Mohanty, Manoranjan, 'On the Concept of Empowerment', *Indian Journal of Social Sciences* 8 (4), 1995.

Mukhopadhyay, Ashim, 'Kultikri: West Bengal's Only All-women Gram Panchayat', *EPW*, 3 June 1995.

Nanda, Amulya Ratna, 'Final Population Totals: Brief Analysis of Primary Census Abstract', *Census of India 1991* Series 1, paper 2, 1992, Office of the Registrar General, New Delhi.

Omvedt, Gail, 'Women Zilla Parishads and Panchayati Raj Chandward to Vitner', *EPW*, 4 August 1990.

Parida, Amarnath, 'A Report on the Socio-Economic Conditions of the Women Candidates Contesting Panchayat Election in a Coastal District of Orissa', submitted to Institute of Social Sciences, New Delhi, as part of the on-going project titled 'Panchayats and Women', 1997.

Saldanha, Denzil, 'Literacy Campaigns in Maharashtra and Goa, Issues, Trends and Directions', *EPW*, 20 May 1995.

Santha, E., 'Participation of Women in Panchayati Raj: A Status Report', submitted to National Commission for Women through Institute of Social Sciences, 1995 (unpublished).

Towards Equality: Report on the Committee on the Status of Women in India, Government of India, Ministry of Education and Welfare, New Delhi, 1974.

3

Ela R. Bhatt

Towards the Second Freedom

Introduction

My most sustained experience since India's independence has been a search for the 'second freedom', i.e., economic empowerment for India's poor and toiling women. The right to vote was not enough for these women. As poor people, they wanted to come out of an existence defined by day-to-day survival. As women, they wanted equal and ample opportunities to learn and to act. As the workers in India's self-employed sector, they wanted to be a part of the labour movement. As Dalits and minorities, they wanted to move in from the margins to the mainstream. They wanted a voice and visibility. This was not possible without access to and ownership of economic resources by the poor women, and their overcoming exploitation by men, society and state policies. They wanted to enjoy the second freedom. Failures and disappointments have met us everywhere in the country since then; although we feel embattled, for me this half century has also been one of constantly renewed fulfilments.

As the struggle for independence came to an end, the atmosphere in the universities and elsewhere was full of an enthusiasm to rebuild the nation. I had joined my efforts with those of the student leader Ramesh, my future husband, like so many young people at that time, to make sense of the recently gained freedom from the British.

In some ways, the yearning for the second freedom overwhelmed us. It pushed us each year to develop adventurous attitudes, enlarge the scope of the search and see to it that the sense of hope and the good humour wasn't diminished in any way.

Gandhi's thinking has shown us the way: a clear direction leading us to commitment, sustained efforts, a gentle but firm belief in women's leadership in social change, and willingness to see beyond the immediate. As I understand Gandhi, economic self-reliance was as important to him as political freedom. He called economic poverty 'a moral collapse' of society. True, political or technological change by itself does not necessarily remove poverty, as it does not remove exploitation. Therefore, the problem of poverty and the loss of freedom are not separate. What has been inspiring about this search is how much we achieved and what we saw ourselves capable of, how effectively we transformed the place and time we went through. What is most inspiring is that it never occurred to us not to.

SEWA is the story of poor women heading towards the second freedom.

Trade Union SEWA

SEWA is a trade union, started in 1972. It has a membership of 2,18,799 women in Gujarat, Madhya Pradesh, Uttar Pradesh, Bihar, Delhi and Kerala and in Durban, South Africa.

In 1971, migrant women working as cart pullers in Ahmedabad's cloth market came to the Textile Labour Association (TLA) seeking help for housing. (The TLA was founded by Gandhiji in 1917.) Next month came head-loader women of the same cloth market feeling agitated over very low rates of payment (30 paise per trip from wholesaler to retailer). Then followed the used garment dealer women in search of credit from the recently nationalized banks. They were paying 10% per day as interest to the moneylender. Women vendors of downtown Manekchowk market came seeking protection from police harassment. And then came Hawa Bibi of Patan, who had been deprived of her work after twenty years by a contractor who first started rejecting 50% of her rolled bidis, complaining they were 'bad', and finally stopped giving her any material at all with which to roll bidis. Hawa Bibi came to the TLA office looking for justice. The Labour Commissioner's office had said to her that she was not, technically, a 'worker' because she was working at home, and on piece rate. That was in 1971. Some of these urban, poor, self-employed women workers came to the meeting I called in a public garden where we formed our 'sangh', i.e. trade union (1972) with the ideological support of the TLA. We called it the Self-Employed Women's Association (SEWA).

Only two things were clear in my mind then. One, when 89% (now 93%) of the working population of the country engaged in the self-employed and informal sector of the economy is outside the labour movement, there is no labour movement worth its name. Two, about 80% of women in India are rural, poor, illiterate or semi-literate, although economically very active. So, in the women's movement of India, we believed that these women should be playing a leading role. Their major concern was economic survival. Unless the issues of urgent importance to them were taken up by the movement, the majority would remain untouched. There was no model or blueprint to follow, but here were these two clear ideas in my mind, and, these, I believe, have kept us on the right track till today. 'You are ahead of your time,' I was told by the International Labour Organization (ILO) in Geneva, in 1974. Though I had not realized it then, overcoming the mental blocks we would face in the coming years proved a Himalayan task.

The Registrar of Unions was not ready to register us as a trade union in 1972, as we did not fit into their definition of a trade union. For them, the garment workers, cart pullers, rag-pickers and forest produce gatherers were not 'workers'. But in 1994, the same Registrar without a qualm would register the National Centre for Labour (NCL), which is a federation of registered trade unions of fisherfolk, construction labour, foresters, contract labour, domestic maids and self-employed workers spread across five states. Of the NCL's members, 60% are women, with the same percentage acting as representatives in the decision-making body, predominantly SEWA women.

I was publicly ridiculed when I talked of recognizing piece-rate home-based workers as 'workers' and providing them legal protection and social security, and this by our own Federation with whom our union was affiliated. That was in 1981. However, on March 18, 1988, the World Labour Congress of the International Confederation of Free Trade Unions (ICFTU) at Melbourne unanimously passed the Resolution mooted by SEWA to recognize and protect the home-based workers, and establish their rights by removing the discrimination between workers in the formal and informal sectors. On June 20, 1996, delegates to the 83rd Conference of the ILO at Geneva voted to adopt Convention No. 177, supplemented by Recommendations on Homework. The ILO Convention has force of law, so it is important. It is important for home workers because it brings recognition at the international level and sets conditions, such as minimum standards of pay, which can be translated into national law and policy. Together with the Recommendations, the Convention has many provisions that go beyond legal protection and can act as a strong instrument for the organization of millions of workers in the world.

It was a great victory for those who had been working with home workers for many years, including SEWA, which took the first step in this direction because of Hawa Bibi of Patan. People like Hawa Bibi are now officially recognized as 'workers' by ILO. There is now available an official definition of 'home worker', 'employer' and 'intermediary', to contest in any court of law.

Of course, we have yet to nationalize the international. The Convention still has to be ratified by the Government of India and that in itself involves a long process of national lobbying.

When SEWA played a leading role in the formation of the NCL in 1994, a journalist described it as a 'mutiny of 290 million'! Indeed it was the culmination of our efforts at organizing the informal sector workers and our grassroots activism; it was a big breakthrough in unionism and voluntarism, when I raised the first flag of the NCL in Bangalore in May 1994 with twenty other union leaders, men and women, standing together.

In fact, it is we who are relevant today as the organized sector is shrinking and unionism in the organized sector declining. The formal sector accounts for only 5% of our work force and even this is declining as production processes and services increasingly get transferred to the unorganized, informal and self-employed sectors. These sectors are important and relevant because about 60% of their work force comprises women, rural and urban. In our experience, in every industrial plant, one-third of the work force is formal; the rest is informal. The formal group, with a standard employer-employee relationship, is legally protected in terms of wages and working conditions, and enjoys representation at various levels of policy-making in the country, while the informal group has no such rights or benefits, in spite of being 95% (290 million) of the country's work force.

Union membership, in general, is stagnant or falling as new foreign investors and family businesses adopt non-union labour policies. This situation leads to further expansion of the unorganized sector and increases the need for its unionization. Of course, there is no need to follow the 'typical' union way of organizing, because it will not work in a sector that is informal, particularly in rural areas. A rural labourer cannot fit into any one definition. She is a combination of worker, producer and entrepreneur, simultaneously or intermittently during the year, and so does not have a fixed target at which to pitch demands. This necessitates innovative approaches, e.g. using tripartite or multipartite mechanisms in the enforcement of laws and implementation of welfare schemes. The Ahmedabad cloth market is governed by the Tripartite Board set up by the State. The union leader of SEWA, Maniben, head-loader of Dhanlaxmi cloth market, sits on the Tripartite Board representing labour along with other representatives of employers, government and labour—all men. Maniben has been instrumental in bringing a group insurance scheme to the head-loaders after much struggle with the employers. 'Economism', the 'curse' of typical union movements, is difficult to sustain in the unorganized sector. Hence innovation becomes necessary.

Given the disparate nature of groups in the unorganized category, it is inevitable to strategize in a holistic way and raise macro policy issues about the overall directions of development. Control over natural resources, income disparities (rather than discrete, specific micro enterprise level issues) and political empowerment in a pluralistic framework are the immediate issues.

The SEWA movement has to go a long way to build up solidarity with other unions, voluntary agencies and people's organizations and thus expand the outreach to achieve major gains through home-based workers' legislations, national living wage, alternative social security coverage and other benefits. The movement has to come from below, through a striving for self-empowerment, and that does not happen overnight.

It is a big challenge. The state must get out of some areas, but it must also get into some. It is not enough that business entrepreneurs and industrialists have freedom; the petty vendors, hawkers, home-based garment workers, contract workers, fisherwomen and forest produce gatherers also need freedom to operate and develop their livelihoods.

Sixty seven per cent of the members are rural; the rest are urban. In a breakdown by trade, 7% are vendors, 35% home-based producers and 58% labour and service providers. One-third of the members are Muslims, and another third are Harijans. SEWA further organizes the members into trade co-operatives (numbering 71 in Gujarat). Joint action of the union and the co-operatives has been the major strategy to make their presence felt in the state economy. All activities aim towards attaining full employment and self-reliance. Efforts are made to achieve these through intense activities in the areas of unionism, rural development, banking, social security (health care, child care, shelter), the SEWA Academy, the setting up of cooperatives, policy research and interventions, and national and international alliances.

Though working class women are not a homogeneous group in terms of caste, class or economic activity, deprivation and discrimination are common to all of them. They suffer from lack of opportunities to work, and low and discriminatory wages. They lack social security, face occupational health hazards, and do not have access to new technologies, skills and information. The vicious circles of poverty, illiteracy and increasing unemployment are all leading to greater poverty. They can be broken only by strong interventions from the government as well as the NGOs. Concepts such as full employment are still a distant prospect.

In 1987, after persistent demands from SEWA, the Government of India set up the National Commission of Self-Employed Women and Women in the Informal Sector to prepare a report on the condition of self-employed women workers and make recommendations on improving their condition. The report, 'Shram Shakti', was submitted in 1988 to the then Prime Minister Rajiv Gandhi and accepted by the Government of India in 1989. It was a milestone in the women's movement in India. It has made working women in the unorganized sector officially visible.

In 1990, the Planning Commission of India concretized some of its major recommendations, namely the setting up of the Rashtriya Mahila Kosh, an exclusive, national-level credit fund for women, and also the setting up of the statutory body of the National Commission of Women. The other recommendations of Shram Shakti, such as the setting up of the National Fund for Creches and the National Fund of Social Security, have also become a reality, officially, though they are yet to be effective. The report has been translated into 13 Indian languages and NGOs use it freely as a guideline. The report has also appeared in German and Japanese. The German government often uses it during its bilateral negotiations with the Indian government. Here again women have taken the lead.

The most significant impact of Shram Shakti is that it has encouraged poor women all over the country to organize themselves into groups whose concerns centre around economic activities and other pressing issues. This very process of forming groups and managing the group's activities is an empowering one. Bashiran Bibi, an agricultural worker in a tobacco field in the Kheda district, said in a public dialogue with Mrs. Hillary Clinton, 'I am not afraid of my landlord, the police or my husband. I now know what is what, and, I believe, I can advise them.'

SEWA Bank

The Registrar of Co-operatives was extremely afraid to register our Co-operative Bank in 1974, as the shareholders were all illiterate women engaged in the 'uncertain' sector of the economy. How can you have banking with illiterate women? Because they are all economically very active. We had recognized the unbankable as 'bankable' in 1974. Today, the Government of India, under the poverty alleviation programme, through RBI's Directive, asks banks to extend credit to poor and rural women all over the country. Throughout, the women's savings and credit groups' activities have proved their bankability, profitability and capability for self-management. Now, all over the globe, for the World Bank and other donors, extending credit to poor families through women has been a popular campaign.

The Registrar was reluctant to register our labour co-operatives of rag-pickers, service co-operatives of child care, midwifery, etc.—as they were unheard of. The video producers' co-operative was not registered because illiterate women 'can't possibly' be producers, or camerapersons or sound recordists. Again, our trading co-operative combining urban vegetable vendors and rural vegetable growers could not be registered because of separate jurisdiction! There were innumerable perceptual blocks that had to be overcome.

SEWA Bank, though registered under strong reservations from the banking system, is an answer to the woman's need for savings and loan facilities. Since then the women have shattered existing myths about banking. Poor illiterate workers have proved to be a viable financial venture. Today the bank has a strength of 60,000 with a total working capital of Rs 12 crore with a record repayment rate of 96%. It is entirely the members' deposits and share amount that made the SEWA Bank totally self-reliant from the beginning.

It is now proved that poor women can run a bank, profitably. When the members own a bank or any programme, they take keen interest in its management and work towards a high repayment rate, maximum surpluses and distribution of the largest possible dividends to the members. Nanuben, an agricultural worker in Mehsana, and her husband Vithal earned Rs 3 per day during the season of six months. For the rest of the year, they almost starved. They migrated to Ahmedabad in search of work in 1978 with a mere Rs 7 and stayed in Nanuben's grandfather's slum on a rent of Rs 5 a month. Nanuben joined her grandmother's tiny business of collecting and repairing used clothes and then selling them in the used garments market. The SEWA Bank Director, Chandaben, introduced Nanuben to the bank. Her first loan, in 1978, was for Rs 500, which she used to buy a basket for collection of clothes, sturdy footwear, buttons and threads for repair and food grains for consumption. She made a surplus of Rs 400 and borrowed Rs 1500 to buy her own sewing machine and to repair the floor of her hut.

The poor are vulnerable to all types of crises. The SEWA bank analysed the factors that lead to the loss of productivity and income. It then decided to run an integrated work security scheme that now covers its members' risks in the event of death, widowhood, accidents, hospitalization, loss of goods and work tools and other emergencies. It even covers the risk of maternity. This is a deposit-linked insurance scheme and is self-reliant and financially viable.

With a long-term relationship with SEWA Bank, Nanuben has borrowed 18 times so far. She bought a house and some furniture, invested in some gold and silver, married off her daughter and has a bank balance of Rs 12,000. 'We were living in a hut and were eating only once a day, sleeping on the floor, when we came to Ahmedabad City. Now we have a *pucca* house, with cots and ceiling fan, a stock of grains and oil, a stove, soaps and woollens. Earlier, I was washing and repairing all the clothes myself. Now we have engaged a tailor and the washerman comes to my house daily for collecting clothes to wash.'

Nanuben now has capital, the capacity to stand in the competitive market, access to social insurance ensuring health care, child care and shelter, and she has a say and share in the decision-making process of the SEWA Bank she owns. Many Nanubens, holding each other's hand, march forward towards the second freedom.

The video story produced by Video SEWA on Nanuben received the second prize in the UN Women's Conference in Beijing.

In the comparative performance criteria laid down by the Reserve Bank of India that shows the financial ratios between public and private sector banks, our SEWA Co-operative Bank tops the list, in terms of stability (capital + reserves/deposits), profitability and liquidity. The bank's figures clearly show that it has a high degree of stability, its ratio of own to borrowed funds being very high. In spite of their poverty, the Board members of the SEWA Bank are always very concerned that the profitability remain high. Madhuben Parmar says, 'When my member, misses one instalment of her repayment, I lose my sleep.' 'How many Boards in the world lose their sleep on such occasions?' asks Nancy Barry, President of the Women's World Banking, New York.

RURAL MEMBERS' INITIATIVES

SEWA's rural development work focuses on the regeneration of sources while creating jobs, rather than merely extracting all the available assets.

SEWA members are spread over 790 villages in Gujarat. The villages are dry, drought-prone, even deserts where it hasn't rained for years. Forced migration is a common problem, especially among the men. Earlier, there were many struggles waged by SEWA for payment of minimum wages to landless agricultural labourers. The organizers were repeatedly attacked in the field and faced innumerable legal cases. However, SEWA learned from these hard lessons. Building capacity and power to bargain are not available to labour in the absence of employment opportunities. Increasing local employment opportunities for women and building the ownership of assets, individual and collective, became our strategy in rural areas thereafter.

Vanlaxmi is a landless agriculture women's co-operative. The members grow crops for cash as well as for domestic food needs. They plant trees for fodder and fruits. The farm uses its own organic fertilizer. The members have harvested rain water into a pond lined with plastic sheets to stop seepage.

Schoolchildren visit Vanlaxmi farm as part of their studies in the environment and ecology.

'My Co-operative has given me a chance to own land. It is our collective property,' Shantaben of Vanlaxmi told the Dean of the Agriculture University.

However, it is not enough to claim the inherited land. Women must have resources to buy land, individually and collectively. Water is also another productive asset. Women must strive to own and control it. Control of water in the hands of women changes most of the power equations in rural life, an asset being safer in the hands of women than their men. In SEWA, we are moving from being water users to becoming water owners.

The tribals of Bodeli lost their roots as the Sukhi Dam submerged their villages. Over a period of four years, the SEWA members of seven villages formed their Sukhi Association to rehabilitate themselves through building assets that the women could own. Their groups learned to raise nurseries and green their new homesteads. They also learned poultry farming. They learned to grow tomatoes of the best quality for the Bombay market, fetching the best possible prices. However, they have yet to feel integrated with the community of the host villages. The Chair of the Sukhi Association, Kavitaben, says, 'Our men come to me asking the price of cement and the name of the Irrigation Minister! I will have to equip myself with every kind of knowledge, it seems!'

It is difficult to explain the organizational chart of SEWA. It is like a banyan tree. The main organization allows for constantly evolving structures. New activities, new services, and the extension of old services to new members often come from the women themselves, who express new needs or cite new dangers. As a result, new societies and organizations are being registered continuously. Smaller groups are constantly in the process of federating themselves to gather more strength. For example, the DWCRA Producers Association of Banaskantha handles an annual business of handicrafts worth Rs 6 crore, which is actually more than that of the State Handicraft Corporation.

Today, we strive for immediate, reliable benefits: full employment at the household level, i.e. employment that ensures income security, food security and social security. For tomorrow, our goal is self-reliance in terms of financial viability and cultivating the ability to take decisions individually and collectively.

Health

How do these women begin to perceive their own health problems? Head-loaders of the grain market experience incessant pain in their back and legs. 'I simply feel like stretching out on the floor all the time.' Women stitching the recycled cement bags in their homes complained of very sore fingers and burning eyes. They wanted the infants in their lap to be protected from the cement dust. The slum women who have to visit the government hospital frequently complained of the loss of work hours. Eyestrain and backache are very common among village artisans. Stone-cutters suffer from severe backache. 'Private doctors are very costly,' they say. Specially hand-picked seeds (HPS) of groundnut that earn high rates of foreign exchange for the State are opened not by nutcrackers but by the women's teeth, leaving their mouth extremely sore; this is in order to keep the tiny shoot intact. Cotton-pod shellers in cotton farms suffer finger-cuts and irregular menstrual cycles. Poor women workers as a rule experience a continuous onslaught on their mental well-being and health.

Insecurity regarding where the next meal will come from, lack of access to family assets, drunkard husbands, rape, harassment by moneylenders, in short, humiliations at every step, are some of the serious factors affecting the mental and emotional well-being of poor women.

What has succeeded in improving their health conditions, in our experience, are the efforts in the areas of community-based integrated primary health run by co-operatives of local midwives and locally trained health care functionaries. Intense, ongoing preventive and curative health education yields good results. Improving women's nutrition through the supply of affordable, good quality food grains is another experiment that has worked. Local savings groups of women run this financially viable scheme called 'Shakti Packet', benefiting 30,000 rural women in the desert districts of Banaskantha and Kutch. 'We work so hard on the desert land to grow food, but end up paying double the amount for food and cooking oil. Droughts force us to migrate in search of food and water. Shakti Packet provides us food that we can afford, and when we want,' said Ranbai of Anternes village.

The savings groups of Kheda and Indore lend for house repairs and upgradation as well as building sanitation and bathing units. Regulations on maximum weight of headloads and cartloads have been laid down by the city authorities at SEWA's instance. The rate of miscarriage during pregnancies has clearly declined.

With the aid of the National Institute of Design and the National Occupational Health Institute, SEWA has tried to redesign handcarts, chairs for garment stitchers, and brooms, baskets, tongs, garbage bags, gloves and masks for cleaners. Here, sadly, arises the problem of the unaffordable cost of redesigned products. There is as yet no provision for subsidy on them.

In some areas, the State has to intervene. With the advent of liberalization, the new drug policy includes price decontrol of life-saving drugs. This has resulted in the increased cost of essential drugs, and a steep increase of four times in the price of anti-tuberculosis drugs. SEWA's health programme records that 63% of the members' families are threatened by tuberculosis. Our health co-operative, which runs drug counters, finds it very difficult to cope with the fast-rising price of such life-saving drugs.

Child care is another aspect of the women workers' economic and health security. They often have to earn their income at the expense of their children. SEWA, through its Sangini child care co-operatives, runs daycare centres for the children of its 6000 members.

The fact remains that nearly six crore children of women in the unorganized sector have no such care. The government-sponsored schemes reach only three lakh children, which is not even 5% of the demand.

In our study of Kheda district, tobacco processing women found that 92% of the mothers who attended SEWA creches reported an increase in earnings from Rs 50 to Rs 300 per month. In Surendranagar, 96% of the salt workers who sent their children to SEWA creches increased their income by 50%. Also, the infant mortality rate fell, instances of malnutrition decreased, and school attendance of siblings increased by 70%.

At present, there seems to be very little budgetary and policy support for child care in India. Our experience shows that child care can be self-financed to a great extent (80% in our case). However, initial support is very crucial. Along with FORCES (Forum for Creche and Child Care Services), SEWA has been asking the Government of India to budget at least Rs 5 per day for the health, nutrition and developmental care of six crore needy children under the age of five. This would be only a hundredth of the nation's GNP. The struggle is on.

Housing

For self-employed women, the home plays a central role in their economic and earning activities. This is true for all urban and rural producers and workers, vendors and cultivators, artisans and ragpickers. Their home is their work place: it is a workshop, a storehouse, a warehouse and a source of inputs such as water and electricity. For them, the house, however dilapidated it may be, is a productive asset, which is why 39% of the loans of the SEWA Bank are for housing.

Hanifa, at the Habitat II Conference, Istanbul, while receiving the World Prize to the SEWA Bank for Best Practice in Housing, said, 'I live on the river bank. I produce *samosas* at home. Due to the improvement in my house, the quality of my *samosas* has also improved. My old mother-in-law spins yarn on the *charkha*. Her productivity has tripled with monthly earnings going up from Rs 700 to Rs 2000. Thanks to the improved floor!'

SEWA Academy

Group training and training for leadership are the core components of the SEWA Academy. It aims at building women's capacities for leadership and self-reliance. It identifies potential leaders from the general membership and trains them in organization, leadership development, teamwork, policy-making and policy-implementation. On the principles of truth, non-violence, dignity and harmony rely SEWA's concepts and strategies of empowerment for the poorest. According to Mahatma Gandhi, every women, as every man, should have the opportunity to become self-reliant, should be able to hold her own against the tyranny of the employer, the State and even her kin.

Panniben, a tobacco processor, after returning from the training course, tells her women, 'Gandhi's life teaches us to tell the truth, to be self-reliant, to be non-violent, to believe in human beings, and to be simple in our habits.'

Credit, though very important, is not adequate for sustained and substantial employment. It is becoming increasingly clear that financial services are no longer enough for poor people to transform their economic activities into profitable ventures. Access to markets, information, technical know-how and social support services is as important as money if the poor are to participate in economic growth.

Strong economic structures for the poor are urgently needed if they are not to be swept off the ground by global market forces. People's economic organizations, if strong and effective, can actually benefit from a liberalized economy.

Where can the managers of our village-level women's savings and credit groups, our producers' groups, our DWCRA groups, and so on learn business planning, financial management, credit assessing and marketing? Where are the local language manuals for them? No business can run without these skills. There is a total absence of educational facilities, big or small, for the managers of the informal self-employed sector. The SEWA Academy and the Barefoot Managers School of the SEWA Bank are meant for just such women. It is a humble effort and there is a long way to go.

Women's Empowerment

For SEWA, women's empowerment translates into full employment and self-reliance, as mentioned earlier. When there is an increase in a woman's income, there is security of work; she has assets in her name, she feels economically strong, independent and autonomous. Her self-reliance is not merely of an individual nature; it is also organizational. She sits on the boards and committees of trade unions and co-operatives and takes decisions. She deals with traders, employers, government officials and bankers on equal terms, where earlier she was a servile worker. She knows that without economic power she will not be able to exercise her political rights in the panchayat. She has learnt to manage these economic organizations on viable terms. However, most important, she has to have employment, work that ensures her a steady income which can then lead to social security, good health care, etc.

Another component of empowerment for poor women is self-reliance. Self-reliance in terms of financial self-sufficiency and self-management, as well as in terms of decision-making. For them collective empowerment is more important than individual empowerment. With collective strength, they are able to combat external exploitative forces like moneylenders or police or black-marketeers. As her economic strength increases, a woman's self-reliance grows, and the respect she commands in the family and the community soon follows.

Kamala, a bidi worker turned senior organizer in SEWA, is today, on invitation, head of the Padmashali Samaj, a governing body in Gujarat, and helping the community take larger decisions.

Her union committee days were a training ground for her public life.

What type of organizations lead to empowerment? Not organizations that are charitable in nature or that are controlled by one person alone. The organization should belong to its women members and be democratically run by them. The dairy co-operative of the women in Rupal village fought severely with the land grabbers of the village who wanted to usurp the co-operative's fodder farm. Vanraji, the Women's Tree Growers co-operative, fought the Bharwads (shepherds) in court to retain the wasteland acquired from the government for collective plantation and fodder. Hariyali, the Vegetable Vendors co-operative, managed their funds so well that they were able to gift a building to the SEWA Union from their surplus. The Union helped the vendors to win a case in the Supreme Court establishing their right of place in the Manek Chowk Market of Ahmedabad, where they had been for the last three generations and were being evicted by the city authorities.

The organization helps the members to overcome their marginalization, and brings them into the mainstream. The SEWA Bank brought the illiterate, poor, women workers and producers into the formal banking system, being able to deal with the Reserve Bank of India at par with other co-operative or government banks. The auditors of the RBI now have to discuss banking matters with the Directors of the SEWA Bank, who represent artisans, labourers, hawkers and vendors, across the same table. This is a unique kind of exposure for both sides. There is no doubt that the SEWA Co-operative Bank would not have been able to perform effectively if there was no SEWA, the umbrella union organization of the self-employed women. Similarly, SEWA could not have fought the union conflicts if there was no stand-by such as the SEWA Bank.

The collectiveness of the organization generates tremendous power and strength for the members in their individual lives. Famidabi of Bhopal, a bidi worker, on her way to attend the bidi workers' meeting in Ahmedabad, dropped her burkha for ever. Karimabibi, leader of the *chindi* workers of Dariapur, openly confronted her own brother who represented the employers while negotiating a wage rise in the Labour Commissioner's office.

When women organize on the basic of their work self-esteem

grows and they realize that they are workers and producers, active contributors to the national income, and not merely wives, mothers, daughters and so on. SEWA Academy's study (done for ESCAP) of the 1200 SEWA field leaders found that 52% of them perceived themselves as the head of their family; 20% saw themselves as joint heads. The same self-esteem is reflected in their responses—'it is necessary to be economically strong,' 'women must own assets,' 'since women work as much as men, they should have equal rights.' All the women said that they worked longer hours than the men in the family.

Within the family, the status of the woman goes higher and her decisions are respected: 32% take decisions while buying family assets; 35% decide on son's and daughter's marriage; all have participated in public meetings and rallies, while only 15% of their men have done so; all have dealt directly with either the police, the municipality, the government and panchayat officials, while only 4% of their men have done so; 87% of the leaders decide whom to vote for and 36% have participated in political meetings.

They noted that social status within their community was also higher than before, owing to their leadership position in SEWA.

When workers/producers form their own organizations, they often break new ground, as when some teachers and mothers formed Sangini, their own child care co-operative. Health functionaries, from doctors to *dais* (midwives), formed their own co-operative, Lokswasthya. They not only 'produce and sell' health services to SEWA members, but also run drug counters at the two municipal general hospitals, thereby propagating the use of generic, rational drugs vis-à-vis drugs with brand names. Saundarya, the cleaner's co-operative, won a historic court case against the company's Employees' Union, establishing their rights to negotiate employment conditions with the company. 'We are not individual workers; we are collectively owners/partners of our co-operatives,' said the Saundarya representative while arguing in court.

Since the government is a big buyer of goods and services, a relationship has to be developed with it. After many years of persistent lobbying by SEWA and other women's organizations, the state government passed a resolution to give preference to women's co-operatives before going to the open market. This has helped to strengthen the existing women's co-operatives and create new ones.

SEWA has also tried to federate women's co-operatives in Gujarat beginning with SEWA's own 71 co-operatives. The Federation provides technical and managerial assistance to the primary cooperatives in the areas of production, storage, acquisition of raw materials, product design and the marketing of goods and services.

For us, the important fact is that the members have, through their SEWA co-operatives and unions, created sustainable employment, eliminating all middlemen. Now for some statistics. In 1995, we created 35,175 new employment opportunities worth Rs 4.5 crore, put an additional cash income of Rs 2.88 crore into the hands of 27,982 women, and built assets worth Rs 1.5 crore for 13,725 women, collectively and individually; 42,903 women benefited from the support services, namely, health care, child care, training, housing and legal aid. All the members are covered under the group insurance scheme. They are no longer dependent on the government's special employment programmes. These women, once organized, want to achieve the second freedom through their own efforts.

Liberalization

India's national economy as a whole will never grow to its full potential unless it makes use of the informal sector and working population, especially the women. It will be to our collective benefit to open up the world of finance and enterprise, and all other opportunities to the informal sector.

'Liberalization' for the small, forest produce gatherers would mean the denationalizing of their forest products and permission to sell directly in the open market. SEWA is struggling with the Forest Development Corporation (FDC) to help the women gatherers interact openly with the market. In the case of the gum collectors of Banaskantha, the gum must to be sold only to the FDC, which pays Rs 8 per kg, when the price in the open market is Rs 26. SEWA's aim is to bring down the 'liberalization' policy to the grassroots micro-enterprise level. The struggle with the Government of India is on.

Similarly, the setting up of nurseries and the planting of saplings, which are exclusive preserves of the Forest Department, have to be released from its clutches. The women who raise saplings for income have to sell them to the Department alone, which pays far below the market rate. Why?

The SEWA women's groups are struggling to be liberalized. They want to sell their saplings in the open market. The demand is to feminize our forests. The women are asking, 'Why should the Government get into nursery raising at all? Leave it to the local women/people,' they say. The nurseries and plantations will support the livelihood of millions of women who will protect and nurture the forests in turn. At the time of writing, one memorandum sent to the Prime Minister by the women gatherers was yet to be attended to.

There is still a long way to go. The forces of competitive markets sometimes appear monstrous. However, we need to constantly evaluate ourselves. We are slow. We need to be strongly united, and expand our base, so as to have enough political visibility and clout to bring change.

Poverty cannot be addressed as long as the poor remain powerless and are not themselves involved in the process. Among the poor, women are the poorest. And poverty cannot be eradicated. In fact, women have become steadily poorer in a scenario of an increasingly merciless struggle over scarce resources, and a dense concentration of wealth at the top of a steep pyramid.

Women and the environment are the 'shadow subsidies' that support all societies. Both are either undervalued or perceived as free, even while the societies continue to profit from them. After all, why hasn't women's work, vital as it is for the national economy, generated wealth for them? One answer is that women do not obtain the full benefit of their own work. They work on land that is not theirs. They manage homes from which they can be driven out at any time. Therefore, if sustainable and equitable development is to be achieved, a priority issue that must be addressed is women's rights to productive assets. SEWA's experience emphatically shows that the single most important factor responsible for the poor woman's transition to sustained self-employment is the ownership of assets. Moreover, assets in the hands of women are far safer than in the hands of men. In the year 1995, the SEWA Bank helped create assets worth Rs 4.45 crore for 33,000 women. The assets include land, work space, wells, houses, production tools, livestock, bank balances and shareholding.

The market responds only to those who have the capacity to participate in it, thus excluding the poor. There is a need to address the markets directly and to move from competitive self-interest to a larger collective that is sustainable and equitable.

Indeed, an economy that appropriates and then locks up livelihood resources through a pricing mechanism tends to breed violence as an alternative means of accessing resources. Unless there is devolution of power and resources into the hands of the people—especially poor women—there is no chance of ever eradicating poverty.

SEWA Co-operative Bank, for its members at least, eliminated the private moneylenders. Sewa's artisans' co-operatives upgraded the wage structure of landless agriculture workers (including men) in the surrounding region of Banaskantha and Surendranagar. Eighty per cent of the forced migration of these poor, assetless rural families to urban centres has been checked, as sustained work opportunities become available to them locally.

Such self-help groups have helped in freeing the poor. It is a sound approach, I think, because the poor people's own strengths and potentials are used. Thus, the base remains sound.

The group has generated the power to bargain and has lent all its members mutual strength. In effect, the women now have access, as a group, to economic areas from which they had been previously excluded.

Policy-makers must begin to recognize the efforts made by grassroots women's economic organizations to eradicate poverty. The poor are not asking for charity. What they want is the capacity to build on their own. They have waited long enough to be equipped with capital, markets, know-how and information.

Certainly, this is a long and painful process. The partners in this journey—government, non-governnment agencies, intellectuals, professions and banks—have to commit themselves to the process, and not treat the women's initiative as merely another project.

For SEWA, the core of the approach is to organize the poor women around their work and income issues, and to form their trade unions and trade co-operatives. Our experience is clear evidence that poor women are willing to build their lives through mutual support. They are keen to be educated so that they can join the mainstream; when given opportunities, they have entered the mainstream and made a difference. There is ample evidence in India, where grassroots women's initiatives have brought about a significant change in the role of education, environment, sanitation and other areas. They have also brought critical developmental issues into the open for public debate.

Movements—A Conclusion

In India, there are social movements of many kinds: the women's movement, the ecology movement, the Dalit movement, the human rights movement, the labour movement, the co-operative movement, and the wide variety of movements for better health and safety and more equitable distribution of economic resources. They all share a resistance to the present process, which has led to economic stagnation, ecological crisis and deepening deprivation.

Ours is the movement of the (poor) self-employed women—a different label again. Today, ours are the bread and butter issues of factory and home workers, farm workers, street vendors. They are all workers, producers, entrepreneurs in their own right, although they remain 'invisible' and 'deprived'. They are struggling to defend their rightful place in the economy, and to make their own decisions at both the household and the macro levels through their representative bodies.

The women must have their own resources so that they are no longer bound to the local moneylenders, contractors, landlords. They must also be equipped to shed inferiority based on gender, caste, illiteracy and poverty, by building their organized strength through self-managed, self-owned and viable economic organizations. It is organized economic strength that helps the poor to exercise their political rights.

In our movement, we constantly challenge the dominant and oppressive structures, concepts and practices.

The SEWA Union structure is developing into the SEWA Movement and changing women's working and living conditions. It owes the change, I believe, to its grassroots origin and to the ability of women to translate their values into working systems. Indian traditions are deeply embedded in these women, and SEWA's point of departure is the women themselves: their strengths, their needs and their limitations. Indian traditions are built as much on economic systems as on socio-cultural ones. SEWA women have managed to recognize the strength of self-employment in the face of the rapidly changing economy and the resulting effect on traditional social values.

SEWA has worked to transform the traditional economy and its people into a modern economy while maintaining the strengths of traditional systems. The SEWA Bank exemplifies just such a traditional-modern union. A regular part of the formal banking sector, it moves with the rhythm of the members. It creates new and vibrant models that cater specially to women—a claim most banks in the world cannot make.

Our experience shows that, whenever we build a new structure relevant to the aspirations and needs of the women, it invariably throws out a movement that gives birth to another structure relevant to the life of the women. Such structures/organizations and the movement have always complemented each other, producing women's leadership at all levels of their public interactions, be it in the area of banking, ecology, social security, legislations or management. Each SEWA intervention has its own chequered history.

How can one sum up this single-minded, five-decade journey? I believe we have all helped to shape this second freedom and set it on its course. We once stood 'against' poverty and inequality; it was much harder to be 'for' the second freedom. One may say, in conclusion, that the journey itself, as opposed to the destination, was our reward.

4

Mukul Mukherjee

Women and Work in India
A Collage from Five Decades of Independence

The Preamble to the Constitution of India promises to secure for its citizens: justice, social, economic and political; liberty of thought, expression, belief, faith and worship; and equality of status and opportunity. It is now increasingly perceived that the aspiration to achieve equality of status for women and their overall development must be rooted in a strong base of economic capability. As we stand on the threshold of a new century after five decades of existence as an independent nation, it is time to pause and take stock of our journey towards economic emancipation of women—through the looking-glass of women's work.

Domain of Women's Work

By and large women's work is spread over:

- self-employment in agriculture and household enterprise for profit,
- self-employment outside the household for profit,
- self-employment in agriculture and allied sectors for subsistence,

resource generation activities for the welfare of the household, and

- home management activities including cooking, cleaning, care of children and care of the aged and disabled.

While few women in the Indian situation would be exempt from the last two areas of work, a very large proportion of women are occupied as unpaid family helpers in agriculture or household production rather than as workers who have a tangible income commensurate with their labour.

Each of the activity categories outlined above is essential for protecting the viability of the household and for maintaining the cycles of production and reproduction for society at large. To this day, the world over, women's work is undercounted and undervalued in economic terms, though as documented in the Human Development Report for 1995, women work longer hours than men in nearly every country and of the total burden of work, women's share is 53% in developing countries and 51% in industrialised countries of the West. Predictably, standard data sources provide only a hazy mirror for reflecting the full spectrum of the work that women do, particularly in a country such as ours where three-fourths of the population is tied to the rural sector. This is mainly due to the restrictive definitions of economic activity or work adopted by data collecting and reporting systems, including our decennial population censuses and the National Sample Surveys (NSS). Since economic activity is generally equated with paid or marketed work, many types of unpaid activity, especially home-based and community-based work, tend to be excluded from national income accounting. As a result, the economic contribution of many groups, primarily women, remains unrecognized and unrewarded. Women's work also tends to be 'invisible' on account of false perceptions in the minds of both surveyors and respondents regarding what is to be accepted and recorded as work or economic activity. Some of the other problems that stand in the way of an accurate documentation of women's work relate to incomplete and outdated information and to the question of comparability of data. To avoid problems of comparability due to changes in key concepts and definitions, we have mostly referred to the census held in India in 1961 and 1991.

Table 4.1: Facets of farm women's work in West Bengal

- **Farm**
  - **Crop production**
    - **Rice**
    - **Other: e.g. betel nut**
      - seed nursery
      - transplanting
      - weeding
      - harvesting
      - threshing
      - cleaning
      - drying
      - parboiling
      - milling
      - storage
  - **Ancillary**
    - Processing of straw
    - Fodder collection
    - Home-stead gardening
    - Food processing and making rice products such as 'muri' 'gur' making
    - Maintenance of fishing nets
  - **Animal husbandry**
    - poultry
    - duck breeding
    - goat
    - dairy
    - aquaculture
- **Non-farm**
  - **Household**
    - Cooking
    - Cleaning
    - Childcare
    - Firewood collection
    - Drinking water collection
    - Preparing cow dung fuel
    - Care of old and disabled
    - Maintenance of dwelling
  - **Non-household**
    - Marketing
    - Bamboo/cane work
    - Weaving

Adapted from: B. Mitra et al., 'Women in Rice-Based Farming System. A Case Study', in C. Prasad and Shri Ram (eds), *Women in Agriculture—Technological Perspective,* New Delhi, International Federation for Women in Agriculture, Delhi 1990, Fig. 2.

Table 4.1 is an attempt to illustrate the wide-ranging diversity of women's work in rural India; it may not have changed substantially in the post-independence era.

Table 4.2 gives worker-population ratios during the last five decades. These ratios reflect the levels of work participation or people's involvement in economic activity and are viewed as important indicators of their socio-economic status, for work yields entitlements to the means of sustaining and improving living standards. Since participation in gainful work confers a measure of economic autonomy, it is also an indicator that influences women's agency.

Table 4.2: Worker-population ratios in India from census data 1951–91

Year	Total pop. (million)		Economically active pop. (%)		No. of women recorded as economically active (million)	Term used to denote economically active persons
	W	M	W	M		
1951	173.4	183.2	23.3	54.1	40.4	'Self-supporting person' and 'earning dependants'
1961	212.9	226.3	28.0	57.3	59.5	Worker
1981	329.9	353.4	20.8	53.2	66.3	'Main workers' working for six months or more and 'marginal workers' working for shorter duration during the year (1981 and 1991)
1991	407.1	439.2	22.3	51.6	89.8	

Source: Relevant census tables.

Table 4.2 is based on information available in various census reports. Census data suggest that there is a secular downtrend in women's work participation in India, especially between 1961 and 1981, even though the definition of worker becomes more inclusive with the 1961 enumeration, implying better coverage for women. There are indications of a slight recovery in recent years but the 1991 ratio of 22.3% is still short of the 1951 figure.

An alternative and perhaps more realistic picture of employment trends can be derived from the results of the periodic National Sample Surverys, as reproduced in Table 4.3 below. Here the work participation rates (WPR) rise with time for the urban population as a whole and for rural males. For rural women, though their gains during the 1980s could not be sustained, their WPR is higher in 1993–94 than in the earlier two decades. Table 4.4 provides estimates of different population groups classified by economic status and rural urban residence in terms of FMR or female-male ratio (females per 1000 males).

Table 4.3: Work participation ratios in India (%) from NSS data (usual status)

Year	Rural		Urban	
	W	M	W	M
1972–73 NSS 27th Round	31.8	54.5	13.4	50.1
1983 NSS 38th Round	34.0	54.7	15.1	51.2
1993–94 NSS 50th Round	32.8	55.3	15.4	52.0

Note: In NSS terminology, 'usual status' refers to the pattern of activity followed by a person for a relatively long period of time.

Source: Central Statistical Organisation (CSO), *Men and Women in India; 1995,* Table 20; National Sample Survey Organisation (NSSO), Revised report No. 406, June 1996, Table 4.2.2.

Table 4.4: Female-male ratio in selected population groups: 1981–91 (all-India)

	1981		1991	
	Rural	Urban	Rural	Urban
Total population	952	880	937	894
Total workers	410	149	477	170
Main workers	289	132	337	150
Marginal workers	5,756	1,715	10,608	2,625
Non-workers	1,583	1,584	1,448	1,592

Source: Govt. of India, *Women in India: A Statistical Profile—1997*, Table 5.1.

Several distinctive features of women's work participation emerge from the preceding tables:

1. The contrast that immediately strikes the eye is the much smaller component of the female population participating in gainful economic activity as compared to males throughout the five decades of independence. This gender disparity in work participation is part of a global phenomenon. In the 1980s, for example, a UN Report shows that the female WPR varied between 21% and 38%, while the male WPR varied between 48% and 60% in Japan, Indonesia and Sri Lanka. According to the same report, even in Sweden, one of the most progressive nations of the world, the WPRs for men and women were closer (at 58% and 48% respectively)—but far from equal. (ILO and INSTRAW, 19, chs 2 and 5).

2. The WPRs are systematically higher in the rural sector for both men and women but the rural-urban gap is more conspicuous in the case of women. This is partly due to limited employment opportunities available to women living in urban areas and their relative invisibility as they become part of the informal sector.

3. The rise in the FMR for main workers 1981–91 is a good augury, for this implies longer periods of regular employment for women even though women are still a small component of the working population.

4. A disquieting finding is the high and steadily rising FMR for marginal workers—those who work for less than 183 days in a year.

The implication is that even after several decades of planning and development, women's economic vulnerability continues as a major handicap.

5. A connected issue is the extent of unemployment among men and women. The unemployment rate is usually defined as the number of unemployed persons per thousand in the labour force (employed and unemployed taken together). According to NSS 50th Round (1993–94) the unemployment rate for rural and urban women was 13 and 83 respectively, the corresponding figures for men being 20 and 45. Rural women as a group thus seem to be seriously affected by chronic unemployment, and the worst affected are those rural women who are educated up to secondary or higher levels. As many as about one-fourth of educated women in the rural sector and one-fifth of educated women in the urban sector were found to be chronically unemployed in the NSS Round of 1993–94. These rates, however, are marginally lower than those observed in the 43rd Round of the NSS held in 1987–88.

Official statistics may create the impression that a large majority of Indian women are non-workers. Yet it is this hidden legion of women, performing a host of resource-generating activities, who more often than not stand as a buffer against economic deprivation, particularly in low-income households. We now have evidence from carefully conducted time allocation studies that a substantial part of what is generally relegated to the background as women's 'domestic duties' in fact belongs to the productive category. (Jain 1996). This would also be corroborated by information gathered in the course of NSS Rounds. In some of the later Rounds, women who are normally described as 'non-working' are classified separately under a special code (code 93), if they are found to pursue certain specified activities. As shown in Table 4.5, these are all critical 'family survival' activities such as collection of food, fuel and water. In 1987–88 (NSS 43rd Round), almost 88% of rural women were classified under NSS code 93. Obviously female WPRs would rise substantially if women formally counted as workers were added to those included in code 93.

Table 4.5: Percentage of rural women (5+) engaged in household duties and also participating in specified activities for household use to total women (5+) engaged in household duties

	38th Round 1983	43rd Round 1987–88
Maintenance of kitchen garden, orchard etc.	14.4	16.3
Work in household poultry	14.5	33.0
Work in household dairy	31.8	
Free collection of fish, small game etc.	24.1	21.2
Free collection of firewood etc.	43.5	40.5
Husking paddy	27.6	17.8
Preparation of gur	2.2	0.9
Grinding of foodgrains	38.2	17.5
Preparation of cow dung cakes as fuel	49.9	51.9
Sewing, tailoring etc.	17.4	19.5
Tutoring of children	3.4	3.6
Bringing water from outside household	63.0	60.8
Bringing water from outside village	33.3	3.0
Any of the above	–	87.7

Sources: S. N. Ray and Paul Jacob, 'A Statistical Profile of Indian Workforce: A Study Based on the NSS 38th Round Employment-Unemployment Survey Results', *Sarvekshana*, September 1990 (spec. no.), Statement 55.6.

There is now an increasing awareness that conventional measures of the national product or national income generated in the economy do not adequately portray the economic contribution of women. As a result, there is also a welcome interest in developing an alternate system of national accounts in which women's contribution to the net national product (NNP) can be shown separately. A recent exercise estimated that if the various facets of women's work are evaluated in money terms, their contribution to India's extended NNP would rise to about Rs 126,000 crore in 1990–

91 (at 1980–81 prices). This figure, equating women's contribution to about 44% of our NNP, is much higher than the corresponding official figure of 17% derived from conventional statistics on national income and is a strong reminder of the innate and abiding significance of women's roles in the economic life of a nation.

Against the backdrop of a consistently low female WPR at the macro level, there are considerable regional differences, even though the male WPR does not show much variation across states. The female WPR varies from more than 33% in Maharashtra and Andhra Pradesh to about 4% in Punjab and 11% in West Bengal according to latest census estimates. The intriguing phenomenon is that the pattern of inter-state variation has tended to persist. While the female WPR in Madhya Pradesh, Andhra Pradesh, Karnataka and Maharashtra usually remains well above the all-India average, in Uttar Pradesh, Bihar, Orissa and West Bengal it is consistently lower. Studies have shown that the spatial disparities with respect to female WPR are not significantly co-related to differences in cropping pattern, per capita income, literacy levels, male participation rates or percentage of SC/ST population. Perhaps the continuity in the location of zones with high and low female WPR is linked to the influence of cultural norms and traditions. Regional value systems have an important bearing on the dimensions of the working population everywhere, more so in an economy with strong rural roots which tend to enforce restrictive norms on the lifestyles of women. Therefore, wherever sociocultural norms discourage visible work participation by women, there seems to be a strong motivation—on the part of both sexes—to confine women's income-generating activities within the home.

Accent on Agriculture and Casual Labour

The sectoral composition of the working population in India during 1951–91 and their distribution by employment status are presented in Tables 4.6 and 4.7 below. These tables draw attention to the following developments in the arena of women's work:

1. As in most developing and formerly colonial economies, India's population has been primarily dependent upon agriculture as a means of livelihood. It is well known that one of the hallmarks

Table 4.6: Distribution of workers in India by industrial categories 1951–91

	1951		1961		1991	
	F	M	F	M	F	M
Cultivators	45.4	51.9	55.7	51.5	34.2	39.6
Agricultural labour	31.4	15.0	23.9	13.4	44.9	21.1
Livestock, forestry, fishing, hunting, plantations and allied activities	3.4	2.8	2.0	3.1	1.6	2.0
Mining and quarrying					0.3	0.7
Primary sector	80.2	69.7	81.6	68.0	81.0	63.4
Manufacturing, processing repairs etc. in household industry	–	–	7.9	5.7	3.5	2.1
Manufacturing etc. as above in non-household industry	6.9	9.8	1.2	5.6	3.9	8.9
Construction	0.7	1.2	0.4	1.4	0.7	2.3
Secondary sector	7.6	11.0	9.5	12.7	8.1	13.3
Trade and commerce	2.9	6.2	1.4	5.3	2.3	9.0
Transport, stage and communications	0.3	2.0	0.1	2.3	0.3	3.5
Other services	9.0	11.1	7.4	11.8	8.3	10.8
Tertiary sector	12.2	19.3	8.9	19.4	10.9	23.3
All sectors	100	100	100	100	100	100

Sources: A. Mitra, *Status of Women: Literacy and Employment*, 1979, Table 19; Govt. of India, Central Statistical Organisation (CSO), *Men and Women in India—1995*, Table 24.

of a nation's transition into higher stages of economic development is a gradual weaning away of the population from the agricultural/primary sector and the parallel expansion of employment in the secondary and tertiary sectors comprising industries and services. In most European countries today, less than one-tenth of the female labour force would be found in agriculture, about one-fifth would be in industries and the very large remainder—about 60%—would be associated with the services sector.

Table 4.7: Percentage distribution of usually employed men and women by employment status, All-India

Period	Employment status	Rural		Urban	
		W	M	W	M
NSS 32nd Round (1977–78)	Self-employed	62.1	62.8	49.5	40.4
	Regular employee	2.8	10.6	24.9	46.4
	Casual labour	35.1	26.6	25.6	13.2
NSS 50th Round (1993–94)	Self-employed	58.5	57.9	45.4	41.7
	Regular employee	2.8	8.3	28.6	42.1
	Casual labour	38.7	33.8	26.0	16.2

Source: NSSO, Revised Report No. 406, June 1996, Table 4.4.

As we look for such signs of structural change, there are positive trends so far as the male working force is concerned. The proportion of male workers attached to the agricultural sector as cultivators and agricultural labour declined from 67% to about 61% between 1951 and 1991. In sharp contrast, the primary sector continues to be the refuge of about 80% of the female working force throughout this period and the proportion of women enumerated as agricultural workers shows an increase from 77% to 79%. However, figures derived from the 1951 and 1991 censuses may not be fully comparable. It is generally accepted that valid comparisons may be based on data from censuses held in 1961 and 1991 and during this period there is a nominal decline in the proportion of women dependent on agriculture. It remains to be seen whether this notional change develops into a steady movement of women workers away from agriculture as anticipated in the course of economic progress.

2. As a corollary to what has been said above, in independent India women's involvement in industries and services has not shown a consistent improvement if we take the long time span of 40 years from the 1950s to the 1990s. This is because the continuous displacement of women from older and often decadent industries or livelihoods has not been fully compensated by their entry into modern industries and services. To take a typical instance, it has

been estimated that in the five states of Tamil Nadu, Andhra Pradesh, Gujarat, Maharashtra and Uttar Pradesh about 2.5 lakh women handloom workers lost employment between 1961 and 1971, whereas women workers in powerlooms operating in these states numbered only about 7000 in 1971 (Jain, 1984).

3. If we look at the shorter time span of 30 years, however, there seems to be a recovery in the proportion of women engaged in the services sector. More detailed study is needed to determine to what extent this represents a shift to better employment options as compared to poorly paid traditional services including work as washerwomen or domestic helpers.

4. Apart from the preponderance of agricultural work, a depressing feature of the female labour force is its growing deployment as wage labour rather than as self-employed cultivator. During 1961–91, the proportion of agricultural labourers in the female work force rose from 24% to about 44%. In 1991, agricultural labourers accounted for a much lower share in the male work force (21%). In a number of states the rising ranks of female agricultural labourers have been very marked: in Andhra Pradesh, Bihar, Orissa and Tamil Nadu more than half of women workers toiled as agricultural labourers both in 1981 and 1991. The reasons are not far to seek. A rapidly growing population pressing on a stagnant land-and-water base has eroded the scope for expanding cultivation and self-employment. At the same time, rising prices and rising costs of cultivation have compelled peasant families to resort to wage labour. As a result, large numbers of women from these families as well as from artisan households have been drawn into wage work in agriculture.

5. There is also a parallel and equally disturbing trend towards casualization of labour. Among rural male workers, the casual labour segment went up from about 22% to 34% between 1972–73 and 1993–94. For women, this proportion rose from 31% to 39%. Table 4.7 points to this transition from the self-employed to the more vulnerable casual labour status, especially noticeable in the case of rural women. Poverty being most rampant among agricultural labourers, particularly those who only have intermittent work as casual labour, women casual labourers are a clear majority among

the population below the poverty line. The rising female presence in low-paid, seasonally fluctuating wage work in agriculture as well as in non-agricultural livelihoods such as construction work or general labour is a rude reminder of the limited options for assetless poor women.

Livelihoods Outside Agriculture

An important aspect of women's employment is the extent of their integration into the organized sector of the economy, comprising government services and public sector undertakings at all levels and private sector establishments employing 10 or more persons. This is because the organized sector falls within the purview of laws and regulations that aim to provide a degree of economic security to the worker as well as scope for collective bargaining. The size of our organized sector has been growing but women still occupy only a small niche. In 1981 this sector accounted for roughly 6% of total women workers as against 11% for men. According to the latest estimates prepared by the government, even though women accounted for 15% of the 27 million employees in the organized sector, they represented only 4% of total women workers.

A stark fact, therefore, is that in India today vast multitudes of women function within the shadowy ambit of the unorganized/informal sector. They do so almost anonymously and often under very oppressive working conditions imposed by multiple layers of intermediaries. A study of the lace-makers of Narsapur in the West Godavari district of Andhra Pradesh illustrates a classic case of the 'putting out' system characteristic of the informal sector. These lace-makers were all women, selling their products for a daily pittance to lace exporters—all men. According to official reports the lace-making industry of Narsapur accounted for about 95% of the foreign exchange earnings from export of Andhra handicrafts in the 1970s. And the irony of the whole situation lies in the fact that in the world of official statistics these women workers did not exist.

Women's employment in the informal sector has increased threefold from about 30 to 90 million in the decades following 1971.

According to the National Commission on Self-Employed Women and Women in the Informal Sector, these 'unprotected' workers fall into several broad categories: (1) home-based producers including artisans and piece-rate workers, paid and unpaid family labourers; (2) petty vendors and hawkers who do not hire labour but take the assistance of family members; (3) contract labour and sub-contract labour; (4) providers of services such as washerwomen, scavengers and domestic helpers; (5) women engaged in processing work in traditional and non-traditional areas; and (6) those doing manual work like construction labour and those working in agriculture and other primary sectors. 'Among these women in petty trades, crafts and personal services, the worst cases of poverty and malnutrition were to be found'—these observations recorded in the Report of the Committee on the Status of Women in 1974 are still largely and sadly true.

As in the case of women's overall work participation levels, there are prominent regional disparities in women's access to non-agricultural employment. It would appear that their work participation outside agriculture is to a considerable extent related to certain basic capabilities that in turn are reflected in their educational attainments and progress achieved in health-related variables such as expectation of life at birth (LEB), infant mortality rate (IMR: number of infant deaths per 1000 live births), maternal mortality rate (MMR: number of maternal deaths per 100,000 live births) and total fertility rate (TFR: total number of children expected to be born alive to a woman). Table 4.8 shows that in the four states of Bihar, Madhya Pradesh, Rajasthan and Uttar Pradesh female literacy rates are much below the all-India average of 39% and the health-related variables are markedly unfavourable as compared to all-India averages (except for IMR in Bihar). In these states, not surprisingly, the percentage of non-agricultural workers in the female working force varies between 9 and 16 both in 1981 and 1991. In contrast, the same percentage rises to 46 and 58 in West Bengal and Kerala, where all the five indicators have attained much higher rankings.

Table 4.8: Socio-economic indicators for India and selected states

	Literacy rate for pop. aged 7+ (%)	LEB for women (years)	IMR per 1000 live births	Estimated MMR per one lakh live births	TFR	Non-agricultural workers as % of total women workers	
	1991	1990–2	1990–2	1982–6	1991	1981	1991
India	39.3	59.4	80	555	3.6	17.8	20.9
Andhra Pradesh	32.9	61.5	71	402	3.0	15.8	17.3
Bihar	22.9	58.3	72	813	4.4	10.2	9.0
Gujarat	48.6	61.3	69	355	3.1	14.5	14.3
Karnataka	44.3	63.6	73	415	3.1	22.1	22.5
Kerala	86.2	74.4	17	234	1.8	45.4	58.3
Madhya Pradesh	28.9	53.5	111	535	4.6	11.3	11.5
Maharashtra	52.3	64.7	59	393	3.0	15.4	17.2
Orissa	34.7	54.8	120	778	3.3	16.2	19.0
Rajasthan	20.4	57.8	84	938	4.6	10.0	12.5
Tamil Nadu	51.3	63.2	58	319	2.2	23.7	15.3
Uttar Pradesh	25.3	54.6	98	931	5.1	14.7	16.0
West Bengal	67.8	62.0	68	551	3.2	34.7	45.9

Sources: Jean Drèze and Amartya Sen, *India: Economic Development and Social Opportunity*, Appendix Table A.3, Govt. of India, *Women in India: A Statistical Profile—1997*.

Occupational Patterns and Earnings

As we review the evolution of women's work over the years, a distinct pattern of occupational segregation comes into focus: crowding of women into a narrow range of occupations marked by physical drudgery, poor reward and little scope for upward mobility. Table 4.9 provides a glimpse of such 'women-prone' concentration—sometimes described as horizontal segregation. Against a low average of about 365 women per 1000 men in the aggregate work force in 1981, the FMR in the sweated occupations of cashewnut processing, bidi-making and match-making was 2903, 1236 and 1173 respectively.

Table 4.9: Women's participation in selected occupations

NIC Code No.	Occupation	No. of women workers (thousand)	Proportion of women in total workers (%)
214	Cashewnut processing	57.7	87
219	Manufacture of food products	310.1	49
226	Bidi-making	1700.0	69
233	Cotton spinning other than mills	112.4	79
235	Handloom weaving other than Khadi	740.9	42
262	Embroidery, lace-making etc.	171.1	55
268	Manufacture of coir and coir products	163.9	77
272	Manufacture of wooden and cane baskets etc.	319.9	46
277	Manufacture of bamboo and cane furniture etc.	156.7	58
317	Manufacture of matches	122.3	80
910	Sanitation services	138.4	45
960	Domestic services	1248.5	76
961	Laundry services	732.9	48

Note: NIC refers to National Industrial Classification.
Source: Gopalan, 1995, Table 3.4.

There is also evidence of what may be described as vertical segregation. Many case studies have confirmed that women's placements generally follow a well-defined hierarchical pattern in that within a given enterprise women are typically found as unskilled production workers with very little access to skill upgradation or positions of authority and decision-making. For instance, a study of the electronics industry of Bombay and Pune noted that more than 70% of women employed in electronics units performed monotonous chores at the assembly line while those with supervisory or managerial responsibilities accounted for less than 10%. Other studies show that in the all-India context women have continued to register only a minimal presence—about 4%—in administrative, executive and managerial positions. Again, this is part of a global pattern: ILO surveys show that in most Asian countries only one woman in a thousand holds a post classified as administrative or managerial and in European countries too the number of women employed in such positions is small, not only in comparison with the female labour force but also compared to the number of men in the same occupational group.

A silver lining is that women are gradually establishing a foothold in modern sectors of India's economy that afford greater diversification and brighter prospects. In the 1980s, women's share in total employment became 17% under manufacture of chemicals and chemical products, 10% under electrical machinery including electronics, 64% under public administration and defence, and 26% under education and scientific research, from small beginnings in the 1950s. Between 1951 and 1994 women's share in university education in engineering and medicine rose from insignificant numbers to 12.5% and 6% respectively. The female-male ratio in the All-India Services was as low as 1: 66 in 1960. In 1992, women officers accounted for about 9% of the total strength of the Indian Administrative Service and Indian Foreign Service. Women have also made their mark in the Indian Police Service and in the higher judicial services. Though women's representation in Parliament and state legislatures is still far from satisfactory, their integration into panchayati raj institutions has been a remarkable phenomenon and their growing participation in decision-making at the grassroots level will surely add a new dimension to Indian women's work experience.

Table 4.10 brings out the present-day disparities in the average daily earnings of men and women in different areas of employment. Despite legislations promising equal pay for equal work, in practice men and women are seldom remunerated at par even when they perform the same tasks. NSS reports show that wage discrimination prevails even in transplantation work in agriculture, universally known as a female-intensive task. The periodical Occupational Wage Surveys too contain enough data to show that women's earnings in different types of industrial establishments usually amount to 50–70% of male earnings.

Table 4.10: Average daily earnings (Rs) of wage/salaried employees by sector (industry) of employment: 1987–88

	Rural			Urban		
	M	W	Parity index	M	W	Parity index
Agriculture, hunting forestry and fishing (0)	14.6	10.7	73.3	27.6	19.0	68.8
Mining and quarrying (1)	38.7	23.8	61.5	46.3	31.7	68.5
Manufacturing (2)	22.8	9.4	41.2	29.8	13.1	44.3
Manufacturing (3)	28.7	13.8	48.1	43.6	33.2	76.1
Electricity, gas and water (4)	36.2	45.2	124.3	50.1	43.9	87.6
Construction (5)	31.6	18.3	57.9	39.2	27.6	47.7
Trade (6)	18.0	18.4	102.2	22.6	18.4	81.4
Transport, storage and communication (7)	32.1	26.8	83.5	41.5	47.2	114.8
Finance, insurance, real estate and business service (8)	46.2	38.8	84.0	62.1	53.9	86.82
Community, social and personal services (9)	38.5	28.4	73.8	46.5	36.3	76.1
All sectors	30.1	21.6	71.8	41.9	34.8	83.1

Note: Parity index shows women's earnings as percentage of male earnings.

Source: Sarvekshana (published by NSSO), September 1990, Table 79.

Emerging Issues

Any survey of women and work in India remains incomplete without reference to several significant issues that have important socio-economic implications. In this account we are more concerned with understanding their impact from the perspective of women who have their own distinctive needs, experiences and priorities.

State Intervention in Favour of Women

Soon after independence, India chose the path of planned economic development. For a considerable time our planning process tended to take a rather narrow view of women's welfare in terms of maternal and child health and family planning. In 1974, the Report of the Committee on Status of Women in India appeared as a major landmark in creating awareness about the deep-rooted disabilities faced by women in all walks of life. A few years later India's Sixth Five Year Plan (1980–85) contained, for the first time, a separate chapter on women and development. Thereafter, the objective of raising women's social and economic status has been reiterated as a policy goal and the government has introduced a series of employment-related programmes with provision for women beneficiaries. These include Jawahar Rozgar Yojana, with 30% reservation for women in wage employment generated; Integrated Rural Development Programme (IRDP) and Training of Rural Youth for Employment (TRYSEM), both with 40% reservation for women in self-employment generated; Development of Women and Children in Rural Areas (DWCRA), fostering self-employment ventures for rural women; Support to Training and Employment Projects (STEP), aimed at assetless rural women; and Rashtriya Mahila Kosh and Mahila Samiriddhi Yojana, aimed at extending credit and saving facilities to women. Despite their small coverage as compared to women's diverse needs, these schemes represent policy initiatives in the right direction.

It is in independent India that the State has taken the first steps to ensure women's access to labour welfare and social security. Landmark legislations that also seek to improve the working conditions of women include the Minimum Wages Act of 1948, Plantation Labour Act of 1951, Factories Act of 1952, Maternity Benefits Act of 1961, Contract Labour (Regulation and Abolition) Act of 1966 and Equal Remuneration Act of 1976. A fairly comprehensive legal framework has thus come into being for delivery of basic amenities to the working population. Implementation, however, remains woefully inadequate.

Some of the factors that contribute to this unhappy situation are known, as recounted below, but not much has been accomplished by way of redressal. First, administration of labour laws is often linked to the identification of an employer-employee relationship, as the amenities are channelled through the employer. Since this relationship is difficult to pinpoint in the informal sector, its large contingent of women workers are ultimately left untouched by beneficial legislation. Furthermore, very often the benefits intended for workers under the Minimum Wages Act or the Equal Remuneration Act also prove elusive because of the rampant practice of categorizing women's tasks as being of a somewhat inferior nature and thus validating the gender differential in earnings. Finally, a paradoxical situation may arise because of two disparate outcomes of labour legislation so far as women are concerned. On the one hand, such laws are an important means of protecting their rights and interests. At the same time, women's employment is likely to be affected because of the legal responsibilities imposed on employers by way of special amenities to be provided for women including maternity benefits and creches at the workplace. Employers are thus prone to recruit women as temporary labour or home-based workers rather than as permanent employees.

The Toll of Technology

Technology can be broadly construed as 'objects, skills, techniques and processes' that facilitate human activity by raising productivity levels and reducing labour time. As technology evolves and advances in different spheres, it tends to have a differential impact on women's lives and may often appear as yet another constraint on economic options and opportunities open to women. Perhaps one of the most telling examples of pruning effect of new technology on female labour is provided by the history of grain processing in India. As manual rice husking—a virtual female monopoly—was overtaken by rice mills and husking machines, women workers were steadily and irretrievably replaced by rising male employment in these modern grain processing units. For India as a whole, while male employment in grain milling rose from 3.5 lakh in 1961 to about 5.1 lakh in 1981, women's employment declined from 2.9 lakh to 0.6 lakh during the same period. Another striking episode of technological change is India's Green Revolution, which gathered momentum within two decades of independence. The attendant innovations in seed, water and fertilizer regimes led to remarkable gains in agricultural productivity. Case studies of the Green Revolution make it clear that as men take over new tasks and processes created by advanced technology (use of tractors, pumpsets, weedicides, insecticides, etc.), female labour that was earlier employed in traditional tasks and processes becomes redundant. The resultant effects on women's earnings and economic status are quite predictable. Even in better-off households that have prospered in the wake of the Green Revolution, women may withdraw from field labour but there is hardly any respite from the heavy workload borne by them because of the extra hours devoted to processing a larger output, cooking for hired labour and managing animal husbandry. Since new technology has the potential of deepening disparities between women and men, it has to be monitored carefully, constantly and with special attention to its gender-differentiated impact.

New Economic Policy and Structural Adjustment

The 1990s have witnessed a reshaping of India's economic policies. This was in response to a crisis situation manifested in a severely strained balance of payments and a steadily rising fiscal deficit (gap between the spending and receipts of government). An integral part of the new approach to the management of the economy is the structural adjustment programme (SAP), based on the general philosophy of reducing the role of the State and strengthening the play of market forces. A number of countries in South America and Africa have now experienced the impact of SAP. Evidence collected from these countries shows that it is women who most often bear the brunt of pressures generated by SAP. As the State reduces support for education, health, housing etc. and livelihoods become insecure due to privatization and deregulation, women are increasingly compelled to stretch their paid and unpaid labour time as a form of compensation. This additional effort, combined with the known gender-based biases in access to nutrition and other resources of the household, has serious repercussions on women and young girls. Processes connected with structural adjustment in India, therefore, need to be analysed and evaluated in the context of women's experience, especially in terms of changes in their employment, earnings, work burden and access to education and health care.

AGENDA FOR ACTION

1. Our brief overview suggests that we now have a fairly large database on many aspects of women's work which can be a valuable guide for policy and programme formulation. Nevertheless, gaps remain and they need to be addressed systematically. For instance, in the absence of scientific studies dealing with women's productivity in different spheres of activity, quite often arbitrary judgements are made about their performance as workers, resulting in lower incomes and lower economic status as compared to men. Secondly, we need many more time allocation surveys for a better understanding of the nature and intensity of women's work, on the lines of existing studies based on this methodology. Thirdly, though researchers have drawn attention to the nutritional deficiencies suffered by women because of their multiple role as parent, producer and home manager, this issue needs much wider exposure as also the issue of health hazards faced by women working under stressful conditions in different occupations.

2. Our review also suggests that mobilization and collective action on the part of women can be an effective mode of promoting their rightful causes. According to the Labour Bureau of the Government of India, about 4600 trade unions were registered in 1951–52 with 6% women members. By 1981, the number of such unions rose to more than 37,000 but membership of women was almost stagnant at 7%.

As underscored in many accounts, workers' unions tend to be preoccupied with issues that carry weight for their male membership. In order to assume a more equitable role, trade union leadership has to respond to women's concerns with greater sensitivity, just as women have to strengthen their involvement in unionization.

3. We have seen that the organized sector of our economy absorbs a very small proportion of our labour force and that the unorganized sector hardly affords a satisfactory work environment, especially where women are concerned. In this situation, group

activity in the shape of producers' co-operatives or self-help groups can become an important alternative in needy women's search for employment, income and autonomy. Organizations such as the Self-Employed Women's Association (SEWA), the Working Women's Forum (WWF) and the Gujarat State Women's Cooperative Federation have already made seminal contributions in this area. Their initiatives need to be replicated widely across regions and vocations.

4. It must now be recognized that women's ability to reach out for more rewarding pursuits is almost always constrained by their involvement in the elemental task of household management—so easily taken for granted by society. Therefore, the concern for employment generation for women must be matched by an equal concern for planning and delivery of 'back up' services that could make a dramatic difference in the life of a working woman—for example, community kitchens and recreation centres, child care facilities, labour-saving aids at home and basic amenities at the work place.

5. Finally, it is quite clear that development of women's capabilities, particularly their skill development, will continue to be a major area of concern whether in the context of new technology per se or of SAP, which often brings more sophisiticated methods of production. When at least primary education is now needed for training and participation in modern occupations, a distressing feature of our female labour force is the pervasive lack of literacy and vocational skills. It must be realized that apart from extending economic opportunities, higher literacy and higher skills also create the capability for resisting oppression and articulating the need for supportive public action—all of which are crucial issues for working women. As the present regime of liberalization opens up new sectors of economic activity and consequently new areas of skill formation, the entire system of providing functional literacy and vocational training for women has to be reoriented so that they are adequately equipped to enter new avenues for employment and transcend barriers based on gender.

REFERENCES

1. Gopalan, Sarala, *Women and Employment in India*, Har Anand, New Delhi, 1995.
2. Gothoskhar, Sujata, 'Women Paid Workers and Labour Unions', in R. Sudarshan et al. (eds), *Sites of Change: The Structural Context of Empowering Women*, Friedrich Ebert Siftung (FES) and UNDP, New Delhi, 1996.
3. International Labour Organisation (ILO) and United Nations Research and Training Institute (INSTRAW), *Women in Economic Activity: A Global Statistical Survey (1950–2000)*.
4. Jain, Devaki, 'Valuing Work: Time as a Measure', *EPW*, 26 October 1996.
5. Jain, L. C., 'The Phenomenon, Scale and Process of Displacement of Women in Traditional Industries', paper presented at Workshop on Women, Technology and Forms of Production, IDS, Madras, 30 October 1984.
6. Kulshreshtha, A. C. and Gulab Singh, 'Domestic Product by Gender in the Framework of 1993 SNA', *EPW*, 26 October 1996.
7. Mies, Maria, 'Dynamics of Sexual Division of Labour and Women Lacemakers of Narsapur', *EPW*, March 1981.
8. Mukherjee, Mukul, 'Impact of Modernisation on Women's Occupations: A Case Study of Bengal', in J. Krishnamurty (ed.), *Women in Colonial India: Work, Survival and the State*, OUP, Delhi, 1989.
9. Ramanamma, A. and U. Bombawala, *Women in Indian Industry*, Delhi, 1987.

5

Leela Visaria

Deficit of Women in India
Magnitude, Trends, Regional Variations and Determinants

Introduction

The deficit of women in the Indian population has been known at least since the first synchronous census was conducted in the British-occupied parts of India in 1881. The deficit has not only continued but has got worse over time according to each successive census, with the exception of the 1981 census, when the masculinity ratio of the total population declined a little. According to the last census, conducted in 1991, there were 32 million more men than women in India, when in most countries of the world, women outnumber men by 3% to 5%. There are 95 to 97 males per 100 females in Europe, the United States of America and Japan, but 88 males per 100 females in the former Soviet Union due to heavy male mortality in the wars (Coale, 1991: 917). India shares with China the phenomenon of deficit of women or masculinity ratio indicating some 6% to 8% more men than women in the population. Both societies have traditionally been patrilineal and men have enjoyed a much higher status than women.

The continued deficit of women in the Indian population has

aroused much attention about the causes or conditions that have led to such a situation. Before examining the causes, or the factors contributing to the masculinity of population, the paper will first discuss the magnitude of the deficit over time, and the regional differentials in the deficit of women in India. Factors leading to the deficit of women or excess of men in the Indian population, such as under-enumeration of women (or over-enumeration of men), sex-selective out-migration of women (or in-migration of men), sex ratio at birth, and higher mortality experienced by women than men at several ages, including the effects of practices such as female infanticide and female foeticide are examined.

MAGNITUDE OF DEFICIT OF WOMEN

The commissioners of the censuses conducted during 1891–1911 in the Indian subcontinent noted that there were about 1.5% to 2% fewer women than men in the population counts of those years. According to the 1901 census, for example, men outnumbered women by about 3.4 million in the total population of 238 million. The census commissioners of that period found the deficit of women to be quite anomalous compared to the situation observed in the European populations with which they were familiar, and they dwelt on this issue at great length in their narrative reports. Not only did they compare the trends in the sex ratios of population over time, they estimated age-specific sex ratios to discern whether there was any pattern in under-reporting or under-counting of women at certain ages and whether it could be attributed to social or cultural practices related to age at marriage, seclusion of women from strangers (or enumerators), etc. Female infanticide, practised by certain caste groups in some areas of the country, was also discussed at great length in several census reports. Similarly, sex ratio at birth and the possible factors that can lead to more masculine sex ratio at birth in the Indian population also received considerable attention in the narrative reports (Census of India, 1971, Census Centenary Monograph No. 6).

Table 1 shows the population by sex, deficit of women in absolute number (or the difference between the total male and female population) and as percentage of total population for

Table 5.1: Population by sex, deficit of women in absolute numbers and as per cent of total population, and sex ratio of population of India, 1901–91

Census year	Total population (in millions) Persons	Male	Female	Deficit of women	% Deficit of women	Sex ratio (males per 1000 females)
1901[a]	238.2	120.8	117.4	3.4	1.4	1029
1911	252.1	128.4	123.7	4.7	1.9	1038
1921	251.4	128.6	122.8	5.8	2.3	1047
1931[b]	278.7	142.9	135.8	7.1	2.5	1052
1941[b]	318.4	163.7	154.7	9.0	2.8	1058
1951	361.1	185.5	175.6	9.9	2.7	1056
1961	439.2	226.3	212.9	13.4	3.1	1062
1971	548.2	284.1	264.1	20.0	3.7	1075
1981	683.3	353.4	329.9	23.5	3.4	1071
1991	846.3	439.2	407.1	32.1	3.8	1079

Notes: [a] Sex distribution of population of Chandannagar in West Bengal, Gonda in Uttar Pradesh, and Pondicherry was not available. The total population figure shown here is exclusive of the population of these territories.

[b] Sex distribution of population of Pondicherry for 1931 and 1941 was not available. The total figures shown here are exclusive of Pondicherry's population.

Sources: Census reports for various census years.

present-day India, beginning with the 1901 census. The table also gives the sex ratio (male per 1000 females) of the population in successive censuses. It is evident from the data that the deficit of women has progressively increased. From a situation when women were a little less than 2% fewer in the total population at the turn of the century, the deficit of women has increased to nearly 4% by 1991. In absolute number, men in the population count have increasingly outnumbered women such that the deficit of women has widened from less than 4 million at the beginning of the century to 20 million in 1971 and to 32 million in 1991. The magnitude of the deficit of women has increased at a faster rate than that of the population. The progressive deficit of women is evident in the sex ratio of the population: the masculinity ratio has increased from 1029 in 1901 to 1079 in 1991.

A slight decline in the masculinity ratio of the population was observed between 1971 and 1981 and was seen as a promising sign that the deficit of women in India was finally beginning to decline. When, on the other hand, the 1991 census reported a small rise in the sex ratio from 1071 in 1981 to 1079, it was widely interpreted as a major cause for concern and indicative of a lack of improvement in the status of women by the demographers as well as women's groups in the country. However, it was important to know, at a disaggregated level whether the deficit was noted throughout the country, whether there were rural-urban differences, etc. before attributing the decline in the number of women to their worsening health status. In the next section, an effort is made to understand the regional diversity in the sex ratio of the Indian population.

Regional Variations in the Sex Ratio

In a continental country like India, there are bound to be variations in the extent of deficit of women just as there are sizeable regional variations with regard to other population parameters such as birth rate, death rate and infant mortality rate. Table 2 shows the sex ratios of the major Indian states for selected census years. They clearly indicate that there is a regional pattern in the deficit of women as well as in the trend over time in the sex ratio within each state.

It is evident from Table 2 that the deficit of women in the southern states of Kerala and Tamil Nadu and to a lesser extent in Andhra Pradesh and Karnataka has tended to be much less than that observed in the northern states of Haryana, Punjab, Rajasthan and Uttar Pradesh. The southern states and the northern states belong to two distinct contiguous regions. The states of Gujarat and Maharashtra in Western India have had a slightly smaller deficit of women than the national average.

Over time the sex ratio has become more masculine (with the exception of the 1981 census, as indicated earlier) in practically all the states with the exception of Himachal Pradesh, Punjab and

Rajasthan. In these states the masculinity of population was quite marked in the earlier censuses, over time it has become less masculine. The improvement in Punjab and Rajasthan is somewhat modest but Himachal Pradesh has shown a remarkable decline in the masculinity ratio. This relatively small mountainous state, whose population until recently depended largely on subsistence farming, has witnessed a marked economic development due to horticulture and tourism. Some population groups in Himachal Pradesh have been practising polyandry and women have traditionally enjoyed equal status with men. The contribution of these factors along with

Table 5.2: Trends in sex ratios in the major states of India, for selected census years between 1901 and 1991

States	1901	1951	1971	1981	1991
Andhra Pradesh	1015	1014	1023	1026	1029
Assam[a]	1088	1152	1116	–	1083
Bihar	949	1010	1048	1057	1098
Gujarat	1048	1050	1071	1062	1071
Haryana	1153	1148	1153	1149	1156
Himachal Pradesh	1131	1096	1044	1028	1035
Jammu and Kashmir[a]	1134	1145	1139	1121	–
Karnataka	1017	1035	1045	1038	1042
Kerala	996	972	984	963	965
Madhya Pradesh	1010	1034	1063	1063	1074
Maharashtra	1022	1063	1075	1067	1071
Orissa	964	978	1012	1019	1030
Punjab	1202	1185	1156	1138	1134
Rajasthan	1105	1086	1098	1088	1099
Tamil Nadu	958	993	1022	1024	1027
Uttar Pradesh	1067	1099	1138	1130	1138
West Bengal	1058	1156	1122	1098	1090
All India	1029	1057	1075	1071	1079

Note: Sex ratios are estimated as number of males per 1000 females.
[a] The 1981 census was not conducted in Assam and the 1991 census was not conducted in Jammu and Kashmir.

Source: Census of India, 1992: 86–86. 102–105.

the rapid rise in literacy and educational levels of both men and women in the last two decades to the declining masculinity ratio needs to be ascertained. Also, one needs to ascertain whether the rapid increase in the level of education has led to increasing migration of men to other parts of the country in search of employment.

During 1981 and 1991, the masculinity of the Indian population increased by between 3 and 8 per 1000 in all the major states of India, except for Bihar, Madhya Pradesh, Orissa and Rajasthan, where the increase in masculinity was over 1%. Bihar recorded a maximum of 3.9% deficit of women during this decade. On the other hand, the situation improved a little in West Bengal and in Punjab, which has had one of the most adverse sex ratios in the country throughout the 20th century. The reasons for the regional differences in the magnitude of deficit of women need to be fully explored.

Reasons for the Deficit of Women in India's Population

Ever since the deficit of women was noted in the population of India, there have been various hypotheses advanced to explain the deficit and various factors have been explored to understand why India's population is masculine. The possible reasons are: under-enumeration of women in Indian population count, out-migration of females, greater excess of males at birth, due to various factors, including female foeticide, and greater mortality, including female infanticide, experienced by Indian women compared to men. The likely contribution of each of these factors in explaining the deficit of women is analysed in the following sections.

Under-enumeration of Women in Indian Censuses

One of the first possibilities explored by the Indian census commissioners to understand the deficit of women in the population related to the differential enumeration of population of males and females. The British census commissioners of the 1891 and 1901 censuses, for example, thought that the 'concealment' of women was not at all unlikely in the Indian setting . 'It is conceivable that females may be omitted from the return, either because their male relatives regard them as of no importance in connection with an enquiry, such as the census, instituted by the Government; or because they have some special reasons for not mentioning them, as in the case of girls who have reached the age of puberty while still unmarried; or because they connect the census with some imaginary ulterior motive on the part of Government, such as the desire to provide wives for its sepoys' (Census of India, 1972: 40).

Although it was hard to find evidence to support any of these hypotheses, the early census reports did notice that the deficiency of women occurred at certain ages. The censuses, for example, reported fewer girls in the age group 10–14, compared to the number of boys. Again, the efforts to understand this peculiar phenomenon led to a hypothesis that in a situation where child marriages are prevalent, there might be a tendency either not to report the presence of young girl who was already married or a child bride in the family to the census enumerators or to inaccurately report her age as older than the real age.

There was some evidence for the latter practice. The number of women in the next age groups of 15–19 and 20–24 tended to be larger than that of the young men. However, the misreporting of ages, done either willfully to conceal child brides and report them as older than their real ages or because ages were not known accurately, cannot lead to deficit of women. It implies that the women 'missing' at certain ages are there in the population; they are included in the older age groups or wrongly counted by the enumerators as older girls.

The possibility of any significant omission of women from the Indian censuses up to 1961 was dismissed after a careful scrutiny of data and evidence by Visaria (1971). However, the issue of the possibility of under-counting of women has resurfaced again after the 1991 census results. The progressive decline in the sex ratio in certain regions of the country has led some scholars to state that there has been an under-counting of women in certain backward states and districts of the country in the wake of decline in their law and order situations. The case in point is Bihar, the second most populous state in India, with a population of 86 million at the 1991 census count. As indicated earlier and shown in Table 2, increase in the masculinity of Bihar's population has been the sharpest among all the major states of India.

In Bihar, the sex ratio rose between 1981 and 1991 by 41 points from 1057 to 1098 (or by 3.9%) and the change was largely confined to rural areas. Almost 51% of the decline in the proportion of women during 1981–91 in the country is attributable to Bihar. It is difficult to postulate a sizeable under-counting of women in Bihar alone, although it is not impossible. The post-enumeration check conducted by the Office of the Registrar General has not shown a significant difference in the net omission rates by gender in the eastern zone, which includes Bihar. The number of households in the sample selected for post-enumeration check was not large enough to make state-level estimates (Census of India, 1991: 9). On the other hand, according to the National Family and Health Survey conducted in Bihar, with a sample of 4748 households, the de jure household population had a more balanced sex ratio (1046 males per 1000 females) (IIPS, 1995: 12, 17) than was reported by the 1991 census (1098 males per 1000 females), implying that females may have been under-counted in Bihar in 1991. Some press reports suggest a practice of female infanticide in parts of Bihar (specifically in Katihar district), but the subject needs detailed micro-level research (Times of India, 1995).

However, the possibility of under-counting of women in the 1991 census in urban areas and in some parts of the country where a volatile political and social climate prevailed prior to the census, continues to find favour with some scholars, especially in the context of faster increase in life expectancy of women compared to men (Srinivasan, 1994).

Sex-Selective Migration

Besides differential enumeration, the ratio of males to females in a population is also affected by different rates of gains or losses due to migration. Typically, urban areas in India have a more masculine population because men tend to dominate the migration flows to urban areas. For the country as a whole, sex differentials in international migration would be an important determinant of the sex composition of the population.

However, relative to the size of India's population, international migration from or to India has been quite small. The small streams of emigration from India have largely been dominated by men, leading to deficit of men in the population. More men than women have tended to emigrate from India both to the developed countries and to the oil-rich Gulf countries. The majority of the men migrating to the developed countries are generally joined by women through marriage at a later date. The migrants to the Persian Gulf region have been mostly men because of the opportunities for unskilled and semi-skilled work in the construction industry in the Gulf region. However, not many of the Indians in the Gulf countries seem to aim at absorption and assimilation in the countries where they work but wish to and do return to the home country, once the contractual obligations are fulfilled.

Immigration from other countries that brings a preponderance of males can result in some masculinity of the population. India has a virtually open border with Nepal, from where people, mostly men, come into the country in search of work. The 1981 census reported about a half million legal Nepalese living in India (the figure from the 1991 census has not yet been published). It is difficult to estimate the number of illegal immigrants from Nepal into India, most of whom are also believed to be men. On the other hand, the influx of people from Bangladesh, where the level of living is lower than in India, has tended to consist of families. The indirect evidence for this inference is based on the fact that the masculinity of population in the border districts of West Bengal, Meghalaya and Tripura has not increased in spite of their high population growth (see Kundu and Sahu, 1991). 'Indian Tamils' have migrated into India from Sri Lanka to escape from a civil war that has raged there for several years. However, no firm estimates are available on the quantum of migration, and the information on the age-sex composition of the migrant population is virtually non-existent.

The total number of migrants into India is believed to be small and is unlikely to account for any sizeable change either in the growth rate or in the observed sex composition of the total population of India. Since the emigration and immigration tend to be to or from certain small regions such as a few villages or a block, their impact on the population of those areas can be quite significant. Immigration of people has typically been to the areas bordering the countries from where the migration takes place. Most of the immigrants from Sri Lanka are concentrated in a few districts in Tamil Nadu because of linguistic and cultural affinity. Similarly, Bangladeshi immigrants are concentrated in the districts neighbouring Bangladesh in Assam, Meghalaya and West Bengal. In spite of linguistic and cultural similarities, the influx of immigrants into these areas has led to some tensions between them and the local residents regarding claims on limited work opportunities and resources.

Sex Ratio at Birth

Besides the differences in sex-specific under-counting, or sex-specific migration, the sex ratio of a population is also a function of the sex ratio at birth and the sex ratio at death. The sex ratio at birth is, however, a biologically or genetically determined phenomenon and ranges from 102 to 107 male births to 100 female births around the world. Unless there is a conscious effort at intervention by human beings, the sex ratio at birth is not found to change even over a fairly long period of time such as a century according to the available evidence.

All the same, the early census commissioners in India, who were intrigued by the deficit of women in the Indian population, explored all possible theories to understand the phenomenon. Excess of males at birth was one issue which received attention from them and besides the genetic or racial factor, they considered factors such as climate, season of gestation, food, or practice of consanguineous marriages or of polyandry, which could possibly influence the sex of the child at conception. However, they could not find evidence in support of any of these factors and therefore dismissed them as not having any effect whatsoever on the sex ratio at birth of the Indian population (Census of India, 1972).

After the result of the 1991 census, however, the issue of sex ratio in India becoming more masculine has resurfaced and serious thought was given to the observation that the proportion of boys among live births or the sex ratio at birth has risen in India at least during the 1980s (Census of India, 1991). The reported change is more likely to reflect the effect of some human interventions including some sex-selective reporting, misclassification or female-selective termination of pregnancy. The contribution of this last factor on the sex ratio at birth needs a more careful analysis of data from various sources, such as those available in the Sample Registration System, census and birth records from hospitals or institutions. Information on about 35,000 births that occurred between 1987 and 1992, in three hospitals in Delhi indicated that the sex ratio at birth went up from 106 in the initial year to 109 in the end year (Raju and Premi, 1992). Whether this reflects a human intervention in the form of some conscious effort to kill female foetuses or normal fluctuations is a moot point because the series is very short and the changes are not dramatic. However, we need more evidence, such as the sex composition of the live births that women already have, to substantiate the effect of sex-selective foeticide on sex ratio at birth.

Female Foeticide

The sex ratio at birth can be altered by identifying the sex of the foetus and then destroying the foetus of the unwanted sex. Technology is available in the forms of amniocentesis and chorionic biopsy, which can, through chromosomal analysis, help detect the sex of the foetus. The chorionic biopsy is a relatively simple test and is available through private sources at many places in India. It has also become relatively inexpensive, can be conducted with a pregnancy of about 8 weeks and is considered to be 90% to 95% accurate. As a result, in areas where discrimination against women is quite widespread, the clinics offering this service have mushroomed.

The feminists, activists and many other concerned citizens have from time to time raised an alarm at the trend of aborting female foetuses after the detection. Some have even voiced their concern that it will have, in the long run, a very adverse effect on the sex ratio of the population (Patel, 1988). However, while raising an alarm against a practice that undermines the value of women in Indian society, the long- and short-term effect of sex-selective foeticide on the sex ratio should be examined as a careful empirical exercise. Also, we need more empirical data on the extent of female foeticide, the demographic, socio-economic status of the women who undergo the sex-selective abortion and other factors. It may be argued that many other processes that are at work should bring about positive changes in the status of Indian women such that practices such as female foeticide are not resorted to.

Sex Ratio of Juvenile Population

Since the technology of amniocentesis has become available on a large scale in the last 10 years, the sex ratio of the population has been calculated from the 1991 census data for the age group 0–6 and 7+ to understand what is happening at the macro level and whether the data reflect the use of such techniques. The 0–6 sex ratios at the state level, as shown in Table 3, present an interesting pattern. (Admittedly, sex ratio is a crude measure to understand the process through which people resort to sex-selective foeticide because the ratio also reflects the traditional measures of discrimination.) The data indicate that in the contiguous area from Kerala and extending up to West Bengal, the sex ratio of children aged 0.6 is very similar and ranges between 103 and 104. In Tamil Nadu, Maharashtra and Madhya Pradesh it is between 105 and 106.

Tamil Nadu is a surprise, because the sex ratio of its total population is much less masculine than that of India, excepting for Kerala. Recently there have been reports from parts of Tamil Nadu and some hard evidence about female infanticide and systematic killing of girl babies (George et al., 1992). How widespread the frank form of female infanticide or subtle form of neglecting the girl babies is, cannot be ascertained. There are no systematic district-level or state-level data to support or refute the prevalence of such practices.

North of Maharashtra and Madhya Pradesh are three major states of Gujarat, Rajasthan and Uttar Pradesh, where the sex ratio of children 0–6 years ranges between 108 and 109. This level of masculinity in sex ratio of children, very likely, reflects the neglect of female children in an open manner. Whether the lowering of the number of female children is achieved through the traditional methods of denying medical care in the event of an illness, or through infanticide or through female foeticide is difficult to ascertain. Very likely, in groups that devalue women, people resort to any or all of these methods. It is interesting to note that in Gujarat the sex ratio of the 7+ population is less masculine and in Rajasthan the two sex ratios are nearly the same. (In the less masculine sex ratio areas, the sex ratios of 7+ population are higher than that of children.) Uttar Pradesh is an exception to this, in the sense that the sex ratio of 7+ population is higher than that of the juvenile population.

Table 5.3: Sex ratio (males per 1000 females) of population by age: India and major states, 1991

Major states	Total			Rural			Urban		
	All ages	0–6	7+	All ages	0–6	7+	All ages	0–6	7+
India	1079	1060	1084	1065	1054	1068	1119	1069	1128
Andhra Pradesh	1029	1030	1029	1023	1021	1024	1043	1040	1044
Assam	1084	1030	1099	1071	1024	1083	1194	1047	1220
Bihar	1098	1040	1113	1085	1041	1097	1185	1052	1215
Gujarat	1070	1080	1069	1053	1068	1051	1103	1100	1103
Haryana	1156	1140	1160	1157	1140	1162	1152	1131	1156
Himachal Pradesh	1025	1050	1020	1010	1047	1002	1203	1106	1219
Karnataka	1042	1040	1042	1027	1038	1025	1076	1052	1080
Kerala	965	1040	953	964	1044	952	967	1044	957
Madhya Pradesh	1074	1050	1080	1060	1046	1064	1120	1068	1131
Maharashtra	1071	1060	1074	1028	1050	1024	1143	1070	1157
Orissa	1030	1040	1029	1012	1032	1008	1154	1053	1173
Punjab	1134	1140	1132	1127	1139	1124	1152	1154	1152
Rajasthan	1099	1090	1101	1088	1089	1088	1137	1101	1145
Tamil Nadu	1027	1060	1023	1019	1058	1013	1041	1047	1040
Uttar Pradesh	1138	1080	1153	1132	1078	1146	1162	1077	1183
West Bengal	1090	1040	1102	1063	1032	1071	1165	1047	1183

* Excludes Jammu and Kashmir.
Source: Census of India, 1991.

The worst areas of India are the twin states of Punjab and Haryana and the union territory of Delhi. Traditionally, this is also the region with highly masculine sex ratio. But a sex ratio of its child population of around 114 boys to 100 girls clearly reflects that the tradition of neglecting female children or finishing them off survives in spite of modernization and economic development. This is also the region where advertisements for sex determination tests and for induced abortions are reportedly seen even in rural areas and facilities for performing them are readily available. Instead of resorting to traditional ways of killing of girls or neglecting them, it is possible that people are taking advantage of the new technology, which may also be more safe. It is, however, a sad commentary on the status of women in this part of India.

Sex Differentials in Mortality

It has been convincingly demonstrated that the primary factor contributing to the deficit of women in India has been an anomalous excess female mortality. The same feature was evident in the past among the Indian communities abroad and other South Asian countries but hardly seen in the developed countries (Visaria, 1972). In Western Europe, the United States of America and Japan, women experience lower mortality than men at most ages and therefore enjoy greater longevity than men. Mortality data from these countries have shown that when the same health care and nutrition are available to children and adults of both sexes, male mortality rates are higher than that of females at all ages (Coale, 1991). This situation arises because women are considered biologically stronger than men, suffer much less from illnesses such as heart ailments, are less prone to accidents and experience much lower mortality arising from alcohol consumption or cigarette smoking. In India, as discussed below, the higher mortality experienced by women from birth almost until the end of their reproductive period has largely contributed to the high masculinity ratio in population, and the discriminatory treatment received by girls and women more than offsets their natural advantage over men.

The evidence for sex differentials in mortality is provided by a comparison of the ratio of the crude death rates of males and females with the ratio of males to females in the populations of each state.

In the states where the female death rates are especially high relative to the male rates, the male population outnumbers the female population by a rather large margin. This phenomenon has persisted even in recent years, as evident from both the 1981 and 1991 census data. In Punjab and Haryana, for example, high masculinity of population is closely associated with higher mortality of females than that of males. On the other hand, the ratio of male to female mortality is nearly normal in Kerala, where women outnumber men in the population.

The persistence of this anomalous situation in India is indicative of the presence of social practices and cultural ethos that undervalue daughters or women. The presence of such traditions is stronger in some states than in others. Among the several practices that adversely affect women's health and lead to deaths, one can list unwillingness to seek health care for young girls or women during illness including at the time of difficult child birth, or seeking care when it is too late. In some parts of the country, female infanticide continues to be openly practised.

There is sufficient evidence from a carefully monitored prospective study undertaken in 11 villages in Khanna tehsil of Punjab that female mortality was lower than male mortality in the first five or six months after birth when the babies are breastfed. Once supplementation begins, female death rates stride ahead of that of males (Wyon and Gordon, 1971). This may arise from not providing enough nutrition to girls and/or not providing timely health care to them in the event of an illness. In a prospective study undertaken almost three decades after the Khanna study was conducted, in rural areas of Gujarat, where children under five years of age were weighed every month for three years, and where all deaths were closely monitored and the causes ascertained, there was no evidence of discrimination in provision of nutrition to boys and girls. What was, however, striking was that among the terminally ill children, girls tended to be treated with home remedies in the initial few days and were taken to a health facility only when their condition worsened. Boys, on the other hand, were rushed to the health care facility almost immediately after an illness was noticed (Visaria, 1988). In the period of 30 years the practices had not changed, girls continued to be undervalued compared to the boys.

Another dimension of the neglect of providing care to girls is brought out by a more recent study in the same 11 villages from the Khanna tehsil. The death rate among girls under five years of age who had an older sister, as opposed to those who did not, was nearly 50% higher than among boys (Das Gupta, 1987). This is indicative of the fact that the neglect of second and higher order female children is behavioural in nature and is willful. The second and subsequent daughters are not wanted by the Kallars of Madurai district in the southern state of Tamil Nadu also, who sometimes resort to poisoning their second-born or higher order daughters (George et al., 1992).

The other side of the neglect of female children or of excess mortality of females is the preference for male children. There is considerable evidence of son preference in India, particularly in the northern region (Miller, 1981; Basu, 1989; Rastogi and Raj Kumari, 1992). The data collected by the National Family Health Survey also confirmed the existence of a strong son preference. Overall, the respondents' preferred family size consists of 1.6 sons, 1.1 daughters and 0.2 children of either sex (IIPS, 1995: 195). In most micro-level surveys, on the other hand, the attitudinal questions on the subject have indicated that the ideal sex composition of children desired by couples is two boys and one girl. The practice of female foeticide is clearly linked to the son preference.

It is sometimes argued that the success of India's family welfare programme, and the decline in fertility, would help improve the sex ratio. However, it is a moot point and needs to be explored with more research. Success in family planning programme or decline in fertility is indicative that parents are having fewer children. However, without being able to influence the son preference or being able to control the techniques by which couples can achieve the children of their choice, the modern measures, which are designed to help couples to have healthy children, can only accentuate the deficit of women (Oldenberg, 1992; Das Gupta and Mari Bhat, 1995).

Conclusion

The evidence presented in this paper indicates that the major factor explaining the deficit of women in India continues to be their excess mortality. True, life expectancy at birth has increased at a faster rate for females than for males, implying that women have gained in real terms from health care. However, compared to many developed countries where female life expectancy is 6 to 8 years higher than that of males, in India we have only recently reached a stage where the life expectancy of females has just about edged above that of males. (According to the Life Tables prepared on the basis of the Sample Registration data for the period 1989–93, expectancy of life at birth for males and females was 59.0 and 59.7 years, respectively). This improvement even extended into Punjab and Haryana, where excess female mortality was particularly marked in the past. Also, female life expectancy exceeded that of males in urban areas throughout India (Office of the Registrar General, India, 1996).

The modest gain achieved in female life expectancy in recent years cannot wipe out the overall deficit of women, which is a cumulative process of neglect of women over several decades. Nationwide, female deaths still exceeded the male death rates at every age from infancy through age 34 in 1991. This pattern was reversed for Indian women aged 35 and over. While maternal mortality is still relatively high in India and does contribute to the deficit of women, excess mortality among young girls in the ages one to four accounts for a much greater share of the deficit. As indicated earlier, baby girls often receive much less health care and attention from their parents than do boys. In families living in or close to poverty, this neglect can have dire consequences. Girls are more likely than boys to become ill and die during childhood, as reflected in their higher childhood mortality rates.

After the 1991 census results were published, a widespread concern was voiced by women's groups and others about the worsening sex ratio of the Indian population. One of the measures initiated by women's groups was to urge the government to ban the use of sex determination tests for detection of the sex of the foetus. The government succeeded in banning the use of sex determination tests for purposes other than the detection of genetic abnormalities, which can be conducted only in approved institutions. In 1994 the Indian Parliament passed the Pre-Natal Sex Determination Technique (Regulation and Prevention of Misuse) Bill. However, without the co-operation of medical personnel, implementation of such legislation has proved a most difficult task. The extent to which sex ratio at birth is being altered through human intervention, however, needs to be carefully studied.

A more long-lasting, although less immediate, solution would be to attack the reasons why parents want to avoid having girls or why they have a preference for sons. Admittedly, the neglect of female children occurs at the household level and it is very difficult to employ any measures to directly influence the behaviour of the members of the household. Preference for sons, for example, cannot be removed easily from the mind-set of people. Only indirect measures such as providing of widespread education to all children, designing a curriculum that is gender-sensitive and emphasizes the worth of daughters or women in family and society, and spreading these messages in innovative ways through mass media, can enhance the status of women in India society.

REFERENCES

Basu, Alaka, M., 'Is Discrimination in Food Really Necessary for Explaining Sex Differentials in Childhood Mortality?', *Population Studies*, 17(2), 1989, pp. 193–210.

Census of India, 1971 *Changes in Sex Ratio*, Census Centenary Monograph No. 6, by D. Natarajan, New Delhi, Office of the Registrar General, 1972.

Census of India, 1991 *Final Population Totals: Brief Analysis of Primary Census Abstract* Series 1, India, Paper 2, Controller of Publications, New Delhi, 1993, pp. 11–12.

Census of India, 1991, Series 1, India, Paper 1 of 1994, *Report on Post Enumeration Check*, New Delhi, 1994.

Census of India, 1992. *Census of India*, 1991, Paper 2 of 1992, New Delhi, Office of the Registrar General, 1992.

Coale, Ansley, J., 'Excess Female Mortality and the Balance of the Sexes in the Population: An Estimate of the Number of "Missing Females", *Population and Development Review*, 17(3), 1991, pp. 517–213.

Dahlburg, John-Thor, 'The Fight to Save India's Baby Girls', *Los Angeles Times*, 22 February 1994, pp. A1–A2.

Das, Gupta, Monica, 'Selective Discrimination Against Female Children in Rural Punjab, India', *Population and Development Review*, 13(1), 1987, pp. 77–100.

Das, Gupta, Monica and P. N. Mari Bhat, 'Fertility Decline and Increased Manifestation of Sex Bias in India', *Population Studies*. 51(3), 1997, pp. 307–15.

Das, Gupta, Monica and Leela Visaria, 'Son Preference and Excess Female Mortality in India's Demographic Transition', in Korea Institute for Health and Social Affairs, *Sex Preference for Children and Gender Discrimination in Asia*, Research Monograph 96–102, Seoul, 1996.

George, Sabu, Rajaratnam Abel and Barbara D. Miller, 'Female Infanticide in Rural South India', *EPW*, 30 May, 1992.

International Institute for Population Sciences (11PS), *National Family Health Survey. 1992–93, India*, Bombay, 1995.

Kumar, Anil K. and S. Rema, 'Sex Differentials in Indian Mortality: Recent Changes and Implications for Sex Ratio', *Janasamkhya* (forthcoming).

Kundu, Amitabh and M.K. Sahu, 'Variation in Sex Ratio: Development Implications', *EPW*, 12 October 1991.

Miller, Barbara D.,*The Endangered Sex: Neglect of Female Children in Rural North India*, Cornell University Press, Ithaca, New York, 1981.

Ministry of Finance, *Economic Survey 1994–95*, Government of India, New Delhi, 1994, pp. 161–62.

Moore, Molly, 'Indian Plan Thwarted by Quest for Sons', *The Washington Post*, 7 September 1994, p. A26.

Office of the Registrar General, *SRS Based Abridged Life Tables, 1986–90*, Occasional Paper, No. 1 Government of India, New Delhi, 1994.

Office of the Registrar General, *SRS Based Abridged Life Tables, 1989–93*, SRS Analytical Studies, Report No. 1 of 1996, Government of India, New Delhi, 1996.

Oldenberg, P., 'Sex Ratio, Son Preference and Violence in India: A Research Note', *EPW*, 5–12 December 1992.

Patel, Vibhuti, 'Sex Determination and Sex Preselection Tests: Abuse of Advanced Technologies', in Rehana Ghadially (ed.), *Women in Indian Society: A Reader*, Sage Publications, Delhi 1988.

Rajan, S.I., U.S. Mishra and K. Navneetham, 'Decline in Sex Ratio: An Alternative Explanation?' *EPW*, 21 December 1991.

Rajan, S.I., U.S. Mishra and K. Navneetham, 'Decline in Sex Ratio: Alternative Explanation Revisited', *EPW*, 14 November 1992.

Raju, S. and M.K. Premi, 'Decline in Sex Ratio: Alternative Explanation Re-examined', *EPW*, 25 April 1992.

Rastogi, S.R. and Raj Kumari, 'Son Preference and Effectiveness of the Family Welfare Programme in Uttar Pradesh', in R.N. Patil (ed.), *Health, Environment and Population*, Ashish Publishing House, New Delhi, 1992, pp. 165–79.

Srinivasan, K., 'Sex Ratios: What They Hide and Why They Reveal', *EPW*, 17–24 December, 1994.

The Times of India, (Ahmedabad Edition), 18 May 1995, p. 8.

Visaria, Leela, 'Sex Differentials in Nutritional Status and Survival during Infancy and Childhood: Review of Available Evidence', Paper presented at the Conference on Women's Position and Demographic Change in the Course of Development, Asker, Norway, 1988.

Visaria, Pravin, *The Sex Ratio of the Population of India*, Monograph No. 10, Office of the Registrar General, Government of India, New Delhi, 1972.

Wyon, John B., and John E. Gordon, *The Khanna Study*, Harvard University Press, Cambridge, 1971.

6

Lotika Sarkar

Reform of Hindu Marriage and Succession Laws

Still the Unequal Sex

During British rule there was a unified criminal law and civil law that applied to all citizens. This was needed by the rulers of the country to administer, and without any hesitation they did away with the laws that had earlier governed Muslims and Hindus. Where family laws were concerned, however, the British rulers left the law as it was because, according to them, family laws governing Hindus and Muslims were of divine origin and therefore should not be touched.

Before independence the law governing the Hindus was Hindu law but that law was in an extremely confused state. There were two major schools—*Mitakshara* and *Dayabhaga*—governing the Hindus and in addition there were a number of sub-schools. Which school would govern a person would depend on the part of the country he belonged to. In addition to these schools and sub-schools, a great deal of importance was attached to custom.[1] It played a fairly important part and could be pleaded in derogation of an established rule of law. In two of the earlier Privy Council cases, the importance of custom was brought out clearly. In *Bhyah Ram Singh v Bhyah Ugar Singh*,[2] the Privy Council clarified this point by saying that the 'Digest (Mitakshara) subordinates in more than one place the language of texts to custom and approved usage.' In another case the same point had been reiterated as the judges said, 'Under the Hindu system of law clear proof of usage will outweigh the written text of the law.'[3] The requirements for a custom to override the written text of the law were that the custom had to be ancient, that is, it should have been followed for a long time; it had to be certain; and it should not be opposed to public policy or immoral. The custom could be of a community or even of a family.

The underlying principle in all the schools governing the Hindus, was the unequal status of the woman and her subordinate position to the male. This was clearly evident whether the law was governing marriage, adoption, succession or guardianship of children.

With the socio-economic changes taking place in the country there was bound to be a tension between the law being followed by the Hindus and the changes taking place in the rest of the country. The first major attempt to reflect some of these changes was a legislation passed in 1937—the Hindu Women's Property Act.[4] It was a law that was applied uniformly to all Hindus irrespective of the school they were governed by.

The Act provided that when a husband died leaving separate property, the widow would be entitled to the same share as the sons in the property. In the case of joint family property, she would be entitled to the same interest in the property as her husband had, including the right to demand partition. The major drawback of the Act was that the widow did not get an absolute right, but the law recognized what is known as the widow's estate. This meant that she was not an absolute owner and on her death the property would pass not to her heir but to the heirs of the last male owner. She would also not have a right to dispose of the property by gift or sale even during her lifetime but would have the right to alienate the property for some specific purposes, such as marriage expenses of the daughter or acts that would confer spiritual benefit upon her husband, for example, gifts to temples. The widow's right to expenses for going on a pilgrimage would also be recognized. But the expenses had to be reasonable.[5] The Act, in spite of this shortcoming, brought about radical changes, as previously the widow had no rights to her husband's property and no rights in her natal home.[6]

This Act also brought about the realization among social reformers and policy-makers that other branches of the family law needed to be reformed likewise. A committee was set up for this purpose under the chairmanship of B. N. Rau. The committee prepared a tentative draft that was widely circulated for responses. On the basis of the replies received, though there were many who were opposed to any major changes, a report was prepared. The committee was opposed to any piecemeal changes and aimed at a comprehensive Code to govern all branches of family law for all Hindus irrespective of the school they belonged to. Their suggestion was to draft a Code by 'bringing the most progressive elements in the various schools.'[7]

The Report was finally submitted in 1947 and it was the intention of the government that it should become law by 1948. But the plan could not be carried out as independence of the country brought about a number of administrative problems and the members of the Constituent Assembly remained extremely busy with the drafting of the Constitution. In 1948, the Report was submitted to a Select Committee under the chairmanship of Dr. Ambedkar, the Law Minister, which made certain changes to the draft of the Rau Committee. Both the Prime Minister and the Law Minister were absolutely committed to having the Hindu Code become a law to govern all Hindus as soon as possible. What neither of them had foreseen was how entrenched the male values were and how tenaciously they would oppose any change to bring about equality for women. The very members who as members of the Constituent Assembly passed the fundamental right of equality and no discrimination based on sex opposed every single suggestion in the draft Code. The changes suggested in the Code were nothing more than an attempt to improve the rights of Hindu women and give effect to the fundamental right that there should be no discrimination based on sex. There was opposition even to making marriages monogamous. Some of the members questioned the right of the Constituent Assembly to bring about drastic changes in the law. They vociferously argued that the members of the Constituent Assembly were not elected members and could not possibly represent the views of the people.

In spite of the tenacity of the Law Minister in carrying on with the debate, the Prime Minister appeared to waver and some of the members got the impression that he probably thought it better to drop the matter, at least for the time being. By 1951, only four of the clauses had been passed. One of them, however, had far-reaching effect as it laid down that the Code will apply to all Hindus irrespective of the school they belonged to.[8] Dr. Ambedkar finally resigned in sheer disgust at the filibustering tactics being adopted by some members to prevent discussion on the draft and the discussion on the Code was temporarily shelved.

Hindu Marriage Act

After the first Parliament had been installed, there was a distinct change in the attitude of the members as far as the draft Code was concerned. For practical reasons it was decided not to take up the whole Code, as it was rather bulky and discussion might be stymied, but to take up the matter piecemeal. The first Bill to be taken up was the part dealing with marriage and divorce. The House after some discussion accepted that all Hindu marriages should be monogamous and husband and wife would have equal rights of divorce with an additional ground for the wife. If the husband had a second wife, even though at the time of his second marriage plurality of wives was permitted under Hindu Law, the Hindu Marriage Act gave the wife, who may be either the first, or the second wife, the right to petition for divorce simply on the ground that he had another wife. This clause perhaps brings out clearly the policy of the government that marriages among Hindus must cease to be polygamous and become monogamous.

Unfortunately, the legislators, having agreed to the principle of monogamy, showed a lack of understanding about Indian conditions by restricting the right to initiate criminal proceedings for bigamy to the 'aggrieved party', which meant in this case the wife. How many wives, even when the husband has married again, would be prepared to initiate criminal proceedings against him and risk social censure if nothing else? The result was that in spite of the government policy of making marriages monogamous, bigamous marriages among the Hindus continued, as was brought out by a census study that showed that Hindu polygamous marriages were more numerous than Muslim polygamous marriages.[9] If the right to initiate criminal proceedings in a bigamy case were given to others, as is done in all major offences, there would have been a consistency in the government stand. The only change that was made in the law was to extend the right to initiate proceedings to family members such as father, mother, brother, sister, son and daughter.[10]

The case for treating bigamy as a serious offence and extending the right to initiate proceedings against the husband was made many years ago in a document brought out by the Ministry of Social Welfare. The recommendation there was that the 'right to initiate prosecution for bigamy should be extended to persons other than the girl's family... to prevent the current violations of this very salutary provision of the law.... The approach should be towards making it a cognizable offence.'[11]

Apart from the short-sighted policy of the legislators, the judiciary, in interpreting whether a marriage is bigamous or not, has adopted a very mechanical approach. This particular reform illustrates clearly the need for a harmonious working of both the legislature and the judiciary; otherwise, the whole purpose of the change contemplated and achieved legally after a long debate is completely defeated.

The law is clear that a second marriage in the lifetime of the first husband or wife is not only void but is also an offence punishable under the criminal law. But the judiciary has adopted the stand that for a marriage to be declared void, it should have been solemnized—that is, all ceremonies required should have been performed. Even when the second marriage has been celebrated before a large number of persons and the couple have lived together as husband and wife and been accepted by the community as such, the judiciary have held that that by itself cannot make the marriage valid and therefore the question of its being bigamous does not arise. The proper ceremonies have to have been performed. But what are the essential ceremonies? There are no set rules as to what are essential ceremonies in Hindu marriages. The law lays down that the marriage 'may be solemnized in accordance with the customary rites and ceremonies of either party.'[12] Can the parents of the girl insist at the time of the marriage that certain ceremonies according to them are essential when the bridegroom's family may completely reject this suggestion?

The late Chief Justice Hidayatullah had pointed out that in insisting on the word 'solemnize' the judges had gone to the extent of saying that 'admission of marriage by the accused is not evidence of it for the purpose of proving marriage in an adultery or bigamy case.'[13] He even cites a case where the Court held 'the mere fact of subsequent registration of the second marriage does not prove the validity of the second marriage.'[14]

Two of the cases chosen illustrate the point of surprising acquittal of the husband in bigamy cases. It is also worth remembering how few are the bigamy cases that come before the court. In *Bhaurao v The State of Maharashtra*[15] the facts appeared to be simple. The husband had married Indubai in 1956 and then Kamlabai in 1962 without divorcing Indubai. The second marriage, it was claimed; was by the gandharva form. On behalf of the State prosecuting the man, it was urged that the marriage was in accordance with the custom prevalent in his community. In any case, the State further argued that for it to be a bigamous marriage, the second marriage does not have to be a valid one and a person going through a second marriage commits an offence. But the Supreme Court brushed aside these arguments and said that there were two ceremonies necessary to be performed in a gandharva form of marriage—invocation before the fire and saptapadi.[16] There was no evidence on record that these two ceremonies had been performed. The court had no difficulty in acquitting the man.

In the second case of *Priyabala Ghose v Suresh Chandra Ghose,*[17] the Court went even further in emphasizing the need to interpret the term 'solemnize' to mean according to all necessary ceremonies. The husband had admitted that he had married the second wife because of the misconduct of the first wife. In addition to this statement the priest who had officiated at the ceremony gave evidence that it was solemnized according to Hindu rites. But both the learned High Court and the Supreme Court came to the conclusion that as 'homa' and 'saptapadi' had not been performed there was no valid second marriage and therefore no offence of bigamy had been committed irrespective of the evidence of the priest.

The palpable injustice done in both cases because of the interpretation of the court of the word 'solemnize' seems to have been overlooked by judges. It is necessary to quote the Late Chief Justice Hidayatullah, who brings out this point so succinctly:

> Thus if one deliberately keeps a small lacuna e.g. instead of taking the seven steps (saptapadi) takes only six steps, while celebrating the second marriage, one can easily avoid the penalty... even though one virtually ruins the lives of two girls. If we are to effectively root out polygamy from this country, we must amend Sec. 494 IPC and Sec. 17 Hindu Marriage Act, in such a way that anyone who goes through a form of marriage during the life time of his or her spouse will come within the mischief of the offence of bigamy.[18]

It is perhaps necessary to mention that neither the suggestion of the late Chief Justice Hidayatullah to amend the law,[19] nor the recommendation of the Department of Social Welfare, made twenty years ago, that the right to initiate proceedings for bigamy should not be confined to the aggrieved wife or her family[20] has had any effect on the government or on the judiciary.

As recently as 1996 the Supreme Court dismissed a case of bigamy brought by the wife. In this case[21] the husband's statement was very clear: 'I have not committed any crime. I have married after ten years of (sic) my wife deserted and went away.'[22] Following the usual reasoning adopted that the marriage was not proved as there was no evidence of necessary ceremonies, the court in a paternalistic manner dissuaded the wife from pursuing the case but very substantially increased the maintenance the husband was paying. The court added, 'Hard realities of the situation require that... the (husband) is not deprived of his job so that he keeps providing the necessary wherewithal to the wife.'[23]

The second case[24] in the same year deals with a case in which the wife went to the National Commission for Women to lodge a complaint against the husband for having married again and secondly for subjecting her to great harassment. She obviously found it easier to go to the Commission instead of the police as she expected a sympathetic treatment from the former. The Commission filed the complaint but the High Court dismissed it, as 'cognizance...

can be taken only if the complaint is made by the person aggrieved.'[25] Obviously the Commission could not be treated as the aggrieved party, and in the usual course the case would have been dismissed. Fortunately, in this case the High Court had overlooked a provision of the law in which if there is a cognizable offence as well as a non-cognizable offence the case shall be treated as a cognizable one.[26] Cruelty to the wife is cognizable and therefore the case could be dealt with even though the National Commission was not an 'aggrieved' party and the case of bigamy was non-cognizable.

One cannot fail to wonder how long it will be before the government decides to amend the law so that effective steps can be taken to root out bigamy among the Hindus.

There is another provision of the Hindu Marriage Act for which it is very difficult to find a rational explanation. This deals with the problem of marriage of girls and boys below the age prescribed both in the Child Marriage Restraint Act and the Hindu Marriage Act. The original requirement was that the bride had to be 15 years of age and the bridegroom 18. The law was amended and now it is 18 years for the bride and 21 years for the bridegroom. This requirement of age is one condition laid down in the section that gives the other conditions required to make a Hindu marriage valid, such as no marriage within the prohibited degree, no bigamy etc. Violation of any of the conditions laid down affects the validity of the marriage and it is either void as in a bigamous marriage or voidable where valid consent could not be given because of the party's unsoundness of mind. In addition to this effect on the validity of the marriage, there is also a punishment prescribed for violating the law. When one comes to the condition in the Act requiring the age of the parties, however, a totally different principle applies. The marriage cannot be challenged and is held to be valid. To add to this, the party or parties to the marriage may be subject to imprisonment and/or fine for having violated the law.[27] The incongruity lies in that there is a general principle of law under which a minor cannot enter into a contract because he or she cannot give consent, but when it comes to marriage consent is presumed and they became liable to be punished for violating the law.

One significant change in 1976 following the recommendation of the Committee on the Status of Women in India was the amendment including the clause on option of puberty in the section dealing with divorce. If the girl was married before she was 15 years old she can repudiate the marriage before she is 18 years old. While the amendment was modelled on the Muslim law of option of puberty, the amendment contains an additional provision, that the young wife does not lose her right to exercise her option even if her marriage has been consummated.[28] To this extent it is more progressive than the original model.

Two more amendments to the section dealing with divorce are the amendments recognizing divorce by mutual consent and the right of the wife to sue for divorce where there has been an order of maintenance against the wife and there has been no cohabitation for more than a year. The addition of both these amendments certainty makes the divorce law more liberal for women.

HINDU SUCCESSION ACT

Though the Hindu succession Act chronologically does not follow the Hindu Marriage Act, as far as radical changes are concerned it certainly compares most favourably with it. As pointed out by Justice Kuppuswami 'the main scheme of the Act is to establish equality between male and female in regard to property.'[29] A close examination of the Hindu Succession Act, however, shows that as in the earlier Act compromises were made to satisfy some conservative members in the House.

The most far-reaching changes that have been introduced in the Act are: (1) giving equal rights to sons and daughters in the property of the father as well as the mother and (2) abolishing the concept of widow's estate under which a woman was never a full owner but was one for life only.

As far as the right to inherit from a male is concerned, the Act lays down that the property will be divided in equal shares among the Class 1 heirs. The Class 1 heirs are the mother, widow, sons and daughters. These four types of heirs inherit by reason of their relationship to the deceased. The other heirs in Class 1 are the heirs of a predeceased son or a predeceased daughter and heirs of a predeceased grandson.[30] Only if there are no heirs among those given in the Act as Class I will it go to the Class 2 heirs. The father is the first heir in this second category, followed by son's daughter's son, son's daughter's daughter, brother and sister, who will take in equal share. These heirs are followed by many others listed in the schedule.[31]

What is intriguing is why there should be a totally separate list of heirs for a woman when she dies intestate. While son, daughter and husband are first to take the property, they are followed by the heirs of the husband. The most unacceptable is that the woman's father and mother come only after that.[32] Why is it that, when in the case of the son, the mother is a Class 1 heir, where the daughter's property is concerned she is third in line and comes only after the heirs of the husband?

It is the inclusion of legal provisions such as this that perpetuates son preference and biases against the daughter. Even the heirs of the mother come last, after the heirs of the father.

The only saving provision is that where a female has inherited property from her parents, then if there are no sons or daughters or children of predeceased son or daughter, it will go to the heirs of her father.[33]

Needless to add, to balance this the Act lays down that any property inherited by a woman from her husband or father-in-law shall devolve, in the absence of sons and daughters including children of predeceased son or daughter, to the heirs of the husband. In effect it amounts to very little as heirs of the husband come soon after the children and the husband, who are number 1 in the second list.

One interesting change made in the Act is the total removal of unchastity as a disqualification. Earlier, unchastity in the case of a widow disqualified her from inheritance. In the case of a daughter also, unchastity was a disqualification under the Dayabhaga school but not under the Mitakshara school. But that too has been removed.[34]

Similarly, remarriage of a widow does not divest her of her husband's property, as was laid down in the Hindu Widows Remarriage Act. When a woman gets a property she becomes an absolute heir, therefore the question of divesting her does not arise.[35]

Perhaps the most radical provision in the Act, even more than that giving equal rights to sons and daughters, is the removal of the disability of a female to acquire and hold property as an owner. Earlier, she remained in control only as long as she lived. If she sold the property for legal necessity, there was always the possibility of its being challenged by the heirs of the husband, who were entitled to inherit the property after her death. What the removal of widow's estate meant is best explained by Justice Koshal in *Bai Vijaya v Thakorbhai Chelabhai*.[36]

> It is a step in the direction of practical recognition of equality of the sexes and meant to elevate women from a subservient position in the economic field to a higher pedestal where they could exercise full powers of enjoyment and disposal of property held by them as owners untrammeled by artificial limitations placed on their right of ownership by the society in which the will of the dominant male prevailed to bring about a subjugation of the opposite sex.[37]

Explaining the provision, Justice Bhagwati said it was done to 'achieve a social purpose by bringing about change in the social and economic position of the woman in Hindu society.'[38]

The abolition of the widow's estate and the whole concept of limited ownership was done not from the commencement of the Act but retrospectively. This extended the change in her status to that of full owner of any property she possessed at the time the Hindu Succession Act became operative. Whether she had acquired the property by inheritance or by gift or in the words of the section 'in any other manner' became immaterial.[39]

In an earlier case, Justice Fazl Ali had explained that the provisions introduced in the Act 'have been couched in the widest possible terms and must be liberally construed in favour of a female so as to advance the object of the Act and promote the socio-economic ends sought to be achieved by this long needed legislation.'[40]

The object of the legal provision is to remove the disability of a female to acquire and hold property as an absolute owner. If she dies intestate, she becomes a fresh stock of descent and the property would devolve by succession to her own heirs.

Furthermore all modes of acquisition of property by a woman known to Hindu law as long as she possessed the property as a widow's estate would be enlarged into an absolute estate.[41]

Possession by the woman was necessary but the possession could be actual or constructive. In the case of *Kalawatibai v Soiryabai*,[42] for example, because she was not in possession as a limited owner, she could not become an absolute owner.

In this case the widow had inherited property from her husband prior to 1956. This meant she had only the right for her life with the right to alienate the property for legal necessity. She gifted the property to one of her daughters. This gift could not be described as a legal necessity, nor as being for 'spiritual or charitable purpose', for which she could alienate the property. Therefore, the 1956 Act could not apply to her to make her an absolute owner. After her death, her other daughter challenged the gift and demanded her share as a reversioner (father's heir). The question was whether the daughter to whom the property had been gifted had become an absolute owner after 1956. The answer was in the negative, as the gift by which she came into the property was one which the mother could give not absolutely, as she was not an owner, but one which would be valid only during the period she was alive. After the mother's death, the alienation could be legally challenged and the second daughter was successful in getting her share.

In another case, the court clarified the point that property to be possessed by the widow at the time of the Act did not mean she had to be actually in possession. Possession could be actual or constructive. The legislators had used the phrase 'property possessed by a female', which is much wider than to be in possession.[43]

In this case the Hindu widow was given the authority to adopt a son, if she so desired. She did but the son died. She then adopted another. This was challenged by her husband's reversioners as not being legal. They further argued that the new Act could not make her an absolute owner as she was not in possession of the property at the time the Act became law. It was the so-called adopted son who was in possession. The court clarified the term 'property possessed', which meant the state of owning or having in one's hand or power. Therefore, if the adoption was held to be invalid, then there was no question that full ownership rested with the widow. If the adopted son was in physical possession, 'his possession was merely permissive and she (the widow) must be regarded as being in constructive possession of it.'[44]

In another case[45] also, the collaterals of the husband, who were going to lose their claims to the land which the widow possessed if she became an absolute owner, challenged the widow's right to absolute ownership. Having first made the point that she had married in the *karewa* form one of the collaterals, thus losing her possession, they dislodged her from the land. As the marriage could not be proved, she instituted a suit for possession. The question the court had to answer was what was her status vis-à-vis the land after the Hindu Succession Act. She was physically not in possession, having been dispossessed. The court reiterated the point that what was required to make her an absolute owner was that the property in question was possessed by her and not at all that she had to be in possession. Therefore, even if the widow was out of actual possession she became an absolute owner and on her death it went to her legal representatives and not to her husband's heirs.

These two provisions go a long way to make equal status of men and women a reality as far as right to possession of property and control over it is concerned. As explained by Justice Bhagwati,

> the object of the legislature (was) to wipe out the disabilities from which a Hindu female suffered in regard to ownership of property under the old Shastric law, to abridge the stringent provisions against proprietors rights which were often regarded as evidence of her perpetual tutelage, and to recognise her status as an independent and absolute owner of property.[46]

But in spite of the efforts of the Supreme Court 'in giving a most expansive interpretation... with a view to advancing the social purpose of the legislation',[47] two other provisions in the Act are definite obstacles in advancing not only the 'social purpose' referred to but also the basic principle of equality of sexes.

The entrenched values of some of the legislators, particularly from northern India, where the Mitakshara school prevailed, clearly sustained the belief in the superior right of the male to control property, excluding women from doing so. Many years ago Gandhiji had written 'Man has always desired power. Ownership of property gives this power.'[48] The truth of this was demonstrated clearly at the time of the debates on the Hindu Succession Act. Ignoring the recommendation of the Rau Committee, the legislators agreed to retain the Mitakshara joint family (coparcenary),[49] which clearly excludes women from having the right to inherit and control joint family property. The property is owned by the father and his sons and their descendants. On the death of any one of them, the remaining members continue to own the property. That is known as survivorship. This is different from individual property, which on the death of a member is opened for succession. The right to become a member of the joint Hindu family (Mitakshara) by birth is restricted to males—completely excluding all female heirs.

Many years before the Hindu Succession Act Jawaharlal Nehru had referred to the joint family 'as a relic of feudal age utterly out of keeping with modern conditions',[50] but the opposition to abolishing the Mitakshara joint family with all its discriminatory rules was too strong within the Congress Party.

It is also to be noted that by retaining this particular institution, the Act moved away from the objective of the draft Code, which was to have a uniform law for all Hindus. Kane, the well-known jurist, commenting on the objective of the draft Hindu Code, had written 'the unification of Hindu law will be helped by the abolition of the right by birth which is the cornerstone of the Mitakshara school and which the draft Hindu Code seeks to abolish.'[51]

The tussle to retain the Mitakshara joint family had to face the vociferous demands of many members who perceived it as a backward step. The disability of the woman, which the law was trying to wipe put, would not only remain, but would remain for some and not for others because the Mitakshara school did not cover all Hindu women. The Dayabhaga school never had this institution.

One compromise was arrived at: when a male Hindu dies as a member of the joint Hindu Mitakshara family leaving Class I heirs, his share of the property, which he would have got if he had asked for a partition, is distributed equally among those heirs. This is what is referred to as a notional partition, so that members such as a daughter will not be completely deprived.

This obviously leads to a difference between what a son gets and what a daughter gets from the father. They inherit equally as Class I heirs by this notional partition but the son in addition to this retains his right by birth in the joint family and will get, if he wants a partition, a share equal to what his father would have got.

It was inevitable that this discrimination and the unequal share of sons and daughters in the joint family property would lead to a great deal of dissatisfaction. Taking advantage of our being a federal government, five states took positive steps to remedy this situation. The first was Kerala, which followed the Rau Committee's suggestion and totally abolished the Kerala joint family. The Kerala Joint Family System (Abolition) Act was passed in 1976. This meant after the Act became law no one would have the right to claim any interest in joint family property founded on the mere fact that the person was born in the family of the ancestors.

Andhra Pradesh, Tamil Nadu, Maharashtra and Karnataka have also taken legislative steps to remove the discriminatory features of the Mitakshara joint family. The last three have followed the Andhra Pradesh legislation.

The Preamble to the Andhra Pradesh legislation states that equality before law is a fundamental right and exclusion of the daughter from participation in the Mitakshara joint family (coparcenary) by reason of her sex is violative of the right. The four states have tried to remove this discrimination between sons and daughters by providing that 'the daughter of a coparcener shall by birth become a coparcener in her own right in the same manner as the son and have the same rights in the coparcenary property as she would have had if she had been a son.' These four states have therefore retained the right by birth but extended it to include daughters. Whether this is preferable to the Kerala model, which totally abolishes the joint Hindu family, may be debatable.[52] But one thing is clear, that the Kerala model helps in retaining the uniformity that the Rau Committee had stated to be one of the objectives of the Hindu Code.

The other provision of the Act, which deals with ownership of the dwelling house, goes a long way in nullifying the equal rights given to sons and daughters in both the father's property and the mother's. The earlier law, that is the uncodified law before the Succession Act, differentiated not only between sons and daughters, who could never demand a partition, but also between daughters. The unmarried daughter often got preference over the married one. But when such radical changes have been made, it is far from clear why if the father or the mother has a dwelling house occupied by the family, the son alone should be given the privilege of demanding partition of it and not the daughters. Drawing their authority from the Hindu Shastras,[53] the legislators felt the right of partition should not be given to the daughter as that might lead to disintegration and fragmentation of the house. It is inexplicable that if a daughter demands a partition it leads to fragmentation but if the sons do likewise it does not lead to any fragmentation. Even the Supreme Court, which is supposed to be the protector of women's rights, justifies this view. According to Justice Ramaswamy of the Supreme Court, 'the object is to prevent fragmentation or disintegration of the family dwelling house at the instance of the female heir to the hardship and difficulties which the male heir may be put to.'[54] The reason therefore appears to be, not to cause any hardship to the male heir, and not really to keep the dwelling house intact. However, the law does provide that if the male heirs have divided their shares in the dwelling house then the right of the female heir arises.[55]

In their efforts to protect the privileged position of the sons, some of the courts have gone to the extent of holding that even when there is one male heir and the question of partition is impossible all by himself, the bar on the daughter continues. The Madras High Court has very clearly articulated its male bias in dealing with such a situation. In its opinion, allowing the partition at the insistence of the female heir would cause 'great injustice to the single male heir and the object of the section would be nullified'.[56] For good measure they add that 'the hardship that would be caused to the female heir... is certainly relatively less than the injustice that would be done to a single male member.' It is the privilege of the judiciary not to have to explain some of their observations. In this case they did not explain how they arrived at the conclusion that the hardship to the female heir will be less. Whose hardship will be greater when a divorced or deserted or separated woman has to live in the same house as her only brother and his family and not have any ownership right, a right that would definitely lead to her empowerment?

Fortunately, not all states take the above view. The Orissa High Court was very clear. To debar a female heir from demanding partition from a single male heir will mean a complete denial of her rights and 'the legislature having the female heirs absolute rights by inheritance on the one hand could not have taken away the same by the other.'[57]

While the right of residence in the dwelling house is given to the female heirs, there is a blatant discrimination among even the daughters. As Class I heir there is no difference among daughters; they may be married or unmarried. But where the right of residence in the dwelling house is concerned there is certainly a difference. A widowed, divorced, separated, deserted or unmarried daughter has the right of residence but not the daughter whose marriage may be one only in name. With the tremendous rise in domestic violence, suicide and murder of young married women, a married daughter needs the shelter of her natal home. The Karnataka High Court in one case even denied the daughter's right to residence in the natal home because she had deserted her husband. It was fortuitous that in this case the father had made separate provision for the daughter and her children so that she was not on the street and did not have to go back to her matrimonial home.

Now, forty years after the Hindu Succession Act was passed, it is time to examine whether these restricted provisions have helped bring about social justice or whether the position of women has remained subordinate.

NOTES

1. According to M.P. Jain, the Hindu jurists always accorded great importance to custom as a source of law. He has argued most convincingly that the sub-schools came about because of the importance given to custom. Jain, M.P., *Outlines of Indian Legal History*, 4th ed., (1981) p. 478.
2. 13, M.I.A. 373, 390.
3. *Collector of Madura v Mootoo Ramalinga* (1868), 12, M.I.A. 397, 436.
4. Prior to this Act, there were two other minor Acts. The first was The Hindu Inheritance (Removal of Disabilities) Act 1928, which did not apply to persons governed by the Dayabhaga School. The other

was the Hindu Law of Inheritance Act 1929, which altered the order in which certain women heirs of a Hindu dying intestate were entitled to succeed.

5. Duncan, Derrett J., *Introduction to Modern Hindu Law,* (1963), p. 435.
6. The Preamble to the Hindu Women's Rights to Property Act 1937 states clearly that 'it is expedient to amend the Hindu Law to give better rights to women in respect of property.'
7. Explanatory statement prefixed to the Draft Code submitted by the members in 1944.
8. Members of the Committee put it beyond any doubt that in respect of any of the matters dealt with in the Code the provisions of the Code should override all existing laws whether based on custom or otherwise unless an express saving is contained in the Code itself. (Clause 4) Report of the Select Committee on Hindu Code (1948).
9. Incidence of polygamous marriages in India, 1961, Census of India (mimeographed).
10. Sec. 198(c) of the Criminal Procedure Code, extending the right to initiate proceedings to family members, was added in 1978. Another addition to the section was that with the permission of the Court 'any other person related to her by blood, marriage or adoption' may also initiate the proceedings.

    Any marriage between two Hindus solemnized...is void if at the date of such marriage either party had a husband or wife living....'
11. Blue Print of Action Points and National Plan of Action for Women, Department of Social Welfare, Govt. of India, p. 26/58(ii).
12. Sec. 7, Hindu Marriage Act.
13. Ratanlal and Dhirajlal, Indian Penal Code, Revised and Revitalised, Justice Hidayatullah (26th ed.), (1987) p. 478.
14. Ibid.
15. *Bhaurao Shankar Lokhande and Another v The State of Maharashtra* AIR 1965 S.C. 1564.
16. Id. on p. 1567.
17. AIR 1971 SC 1153.
18. Supra n. 13, p. 479.
19. Supra n. 13.
20. Supra n. 11.
21. *P. Satyanarayana and Another v P. Mallaiah* (1996) 6 S.C.C. 122.
22. Id. on p. 123.

23. Id. on p. 124.
24. *State of Orissa v Sharat Chandra Sahu* (1996) 6 SCC 435.
25. Id. on p. 437.
26. Subsection (4) of Sec. 155, Criminal Procedure Code, 1973.
27. Sec. 18 (a). In the case of contravention of the condition in clause iii of Sec. 5 (which deals with the age of the bride and bridegroom), with simple imprisonment up to 15 days or with fine up to one thousand rupees, or with both. Justice Jain has pointed out that 'penalty is provided for the marriage of a person below the age specified but neither father or the mother or other relatives who bring about such a marriage, or the priest who performs the marriage ceremony will be held guilty of abetment.' Jain, S.C., *Law Relating to Marriage and Divorce*, 4th ed., (1996) p. 163
28. *Towards Equality*, Committee on the Status of Women, p. 113, 4.68.
29. Mayne's Hindu Law & Usage revised by Justice Kuppuswami, 14th ed. (1996), p. 1043.
30. The other heirs in Class 1 are by virtue of their representation as applied in the case of a predeceased son or of a predeceased daughter. Sec. 8 gives the complete list of heirs of Class 1 in the Schedule.
31. The list of Class 2 heirs is given in the Schedule. They are 9 in number and they inherit in the order the list is given, unlike Class 1 heirs, who take simultaneously. Failing heirs in Class 1 and Class 2, the property will go to the agnates and then to the cognates. A person is said to be an agnate of another if the two are related by blood or adoption wholly through males. A person is said to be a cognate of another if the two are related by blood or adoption but not wholly through males. They may be related through one or more females. Mulla, D. F., *Principles of Hindu Law,* 12th ed., p. 957.
32. Sec. 15:
    (a) upon the sons and daughters (including the children of any predeceased son or daughter) and the husband
    (b) upon the heirs of the husband
    (c) upon the mother and father
    (d) upon the heirs of the father
    (e) upon the heirs of the mother
33. Sec. 15(2)(1).
34. *Supra* n.5, p. 374.
35. Hindu Widows' Remarriage Act 1856, sec. 2.
36. (1979) 3 SCC 300 on p. 307.

37. Id. on p. 307.
38. Id. on p. 314.
39. *V. Tulasamma v Sesha Reddy* (1977) 3 SCC 99 on p. 135.
40. Ibid.
41. According to the Explanation of Sec. 14, 'property' includes both movable and immovable property acquired by a female Hindu by inheritance or devise, or at a partition, or in lieu of maintenance or arrears of maintenance, or by gift from any person, whether a relative or not, before, at or after her marriage, or by her own skill or exertion, or by purchase or by prescription, or in any other manner whatsoever, and also as such property held by her as 'stridhana' immediately before the commencement of the Act.
42. (1991) 3 SCC 410.
43. Gummalapura T.M. *Kotturuswami v Veeravva* AIR 1959 S.C. 577, 582.
44. Ibid.
45. *Mangal Singh v Rattno* AIR 1967 S.C. 1786.
46. Supra n. 39 on p. 139.
47. Ibid.
48. *Young India*, 17 October, 1929.
49. Coparcenary is actually a narrower body than the joint family. It includes only those persons who acquire by birth an interest in the joint property. Mulla, *Principles of Hindu Law*, 16th ed (1990), p. 239.
50. Gopal, S. (ed.) *Selected Works of Jawaharlal Nehru*, Vol. 3, (1993), p. 395.
51. Quoted by B. Sivaramayya in his article 'Coparcenary Rights to Daughters: Constitutional and Interpretational Issues' (1997) 3 S.C.C., Journal Section, p. 25.
52. Critically commented by Sivaramayya. Ibid.
53. 'The disability of female to claim partition when the male members are not willing to effect a partition is an echo of the law that prevailed prior to this Act under the Mitakashara under which no female is entitled to share on a partition....' *Narashimaha Murthy v Susheelabai* (1996) 3 S.C.C. 644 on p. 654.
54. Id. on p. 651.
55. Sec. 23: 'the right of any such female heir to claim partition of the dwelling heir shall not arise until the male heir choose the divide....'
56. Madras High Court in 1981 Mad. 62.
57. Orissa High Court in 1993 Orissa 36 commented by Paras Dewan in *Annual Survey of Indian Law*, 1993, p. 166.

7

ZOYA HASAN

Muslim Women and the Debate on Legal Reforms

The past decade has witnessed a renewed debate on legal systems governing family life. The central and long-standing issue is whether religion-based personal laws should be continued or a uniform civil code instituted. This controversy underscores the conflicting pulls of secularism and minority identity and the tensions between the demands of equity and cultural difference.

The urge for greater economic and political participation of women in society leads to the quest for legal rights. There can be no doubt that legal reforms and formal equality are essential aspects of social emancipation. Legal reforms per se do not neccesarily challenge the deeper inequalities of society, but they signify an important step in that direction. And at the heart of this quest for change is the status of Muslim women and their rights under the Muslim Personal Law (MPL).

This paper explores the official discourse of the state on legal reforms of personal laws in order to unravel the relationship between state and religious communities in post-colonial societies. It attempts to probe the changes in the relationship between gender, religion and legal reforms and map the general contours of the debate and the shifts in these relationships in the post-Ayodhya period.

I

Women's equal rights are no doubt guaranteed in the Indian Constitution, though denied in actuality. The Constitution also reformed property, inheritance and marriage in Hindu laws. Muslim or Christian women, however, have not been similarly served. For example, divorce is still not easy for a Christian woman. A Muslim woman, on the other hand, can be divorced all too easily or may sometimes have to live in a polygamous household. Moreover, there are serious impediments in seeking a divorce. An important obstacle to establishing equality before the law is the absence of reforms in family laws. Personal laws govern marriage, divorce, maintenance, guardianship, custody and adoption. In the case of Muslim women, the Muslim personal law, although not the only form of discrimination, constitutes a significant source of disadvantage. Their unequal rights are a crucial factor in maintaining their subordination to men and a sanctioned device for limiting their access to property and inheritance.

Much of the discussion on law reforms since independence has focussed on the role of the State in initiating reforms of Hindu laws, while the debate on obstacles to law reforms has revolved around MPL. There is no denying that reforms of property, inheritance and marriage laws introduced by the Hindu Code Bill, combined with economic and educational changes, have contributed to greater women's participation in the public domain. In a space of two years from 1954 to 1956, the Hindu Marriage Act 1955, the Hindu Succession Act 1956, the Hindu Minority and Guardianship Act 1956 and the Hindu Adoption and Maintenance Act 1956 were enacted. As is well known, the Hindu Code Bill faced tremendous opposition both inside and outside Parliament and many Congressmen were among its severest critics. They condemned the proposals for subverting Hindu ideas, culture and religion. Every single clause of the Bill was opposed, the cry of religion in danger was raised. Clauses giving property to daughters were most vehemently opposed, as was the abolition of polygamy.

Many of the arguments were, however, brushed aside by Jawaharlal Nehru in his pursuit of legal equality for Hindu women. The pace and content of Hindu law reforms was thus defined by the State and not by pressures for change from within. Legitimizing its actions with reference to the need for social progress, the Nehruvian State appropriated the authority of social reforms and defined law as the key instrument of change. Reform of Hindu laws was justified on the grounds of equal rights for women, which were at the heart of the provisions and philosophy of the Constitution. Acknowledging the special disabilities suffered by women, Article 15 of the Constitution had guaranteed equal rights to women. Women, along with other socially and educationally backward classes such as the Scheduled Castes and Tribes, were perceived as a disadvantaged group who needed social compensation through State intervention.

What is perplexing is why questions regarding the position of Muslim women have not aroused the same reformist zeal? How does one interpret the differences in the State response?

State policy with regard to the civil status of Muslims has been generally cautious. The official policy is based on a strict adherence to the principle of separation of public and private spheres with regard to the Muslim community, in effect acknowledging that the State cannot initiate change in the private sphere of Muslims without their consent. By contrast, the Nehruvian State had dispensed with this distinction in case of the Hindu legal reforms in the post-colonial period. In the event, State intervention succeeded in providing the Hindu woman a measure of legal equality but failed to initiate a similar process of legal change that could lead to the emancipation of Muslim women. This approach was inconsistent with the welfare argument put forward by the Congress government in supporting the Hindu Code Bill, that legal reforms were necessary to enhance the contribution of women in society and alleviate their sufferings. The government's reluctance in the case of Muslim women was basically influenced by the strong opposition of the Muslim leadership to any change in the personal laws. The government conceded the ground to the Muslim leadership on this vital issue in the hope that this would ensure their loyalty and support. Thus, both the reform of Hindu personal laws and denial of legal equality to minority women were guided by political considerations of national unity and integration. In neither case was the issue of equality a prime consideration.

II

The popular perception of MPL is that it is rigid, inflexible and immutable. In actual fact, the MPL was radically transformed during the colonial period. Until the introduction of the Shariat Act in 1937, legal and social codes observed by Muslim communities in different parts of the country were varied and diffused. Despite centuries of Muslim rule, the community did not adopt the Shariah as the basis of law, while women's rights in the Shariah were seldom complied with or enforced. As a result, the opportunities they had in exercising their Quranic prerogatives, especially in claiming ownership of landed estates and property, were denied to them. Indeed, the primacy given by Muslims to custom was a source of embarrassment to the Muslim priests and politicians.

Thus began an effort by the *ulama* to work for a complete supersession of non-Islamic customary practice and compulsory enactment of an Islamic legal system. The enactment of the Muslim Personal Law Shariat Application Act 1937 signalled the acceptance by the State legal system of the principle that in all personal matters, such as marriage, divorce, maintenance, inheritance and custody, Muslims would be governed by the MPL. Similarly, the Dissolution of Muslim Marriages Act 1939 represented yet another attempt by the *ulama* to rectify what they perceived to be a lacuna in the existing laws that had left Muslim women without the option of divorce, except through apostasy from Islam. The Act enumerated the grounds and circumstances under which Muslim women could seek divorce and provided for authorized court personnel to dissolve a Muslim marriage. The *ulama* were, however, unhappy that the Act did not specify that only Muslim judges were empowered to dissolve Muslim marriages; in fact, they argued that a divorce granted by a non-Muslim judge was not invalid. For the first time, this Act gave Muslim women the right to seek judicial dissolution of marriage. At the same time, it raised the question of whether the value of group identity was being supported by the colonial State in accordance with modern ideas of divorce and gender equality or some other value supported by the traditional schools of Islamic law.

After independence, the government made no attempt to reform the MPL. Rather, it has consistently remained non-interfering in the regime of personal laws. This policy, strengthened by the verdict of legal courts, has worked with two basic propositions. First, Muslims constitute a community. Second, all Muslims, regardless of region, sect and class, adhere to a single body of law. 'Though both ideas concur with those of Muslim reformers, consistent application of those principles by the courts has given those propositions greater reality in the past century than they had in "traditional" Muslim states'. This recognition is a sequel to the acceptance of the rights of the communities to their cultural identity by the post-colonial State.

The post-independence State responded to the Muslim community in much the same way as the erstwhile colonial government, with its policy of non-interference in the domestic and religious affairs. The MPL, which is defended as the basis of community identity, was constructed through the Shariat Act of 1937 and the Dissolution of Muslim Marriages Act 1939. Its codification between 1937 and 1939 defined the boundaries of the Muslim community. Once this was done, the religio-political leadership of Muslims strongly opposed any change in the personal laws. The Jamiyat-al-ulema-i-Hind took the lead, stressing always the need to safeguard the Shariah, the main symbol of Muslim identity.

The Directive Principles of State Policy envisioned a Uniform Civil Code applicable to all citizens. Article 44 was incorporated in the Constitution in order to introduce a uniform law in the interest of national unity and integration. It assumed that there was no basic corelation between religion and law in a civilized country. The question of personal law had come up for debate on several occasions in the Constituent Assembly. Muslim members argued that personal law of marriage, divorce and maintenance cannot be changed because that would be in violation of the fundamental right to religious freedom. In fact, it was proposed that the right of a community to follow its personal law should be made into a justiciable fundamental right of the community and that no change should be undertaken without the consent of the community. Their basic argument was that secularism implied non-interference in the realm of religion, which belonged to the domain of citizens' private practices. They opposed a uniform law on the ground that the Islamic community, rather than the State, should initiate legal changes. The same position was taken later in opposition to the application of the Special Marriages Act and the Adoption Bill 1972.

The main objection was similar to the points raised by the *ulama* in opposition to the Shariat Act. Their insistence then and later was that the *ulama* were competent to approve, interpret and, if necessary, reform the personal laws. Religion and legal codes were inextricably interwoven and the Muslims constituted a distinct community on the basis of legal principles and doctrines. The government accepted this view and, in effect, conceded that the Parliament or State assemblies could not legislate in matters concerning the MPL.

In view of the strong resistance from several quarters, the Congress government was not willing to moot the idea of reforms or to enact a common civil law. Jawaharlal Nehru was reluctant, because he felt his govenment in the aftermath of Partition should make the Muslims feel secure and avoid any step that would offend their religious susceptibilities and heighten their anxieties regarding their status in independent India. Hence, the policy of merging religious communities in a single citizenship was qualified by restricting legal reform initiatives to the Hindus. In his keenness to win their confidence, Nehru failed to ensure the equality before law of all Indians. He said, 'If anybody brings forward a civil code bill, it will have my extreme sympathy. But I confess I do not think the time is ripe in India for me to push through it.'

In 1961, the Union Cabinet received suggestions to survey and reform the MPL. The Law Ministry was asked to 'process' and make appropriate suggestions. This led to public outcry. A gathering of Muslim members of Parliament, chaired by Vice President Zakir Husain, urged the government to desist from taking any initiative to change the MPL. They wanted changes in administrative and legal matters, consistent with the principles of the Quran and the *Hadith*, to be left to the Muslims. From this perspective, reform initiatives by the State were deemed morally unacceptable constraints on religious freedom of the community.

The governments that followed Nehru found it more difficult to contemplate legal reforms. It was too much of a political risk in electoral terms. State intervention was possible during the Nehru era, but much more complex after that; not surprisingly, it has been completely ruled out. So that when the State intervened in the controversial *Shah Bano* case in 1986, it did so with an eye on the Muslim vote. This was a logical consequence of drawing the *ulama* into the debate, accepting the authenticity of their version of community identity and community laws, and recognizing the All India Muslim Personal Law Board (AIMPLB) as the sole representative on legal matters.

The turning point in the debate on legal reforms was the *Shah Bano* case, which provoked a countrywide furore among Muslims. To soothe ruffled feelings, Parliament enacted a legislation called the Muslim Women (Protection of Rights on Divorce) Bill 1986, to reverse the Supreme Court's decision that had granted maintenance to destitute Muslim women under provisions of the Criminal Procedure Codes. The State-led negotiations to preserve the MPL culminating in the Muslim Women's Bill was reminiscent of similar negotiations and debates on fundamental rights and minority rights in the Constituent Assembly and on the Uniform Civil Code during the passage of the Hindu Code Bill in the Lok Sabha.

The government's overall strategy was laid down in the debate in the Constituent Assembly and was reflected, furthermore, in the commitment made by the Congress party that personal laws would not be changed without a consensus among the Muslims. It was accepted that personal laws belonged to the domain of citizens' private practices, and the State ought not to concern itself with them. There was no recognition of the potential tension between individual freedom and community practices restrictive of such freedoms. It also assumed that there was a consensus within the Muslim community on the issue, reflecting how personal law served as a unifier and a marker for the community's identity.

Enunciating the policy of the government in the Lok Sabha, the Law Minister had stated that the MPL was based on the Shariah;

so the Supreme Court judgement transgressed the limits of the MPL. This interpretation echoed the position of the AIMPLB; it showed no recognition of the fact that Muslim leaders (many of whom helped to reinforce the Congress view) were manipulating issues of religious identity to serve their own ends. In reality, provisions of maintenance for destitute women did not amount to an interference in personal law; nor did minor modifications constitute an attack on Islamic tenets. But having uncritically accepted the notion of the divine immutability of the Shariah, the Congress government, backed by party functionaries, was constrained to introduce the Muslim Women's Bill. These considerations were summed up by the Law Minister, who declared: 'We have to tread very carefully, for Muslim personal law is linked to the Muslim religion in the minds of most Muslims.... we must look at it from the point of view of Muslims... and then try to find out what is the law which governs the Muslims and which according to them is not merely a law of man's making but a law ordained by God. This is the belief of Muslims.'

The continuation of personal law was defended on the ground that this was something the Muslim community felt very strongly about, so it should be conceded irrespective of the opinion of other communities or society at large. Further justification for the new legislation was developed within the ambit of the religious sanctity of personal law. In this way, the Congress established an equation between law, scripture and community identity as the centrepiece for the integration of minorities into national life.

The hallmark of its policy was to observe neutrality in areas that were defined and accepted as being within the religious domain. Opposition to personal law derived from the argument that such laws impede common citizenship and their continuation perpetuated divisions that were not in consonance with national unity and integration.

The government's policy of non-interference implied that it did not have the authority to interfere in the sphere of religion, of which personal law was a part. Allowing personal laws to continue conflicted with the State's obligation to establish equality before the law for all citizens and prohibit discrimination on grounds, for instance, of gender. The State was complicit in permitting inequalities between communities and within communities. It ignored the foundational problem in personal laws that deny to women the rights that the communities claim for themselves. The democratic principle, i.e. that various communities should be given the space to practise their personal laws, has been used to subordinate and dominate women. The internal domination and restriction, based on the same logic of exclusions, calls into question the very idea of an autonomous space for communities to follow their personal law. Second, the personal laws discriminate against women because they apply to all members of a community. This rules out any choice for individual citizen who do not wish to be governed by these laws.

The debate generated by the Shah Bano issue made it clear once again that Muslim political identity is derived from the legal identity and that this politico-legal identity is significant in modern India. As in the case of the Shariat Act of 1937, it is difficult to say whether the State was affirming an independently existing identity of Muslims or asserting its own values. Again, as in the earlier case, Muslims lobbied the government and the Congress government supported their stand for pragmatic political considerations. The implications of this for women are clear. From the women's standpoint, the difficulty lies in marking the identity of the Muslim community exclusively by defining its women. Failing to define the community in broad terms, the Muslim leadership has succeeded in identifying only one area as the essence of the community identity: the private sphere. Thus, all efforts at continuance and perpetuation of the community are predicated on protection of MPL, which has become, as it were, the last refuge of Muslim leaders and politicians. By defining Muslim identity entirely with reference to a strict code of laws, any change is ruled out because the survival of cultural identity depends on a codified identity. This form of minority identity leads to a definition and redefinition of women primarily as Muslims and as members of the minority community. Overlooked in the process are the stakes of Muslim women in equal rights. The reforms of personal laws does not mean the end of community or community identity, because there are a vast array of things that constitute the identity of the community, including language, religious rituals, pilgrimage to Mecca, *roza* (fast) and *namaz* (prayers).

The controversy over the MPL underscores the important part played by the State in endorsing an overlapping nexus of patriarchy and codifiable notions of community. Thus, the major impediment to legal reforms comes from the conflation of what Akeel Bilgrami calls the normative and descriptive understandings of minority in the State discourse. The normative understanding means the attitude that the community is worth preserving as it is in order to preserve its ways of life. Many who do not share this normative regard nevertheless recognize it as a descriptive fact wherever it exists or wherever it has been created in the minds of the people. The descriptive recognition should not mean that minorities can perpetuate themselves and retain their narrow communal identities in a modern and secular policy. The latter position suggests that the State and official discourse can and should acknowledge the descriptive fact of community, because Muslims and many others might value community identity, but this descriptive recognition of community should not translate into an acceptance of community and communal politics of the Muslim leadership.

The problem of legal change is complicated because of the State's insistence that reform of MPL must come from within the community. Sure enough, if this were to happen it could advance the process of secularization and democratization of the Muslim community. But the official discourse takes this too far to imply that the reform of MPL can and must happen internally, and hence the process of change cannot be started by the State. While it would be just and appropriate for Muslims to work for reforms within the community, this still does not release the State from its responsibility to reform laws that are unjust to women in a secular nation. That responsibility requires the State to hear and respond to different voices within the community and not to accept the AIMPLB as the sole spokesman of the community. From the standpoint of Muslim women, the AIMPLB is not an appropriate arena for debate on community and gender issues precisely because it is marked by an unequal exchange among men and women. The demand for reform of MPL from liberal Muslims, women's movements and Left parties, on the other hand, enjoys a certain legitimacy and credibility. But the same demand made by the Hindu Right has an entirely different implication in the context of the heightened communal mobilization since the mid-1980s. The protagonists of Hindu majoritarianism have condemned the State's failure to bring about a Uniform Civil Code (UCC) as an affront to Hindus compounded by the government's reluctance to enforce any change in MPL. Precisely because Hindutva has launched such a strident critique of MPL and demanded its replacement by a UCC, it has turned gender equality and legal reforms into an issue of Muslim identity.

III

The idea of a UCC was first put forward during the debate in the Constituent Assembly. Although its outlines have never been spelt out and the particular package of laws that would form part of it has never been made clear, it was nevertheless accepted as an important part of the effort to create a unified national identity and achieve some degree of legal assimilation and integration of the communities. The national integration dimension has been consistently emphasized by successive Supreme Court judgements on MPL that different personal laws are detrimental to national unity.

The debate on the UCC is dominated by the inadequacies of the MPL and not lacunae in, say, the Hindu Code Bill. This has created the impression that a UCC is primarily meant to override the MPL. It is therefore not surprising that the vocal critics of a UCC are the religio-political leaders of Muslims. Viewing the issue primarily as a matter of community rights, they have refuted the liberal conception of individual citizens as the sole legitimate subject of rights and advocated, instead, the entitlement of cultural communities to collective rights. The emphasis on community rights derives its force from the overall significance attached to political and religious freedom in Indian democracy, and rests on the notion of negative freedom or State abstinence (restricting the State from interfering with the liberty of citizens) as against the radical view that economic and social justice is central to the rights discourse and that all notions of freedom involve an inescapable and central commitment to some form of equality. The conflict between the two contending notions of rights originates in the tension between individual and collective rights in the Fundamental Rights of the Indian Constitution. The individual citizens are granted collective rights in Articles 14–24 and they are, moreover, sanctioned by Articles 25–30.

From the early 1990s, the debate on legal reforms has been more closely aligned with the larger issue of gender justice. This shift is prompted by the intervention of women's groups, with their emphasis on the primacy of women's rights and gender justice. The accent on gender justice is quite different from the Shah Bano controversy, where women's rights were not a major concern. The official discourse had focused entirely on minority rights and ignored the issue of the everyday experience of the minorities, particularly Muslim women. The Hindu Right mounted their attack on the Muslims through a focus on the unequal treatment of women without taking into consideration their fears and anxieties. These two strategies were not mutually exclusive, though their conspicuous feature was the marginalization of Muslim women and the trivialization of their rights in a discussion that was supposedly centred around their rights. Hence, the debate during the period virtually sidelined the issue of women's rights. Some women parliamentarians tried in vain to raise the problems of women's rights in the course of the Lok Sabha debate in 1986, but it aroused no serious interest among their fellow members. The result was the failure to stress women's rights, which inescapably made MPL the key issue in the controversy.

The arguments have taken a new turn in the aftermath of Ayodhya. Three kinds of interventions have been made with regard to legal reforms. First, there are attempts by women's groups all over the country to evolve a common package of laws that are free of gender bias. Second, there is an effort to reform from within communities. Third, a number of judicial interventions have addressed themselves to discrepancies in law. For example, a recent Supreme Court judgement gave the widow and daughter of a deceased coparcener equal rights to property left by him. Another judgement granted a divorced Hindu woman the right to sell, use for income or dispose in any way she likes the land given to her in lieu of maintenance. In another case, the widow was granted full ownership rights of the premises given to her as part of her maintenance. Such verdicts have greatly helped to reduce the existing inequities between men and women in matters of inherited property.

These initiatives are underwritten by a strong concern for gender justice. This conceptual shift has impelled a rethinking on the demand for a UCC in the light of the concurrent critique of UCC and personal laws and the recognition that introducing a UCC was a difficult proposition in a multicultural society. That is why successive governments were reluctant to push the issue despite the constitutional mandate. Today, most women's groups have relinquished the idea of uniform laws as the central plank of women's equality. Instead, they articulate an alternative position based on the principles of gender justice and women's rights. The shift is also visible in the repudiation of the UCC by almost all political parties, except the BJP. The change is explicit in the case of the All India Democratic Women's Association, the largest women's organization in the country, which has advocated a gradual approach to social reforms: reform of personal laws from within the communities and fresh legislation with regard to matrimonial property and the custody of children.

A number of proposals have been mooted to enlarge the scope of individual choices. One is to devise genuinely egalitarian or secular laws and allow people to opt for them. Such an idea was put forward as early as 1945, when it was suggested that the UCC be made optional. After independence, the Special Marriages Act or the Indian Succession Act offered a number of options. Yet the government did not endeavour to create a machinery for implementing an optional code. Had it done so, it may well have expanded the ground of secular laws, besides building up pressure for reforms within community laws. More recently, attempts have been made to move the debate from the comparative rights of communities and the nation to the rights of women as citizens. A Delhi-based women's rights group has argued in favour of a comprehensive package of legislation providing equal rights for women in terms of access to property, guardianship, right to matrimonial home, equal rights in the work place, and anti-discriminatory provisions in recruitment and promotions. It was further suggested that all Indian citizens would come under the purview of common laws but enjoy the right to choose at any point to be governed by personal laws, if they so desired. Such options would, thus, turn the regime of personal laws into something voluntary. However, the impasse between legal pluralism and legal uniformity would be seriously broken only if the State does not intervene in civil disputes between citizens and it does not provide constitutional protection to inequalities of personal laws.

The dichotomy between public and private, nation and religious minority, uniform and personal, group and individual, has made it difficult to reconceptualize the relationship of State and equal citizenship. The real problem is to arrive at a conception of democratic citizenship that provides space for the articulation of both identities without undermining either equality or justice. Recasting the debate in ways that ensure the principle of democratic choice guarantees equal rights without jeopardizing minority rights. This could, arguably, redress gender inequalities without coming into conflict with communitarian claims.

The emphasis in the contemporary context is more on the interrelationship of secularism, equality and rights, and reconceptualizing it in ways that support rather than undermine social equality and cultural identity. Highlighting the question of rights, which were until recently external to the debate, women's groups have brought to the fore the radical notion of rights in which women's equality should more appropriately be grounded.

REFERENCES

Bajpai, Rachana, Recognising Minorities: A Study of Some Aspects of the Indian Constituent Assembly Debates, 1946–49, M. Phil. Thesis, University of Oxford, 1997.

Bilgrami, Akeel, *Minorities in India*, Rajiv Gandhi Institute of Contemporary Studies, 1997.

Chhachhi, Amrita, Uma Chakravarti, Zoya Hasan, Farida Khan, Neeraj Malik, Nivedita Menon, Ritu Menon, Gautam Navlakha, Kumkum Sangari and Tanika Sarkar, 'Reversing the Option: Civil Codes and Personal Laws', *EPW*, 18 May 1996.

Fyzee, A. A., *Outlines of Muhammadan Law,* Oxford University Press, London, 1964.

Gilmartin, David, 'Customary Law and Shariat', in Katherine Ewing, *Shariat and Ambiguity in Indian Islam*, Oxford University Press, Delhi, 1988.

Hasan, Mushirul, *Legacy of a Divided Nation: India's Muslims since Independence*, Hurst, London, 1997.

Hasan, Zoya, 'Minority Identity, Muslim Women Bill Campaign and the Political Process', in Zoya Hasan (ed.), *Forging Identities: Gender, Communities and the State*, Kali for Women, Delhi, 1994.

Kishwar, Madhu, 'Codified Hindu Law: Myth and Reality', *EPW,* 13 August 1994.

Kozlowski, Gregory, 'Muslim Personal Law and Political Identity in Independent India', in Robert Baird (ed.), *Religion and Law in Independent India*, Manohar Publications, Delhi, 1993.

Mahmood, Tahir, *Muslim Personal Law: Role of State in the Subcontinent*, Asia Publishing House, Bombay, 1972.

Omvedt, Gail, 'Towards a Non-Sexist "Civil Code"', in Indira Jaising (ed.), *Justice for Women: Personal Laws, Women's Rights and Law Reforms*, The Other India Press, Mapusa, Goa, 1996.

Parasher, Archana, *Women and Family Reform in India,* Sage, Delhi, 1992.

Smith, D. E., *Nehru and Democracy: The Political Thought of Asian Democrat*, Longman, Calcutta, 1958.

8

APARNA BASU

Women's Education in India
Achievements and Challenges

Women's education has often been regarded as 'the key of keys' to bring about the required social revolution. It is a sad commentary that fifty years after independence only about 50% of India's population and less than 40% of the female population is literate. India's record on literacy is no better than that of sub-Saharan Africa. In the human development index (1997), India ranks 138, and in the gender development index, 118, an improvement on HDI, but way below China, Indonesia, South Korea, Malaysia, Thailand and even Myanmar and Sri Lanka.

HISTORICAL BACKGROUND

Exclusion of women from formal education has been a strong and long-standing tradition in India. Early in the Vedic times (2000–1500 BC), the country did produce a few learned women scholars. However, women's access to education subsequently declined so miserably that by 200 BC Manu, the lawgiver, declared them, together with the untouchables, as unfit for learning. Feminist research now reveals that despite this, women from some scholarly Brahmin and Kshatriya families, particularly royal families, were often learned. But these were rare exceptions, and women's access to formal education remained very poor. By the time the British established themselves as rulers in India, women were not only excluded from education but subjected to oppressive practices such as sati, female infanticide, child marriage, denial of right to property, and denial of right to remarriage for widows.

Women's education did not interest the East India Company in its early years; it was primarily a trading corporation and, at this time, the government in Britain was not concerned with education either. The surveys of indigenous education undertaken by the governments of Bombay, Madras and Bengal in the 1820s and 1830s revealed an almost total absence of girls from the traditional village schools as well as from the schools of higher learning. Adam in his surveys of indigenous education in Bengal wrote of the deep-rooted prejudices against girls' education (Adam in Di Bona, 1983). The only women he found literate were daughters of zamindars, especially if they had no brothers, courtesans and Vaishnavis, i.e. followers of the sixteenth century Bengali saint Shri Chaitanya. Christian missionaries were the first to start schools for girls in the nineteenth century. Some liberal official and non-official English men and women also helped in this effort. David Hare, for instance, established a school for girls near Calcutta in 1820. Professor Patton of Elphinstone College, Bombay, started a Students' Scientific and Literary Society in 1848 that ran several schools for girls. John Drinkwater Bethune, the Law Member in Lord Dalhousie's Council, established a school for girls in Calcutta in 1849, which was named after him and today is Bethune College, the oldest women's college in India.

It was only in Wood's Despatch of 1854 that the government for the first time expressed an interest in female education. Following the missionaries, Indian social reformers took up the cause of women's education. It was held that an educated woman would make a better wife and mother. Educated men felt a lack of communication with their wives and also realized that their access to the inner social circles of British society would improve if their wives spoke English and acquired European manners. But they also felt that women's position and status would improve if they were educated. Ishwarchandra Vidyasagar set up 35 primary schools for girls in the rural areas of Bengal in the 1850s and reformers in other parts of India followed suit. The Arya Samaj played an important role in spreading women's education in North India and Swami Dayanand, its founder, declared that women could read the Vedas.

While these early efforts were restricted to a small section of upper caste/class urban women, nevertheless, the fact of a few women breaking the traditional barriers was a big step forward. Jotiba Phule started in Poona, in 1851, a school for Scheduled Caste girls and Savitribai, his wife, whom he educated, was the headmistress of the school. Educating young widows to make them economically independent was another task undertaken by reformers such as Maharshi Karve, who opened a Hindu widows' home in Poona that later developed into the first women's university in India. In 1906, Sheikh Abdullah and his wife started a school for Muslim girls at Aligarh. The Parsis had already started educating their girls. It was not only men who worked for educating women. The first few women who received education were deeply committed and felt it their duty to educate their sisters. Pandita Ramabai Saraswati and Ramabai Ranade in Maharashtra, Swarnakumari Debi, Saraladebi Chaudhurani, Abala Bose and Sarala Ray in Bengal, and Vidyagauri Nilkanth and Sharada Mehta in Gujarat were some of the pioneers in the field of women's education.

In the first phase of the women's movement in India, as elsewhere, education was an area of crucial concern, and women's associations took up the cause. The All India Women's Conference was founded in 1927 primarily for promoting activities concerned with the education of girls and women and started an All India Women's Education Fund Association.

To begin with, there were only primary schools for girls as they got married by the time they were 11 or 12 years old. But gradually a few girls wanted to study further and high schools were opened, and in due course women were admitted to universities. The first women graduates were Kadambini Ganguly and Chandramukhi Basu from Calcutta in 1882 and Cornelia Sorabji from Bombay. In 1901, 169 girls were enrolled in colleges all over India. Till the 1920s progress in women's education was, however, very slow and the Hartog Committee (1929) pointed out that only 10% of girls of school-going age were enrolled in schools in British India.

With the coming of Mahatma Gandhi on the political scene and his appeal to women to join his satyagrha, women came out of their homes in large numbers to attend political meetings, march in processions, picket shops selling foreign cloth and liquor and go to prison, and this weakened the traditional bondages. In recognition of their role in the freedom struggle, the Indian National Congress in its resolution on fundamental rights adopted at the Karachi Congress in 1931 declared that 'all citizens are equal before the law irrespective of religion, caste, creed or sex in regard to public employment, office, power or honour.' The National Planning Committee appointed by the Congress also passed a resolution that in a planned society, women's position shall be equal to that of men. Indian leaders time and again declared that women's education was essential for national development. Thus, by the time of independence, the commitment to women's education was established.

Government Policy Post Independence

The framers of the Indian Constitution viewed education as an instrument of social change, individual mobility and social equality. Article 45 enjoined that 'the state shall endeavour to provide within a period of ten years from the commencement of the Constitution, compulsory education for all children upto the age of 14.' Article 15(3) makes a special provision enabling the State to take affirmative action in favour of women and children and Article 15(A)(e) imposes a fundamental duty on every citizen to renounce practices derogatory to the dignity of women.

In the first two decades after independence, rapid economic growth and self-reliance in industry, agriculture and technology were regarded as the first priority. Planners and policy-makers, therefore, emphasized technical and professional education at the higher level. The Indian Universities Commission (1948–49), headed by Dr. Radhakrishnan, noted the importance of women's education and the need to provide opportunities for women to express themselves in different fields. The first two Five Year Plans sought to link women's education to training women for professions and occupations. The Secondary Education Commission (1952–53) had no separate chapter on women's education but was gratified to see women joining faculties of engineering, agriculture, medicine and commerce. While it insisted that girls should be given the same education as boys, it laid special emphasis on the teaching of Home Science to girls as it would prepare them for their life after school. The Second Five Year Plan emphasized the need to educate public opinion on the importance of girls' education. It suggested the appointment of more women teachers, free accommodation for women teachers in rural areas, scholarships for girls, condensed courses for adult women, etc. but with little resource support. The Third Five Year Plan (1960/61–1965/66) has little to say about women's education.

The first effort to focus exclusively on women's education was the appointment of a national committee under the chairmanship of Durgabai Deshmukh in 1958. The committee recognized that women's education was a special problem and 'a bold and determined effort should be made to face its difficulties and magnitude and to close the existing gap between the education of men and women in as short a time as possible.' It recommended that more funds be given for girls' primary education, that a National Council for the Education of Girls and women be set up, and that a special unit dealing with the problem of girls' education be created in the Ministry of Education. The state governments were also asked to take greater interest and to enlist the co-operation of voluntary organizations and the public in the promotion of women's education. It suggested a campaign against the traditional prejudices against girls' education, appointment of women teachers, separate schools for girls at the higher secondary stage, if required, provision of free books, writing material and uniforms, and construction of hostels.

As recommended by the Deshmukh Committee, a National Council on Women's Education was set up in 1959, which in turn constituted a Committee on the Differentiation of Curricula for boys and girls (1961). This committee found no justification to divide school subjects on the basis of sex and proposed a common curriculum for boys and girls up to the primary stage. It rejected the traditional argument that the existing division of labour between men and women is based on their different psychological traits, which in turn arise out of sex differences. The National Council appointed another committee in 1963 to look into the causes for the lack of public support, particularly in rural areas, for girls' education and to enlist public co-operation.

The Education Commission (1964–66) fully endorsed the recommendations of these earlier committees and observed that the role of women outside the home had become an important feature of India's economic and social life. The elite bias of these commissions and committees is shown by the fact that they fail to note that poor women always worked outside the home. It asserted that education of girls should receive attention, not only on grounds of social justice but also because it accelerates social transformation. The National Education Policy Resolution of 1968, while rejecting a gender-differentiated approach to the content of education, remained silent on the instruments and strategies for implementing a common curriculum. Thus, in the first 25 years after independence, the emphasis was on women's higher education, the focus being on urban middle class women, but here also more was said than done. Women were treated as a homogeneous category, as if the needs of all women were the same.

The Committee on the Status of Women (1971–74) found that in the Census 1971, about 68% of women in the age group 15–25 years and nearly 87% in the age group of 15 years and above were illiterate. It also drew attention to the high rate of dropouts. The committee accused the planners and policy-makers of an urban middle class bias and wrong assumptions regarding women's roles, needs and priorities. It recommended a common curriculum for boys and girls, pre-school education, co-education, part time education for girls who could not attend school full time, free education for girls up to the secondary stage, and multi entry for girls, among other things. The committee found that the acceptance of the need for education of girls was highest among the urban middle classes.

WOMEN'S MOVEMENT AND WOMEN'S EDUCATION

The Report of the Committee on the Status of Women and the United Nation's declaration of 1975 as the International Year for Women, beginning with the First World Conference on Women at Mexico, generated a new interest and debate on women's issues. There was a resurgence of the women's movement that found expression both in activism and in academia. It was the women's movement that demanded that education had to play 'a positive interventionist role' in changing social attitudes to one of acceptance of gender equality and empowerment of women. As a result this aim was incorporated in The National Policy on Education (1986). The whole emphasis on women's rights and equality opened up new vistas. As countries struggled for gender equity and for recognition of women's role as vital, the question of women's education also assumed importance. The eruption of the women's movement in the 1970s had its impact on women's education in India. The Indian Association of Women's Studies was established in 1982 to bring together those engaged in teaching, research and action programmes. Women's illiteracy and lack of education began to be treated not just as a failure of education policy but as systemic to Indian society. The new generation of women activists began to treat it as an unjust effect of patriarchy. Much of the new experimentation in women's education went beyond the problem of literacy to the root cause of women's oppression and focused on tackling issues of low status and lack of economic independence. A number of non-government organizations shifted the agenda from simple literacy classes towards programmes of self-help through which women could get gainful employment and financial independence. Groups such as the Mobile Creche for Women in Delhi, working on construction sites, started non-formal education classes around issues of health, nutrition and practices of everyday life during work breaks. Formal literacy classes were held five nights a week after work for two hours in the slums where the women lived. The Baliga Foundation, a voluntary agency, opened literacy classes for women in Dakshinapuri, a working class suburb of New Delhi. These were combined with teaching women income-generating skills.

The Rural Development Society in Chingleput district of Tamil

Nadu was formed in 1979 and its schools started functioning soon afterwards. It worked in villages where women's groups or sangams were formed which, apart from local developments and problems, also discussed gender-related issues specific to rural women. The activities included encouraging non-literate women to enrol in literacy classes, health training, 'cradle programme' to prevent female infanticide, and campaigns against child marriage, illicit arrack, dowry and violence against women.

NON-FORMAL EDUCATION

A number of creative experiments in non-formal and innovative education have taken place in the last few years, while the issue of female literacy and education has grown in prominence. The draft Sixth Five Year Plan (1978–83) admitted that the benefits of education had failed to reach the majority of the population. The Sixth Five Year Plan (1980–85) emphasized eradication of illiteracy, universal primary education and introduction of job-oriented education. The plan for the first time had a chapter on 'Women and Development' that dealt with education, health and employment of women. It said that efforts should be directed towards enrolment and retention of girls in schools, income-generating work for girls outside the school hours for supplementing the family income, increase in number of women teachers, etc. The Seventh Plan (1980–90) envisaged similar measures. In 1985, a document, 'The Challenge of Education', was published by the government to elicit widespread debate in arriving at a national policy on education. It was a reflective paper that highlighted the experience of NGOs and drew attention to the drawbacks in educational management. This resulted in the National Policy on Education (1996), which for the first time recognized gender inequalities in education as a priority area, with government seeking an active role in women's empowerment through education. Participation of the people through local bodies, particularly the involvement of women, was recognized as crucial. The Programme for Action updated in 1992 stated that education would be used as an agent of basic change for the equality and empowerment of women. The removal of women's illiteracy and obstacles to their access to and retention in education were given top priority through provision of special support services, setting up of time targets and effective monitoring. Major emphasis was laid on women's technical, professional and vocational education at all levels.

One of the outcomes of the National Policy of Education 1986 was the setting up of 22 centres for women's studies in various universities by the University Grants Commission. The goals of these centres are in five major areas: teaching, research, training, extension and documentation. This involves curriculum development removal of sexist bias from textbooks and syllabus formation.

The National Perspective Plan 1988–2000 AD reiterated the NEP's view of the role of education in empowering women in order to overcome inequalities and disparities. With this in view, several new programmes were launched.

The National Literacy Mission (NLM) was launched in 1989 with the aim of imparting functional literacy to around 80 million illiterates in the age group 15–35 by 1995. Later, the 9–14 age group was also included, raising the target by another 17 million. According to NLM's 1993–94 report, 225 literacy campaigns and 7 post-literacy campaigns have been run in 275 districts, relying to a considerable extent on voluntary support. An attempt is made not only to achieve self-reliance in literacy and numeracy but also to inculcate values such as women's equality.

The Total Literacy Campaign (TLC) emerged as the most favoured strategy and also an effective and viable model for education of adult illiterates. In 1989, a voluntary agency, the Kerala Shastra Sahitya Parishad, asked the NLM for financial assistance for a mass campaign in Eranakulam district for launching a 'sampurna saksharta yagnam' or total literacy campaign. The movement involved cultural shows, processions, plays, songs, puppet shows, padayatras, etc. The objective was to generate awareness and create a favourable climate for literacy. By 1990, Eranakulam became the first fully literate district and from this developed the TLC model that is now being implemented in 366 districts. The Bharatiya Gyan Vigyan Samiti set up in 1989 conducted jathas right across the country between 1990 and 1992. Pudukottai in Tamil Nadu had, according to the 1991 census, 6.62 lakh illiterates out of a total population of 13.22 lakh and the gap between male and female literacy was highest in this district, 24.3%. The Pudukottai Mavatta Arivoli Iyakkam, a voluntary society, launched a total literacy movement here in which women's literacy was specially emphasized and literacy programmes were accompanied by income-generating activities to motivate women to learn. Women were taught to cycle as part of the literacy campaign. About 60,000 women learned cycling and this not only helped them in their daily chores such as fetching water, going to the ration shop or going to the hospital, but also boosted their self-confidence and leadership qualities. In Sivaganga district of Tamil Nadu, women were taught karate and this helped them to realize their own strength and overcome their fears and inhibitions.

In Nellore (Andhra Pradesh) the Akshara Deepam, a government-initiated programme to eradicate illiteracy taken up in each district, played a prime role in making women aware of social issues and leading the agitation against arrack distillation. With education, women were in a position to prevail upon village elders and contractors to close arrack shops, take care of their subsistence and send their children to school. Chittoor in Andhra Pradesh is another district that has taken full advantage of the TCL programme, which started in 1991 with about 60,000 volunteers teaching some 600,000 learners, 85% of whom were women. In Bhemai village, in the largely tribal district of Dungarpur in Rajasthan, the age of marriage rose and so did social awareness as a result of women's literacy.

A total literacy project was taken up by Delhi Saksharta Samiti, a voluntary society, in 1991 in Ambedkarnagar, a resettlement colony in south Delhi. Living conditions here are abysmally poor. There is lack of proper sanitation, inadequate drainage, limited and irregular water supply, and immense pressure on basic facilities such as milk supply. The literacy campaign was launched in a phased manner by first building up an environment in which several activities were conducted concurrently. 'Kala Jatha' troupes went around singing songs and performing street plays on the theme of illiteracy and the problems faced by adults due to illiteracy. After that, literacy classes were started in which initially 10,000 learners were enrolled. The women felt that they had gained self-confidence, were less shy in articulating their problems and thoughts, and were better able to manage their business and help children with their homework. The findings of this study corroborated the findings of other studies that women's motivation for literacy is very high. In a city like Delhi, the inability to use the public transport system efficiently or the inability to keep accounts or write an occasional letter or read written communications often becomes the reason for joining literacy classes. Given the poor quality of teaching that is provided in government schools, mothers of school-going children feel the need to become literate to help the children with their studies and monitor what is being taught in schools. The reasons given by women for joining literacy classes are conditioned by the socio-economic milieu in which they live.

The campaigns have now become operational in more than 250 districts in the country. The strategy deals exclusively with imparting skills of reading, writing and numeracy to the non-literate, most of whom are women. Women have invariably been the large majority of participants after constituting 75–80% of the learners. By and large, however, TLCs have paid little attention to specific issues relating to women's literacy. While the TLCs in many areas have been quite successful, usually when people have been involved through voluntary agencies, they have so far not been able to fulfil their targets. They generate initially considerable excitement and enthusiasm that cannot always be sustained over a long period.

Post-literacy centres are part of the literacy mission, as there is always the danger of people lapsing back into illiteracy unless follow-up efforts are made. By February 1994, 80 post-literacy centres had been launched. Jana Shiksha Nilayams and Jana Vidya Kendras were set up in many TLC districts to provide access to appropriate materials including books, periodicals and newspapers. One such centre is supposed to provide for five villages with a population of about 5,000 and provide for a reading room, library and other facilities.

It was in order to focus attention on gender issues in TLCs that SAMATA, a gyan vigyan jatha for women, literacy and peace, was launched during early 1993. For one month, eight cultural troupes consisting of young men and women travelled through the countryside performing street plays, singing songs and generally raising people's awareness on gender issues. While SAMATA was short-lived and its gains limited, it showed one direction for furthering the cause of women's literacy by making an attempt to link it with the larger women's movement in the country.

The Mahila Samakhya project was launched with the assistance of the Government of Netherlands in 1992 to promote women's equality and empowerment through education. It is now in operation in 14 districts in 4 states—Gujarat, Karnataka, Andhra Pradesh and Uttar Pradesh. In over 1200 villages there are Mahila Sanghas or women's collectives that mobilize women and motivate them to become literate. Sahayoginis (guides) are the initiators and members of the sanghas who co-ordinate and facilitate the work. The sakhi (friend) is the focal point of the work in the village. Mahila Samakhya was conceived not just as a literacy programme but as a programme of total education by which women would get confidence and control over their lives.

A team that evaluated the programme in Karnataka in 1991 found that it had reached the poor and socially oppressed groups of women, while the evaluation team in Gujarat did not find it very successful. Quantitatively, it was small and had not yet picked up till September 1993. The under utilization of funds and the vacant key posts indicated that the programme was not properly backed up by the kind of commitment it needs. Qualitatively, the programme had achieved some success in creating awareness and a desire for literacy. The team held that gradual bureaucratization of the Mahila Samakhya programme had alienated a large number of women's organizations, activists and academicians and for its success it had to be an autonomous programme. An evaluation of the programme in Uttar Pradesh revealed that the workers were enthusiastic and motivated and that the potential in women was sparked by just minimal education and exposure to the outside world. This team also felt that greater autonomy was necessary for the programme to be successful. It could also be that the approach is faulty. These programmes are built on the traditional model of adult literacy programmes, which hold that literacy training is a transfer of a set of independent skills from literacy instructors to ignorant women and income-generating skill programmes are often based on the same premise. The needs and priorities of the women concerned are not always taken into account.

The Bihar Education Project, started with the assistance of UNICEF in 1993 for universalizing primary education in certain districts, had as one of its goals to make the education system more responsive to the needs of women and to ensure that it promotes equality for women and facilitates their empowerment.

The District Primary Education programme was started in 42 districts of 17 states where female literacy was below the national average and where the TLC had generated some demand for education. Its focus is on the reduction of gender disparities in education and particularly on girls from socially and economically disadvantaged groups. The aim is to provide access to education through either the formal or non-formal system.

The Lok Jumbish (movement of the people) was launched in 1992, supported by the Swedish International Development Agency (SIDA). It began in Rajasthan, where 80% of women are illiterate and of every 100 children deprived of primary education, 70 are girls. It tries to harness the power and network of government structure to experience and skills of NGOs.

The Shiksha Karmi Project, also funded by SIDA and the Government of India, aimed at revitalizing and expanding education in about 2000 remote and socio-economically backward villages in Rajasthan. The project aims to solve the problem of poor enrolment, particularly of girls, high dropout rates, teachers' absenteeism and poor local relevance of the curriculum. The crucial innovation in the project is the substitution of the primary school teacher by a team of two educational workers, 'shiksha karmis', who are local persons living in the village. They are supposed to teach 40 to 50 children for two to three hours per day and in addition have evening classes for children who cannot attend during the day. Aangan pathshalas (courtyard schools) were set up for girls. Another imaginative innovation was to use elderly women as helpers to escort girls to schools in difficult areas and to take care of younger siblings.

The government has also started programmes to upgrade the skills of poor, assetless women and train women in modern trades such as electronics and computer programming. The schemes are, however, on a small scale and have not been very successful because of bureaucratic control and delays in releasing funds. They are implemented through NGOs, who are often hesitant to take them up because of these reasons.

Literacy

Despite all the recommendations of committees and commissions, policy initiatives and plans of action during these five decades, progress in women's literacy has been very slow. No doubt there has been some advance. In 1951, only 8.6% of Indian women were literate, as against 39.42% in 1991. Male literacy rate has gone up from around 27% to 64% in this period. The definition of literacy has, however, changed and today anyone who can simply write his or her name or any sentence without even understanding what is written is regarded as literate. Also, the literate population is now counted for those above the age of 7. While the percentage of illiterate women declined by 10% in the decade 1981–91, the total number of illiterate women in the age group 7+ increased from 76.9 million to 197.34 million in this decade.

There are, of course, vast regional variations. In 1991, Kerala was leading with 86.93% literate women, while Rajasthan was at the bottom with 20.84%. Female illiteracy is concentrated in certain states: 155 of the 247 districts where female literacy is lower than the national average are concentrated in the four states of Bihar, Madhya Pradesh, Rajasthan and Uttar Pradesh. Kottayam district in Kerala has the highest female literacy, 96%, and Jhabua in Madhya Pradesh has the lowest, 19%. These disparities are due to geographical, social and historical reasons. Kerala is a fertile state with no water shortage, whereas Rajasthan is desert land with acute water scarcity. The backwardness of Jhabua is largely due to the fact that it is in an extremely arid region where the main problem of women is to get water. Literacy is not their first priority. Some communities in Kerala, Mizoram and Meghalaya have a matrilineal system in which the status of women, is high and property belongs to women. There is no seclusion of women, unlike in Rajasthan or some of the other states of the Gangetic heartland. There are no instances of sati recorded in Malabar. Kerala has not been subjected to repeated invasions unlike the northern states where, as a result, women were kept in purdah. Kerala also was fortunate in having rulers who promoted women's education. Also, early in its history it had Christian missionary schools. The urban/rural divide in Kerala is also not as sharp as in some other states and communication is easy.

Urban/rural disparities in literacy are striking in India. In the country as a whole, in 1991, female literacy rate was 30.6% for rural areas as against 64.1% in urban areas. Twenty-seven districts had less than 10.5% literacy (15 in Rajasthan, 7 in Uttar Pradesh and one each in Bihar and Orissa). There are 134 districts, i.e. 30% of the total districts in India, with a female literacy rate of less than 20%. Scheduled Caste and Scheduled Tribe women are at the bottom of the heap, the former having a literacy rate of 24% and the latter 18%. In Uttar Pradesh, the S.C. female literacy rate was 10.69%, in Rajasthan 8.31% and in Bihar the lowest, 7.07%. Scheduled Tribe female literacy rate was lowest in Rajasthan, 4.42%, followed by Andhra Pradesh, 8.68%. The highest was in Nagaland, 54.51% (Census 1991). Rural female literacy is less than 10% in 27 districts, 10–20% in 107 districts, and 20-30% in 99 districts.

ENROLMENT

There has been a spectacular growth in the number of schools and colleges and enrolment at all levels. Girls' enrolment at the primary level has grown from 5.4 million in 1950–51 to 47.37 million in 1995–96. The corresponding increase at the middle level has been from 0.5 million to 16.5 million. In 1995–96, 93.3% of girls in the age group 6–11 were enrolled but enrolment decreased to 54.9% at the middle level, i.e. in the age group 11–14. In 1990, only 16.3% of the girls in the age group 14–17 were enrolled in high schools.

Although girls' enrolment has grown at a faster pace than that of boys, they continue to lag behind, with their proportion to the total going down with every successive higher level. In 1995–96, girls form 40% of all students in the education system, 43% at the primary stage, 39% at the upper primary stage, 36% at the secondary stage, and 34% at the higher level.

Interstate disparities are wide. High female literacy states (above 50%) have universalized primary enrolment among girls with the exception of the union territory of Chandigarh, where though the female literacy rate in 1991 was 74%, girls' enrolment in primary schools was only 59%. Girls' enrolment at the primary level is highest in Pondicherry, Lakshadweep, Mizoram, Goa and Kerala. These states fare very well at the upper primary level also. The gender gap in primary level enrolment is minimal in Kerala, Nagaland, Meghalaya, Mizoram, Lakshadweep and Delhi. In states where female literacy is 40–50%, girls' enrolment is high at the primary level but there is a steep fall at the upper primary level. In states where female literacy is 20–40%, girls' enrolment in primary schools is very poor, specially in Bihar, Uttar Pradesh, Rajasthan and Jammu and Kashmir. Half the country's population resides in these states.

Girls in rural areas are far behind those in cities. They constitute 74.1% of all girl students at the primary level but this drops to about 30% at the higher secondary level. Only 8.22% of villages were covered by secondary schools and 1.98% by higher secondary schools in 1993, with the result that only 42% of rural girls in the age group 10–14 attend schools and hardly any go to college (Sixth All India Education Survey, NCERT, 1995). The state of many primary schools in villages is abysmal: there are no chairs, no tables, no blackboards, no chalks, often no buildings. Teacher absenteeism is endemic and in Uttar Pradesh it is reported that two-thirds of the teachers fail to attend school regularly. Even in schools where regular classes are held, the quality of teaching leaves much to be desired.

While enrolment rates have increased, a large number of children drop out of school before even completing their primary education and the majority of those who do so are girls. The dropout rate between classes I and V was 35.5% for boys and 38.57% for girls in 1993. For Scheduled Castes the figures in 1988–89 were 47% for boys and 55% for girls. In the same year, 64% S.T. boys and 70% S.T. girls enrolled in class I dropped out before completing class V. The reasons for the high rate of girls dropping out are by now fairly well known. Poverty compels girls to help in household work such as cooking, fetching water and fuel, looking after younger brothers and sisters, as well as to earn an extra income by working outside the home. Early marriage is also a deterrent. According to the 42nd round of the National Sample Survey (July 1986 to June

1987), a little over one-fourth of all dropouts gave 'not interested in further education/study' as the reason for leaving school. This is because of the irrelevance of the curriculum specially for rural and urban poor girls. Apart from the curriculum being irrelevant, the quality of teaching is also poor. Rural schools do not have toilets for girls which is another reason why girls drop out.

The strategies and means for attracting and retaining girls are known. They include reducing the cost of schooling, having schools closer to the community so that girls do not have to walk long distances, increasing the number of women teachers, adopting more flexible schedules, providing midday meals and making the curriculum more relevant to the lives of the students. The problem is not that policy-makers do not know what to do but that they fail to implement policies.

HIGHER EDUCATION

The higher education system has grown steadily since independence. From 35 universities in 1947 and 700 colleges for general and professional education (1951), in 1996 there were 226 universities, institutions deemed to be universities, and institutions of national importance and over 9000 colleges. There was only one women's university at the time of independence, the SNDT Women's University; today there are five, and 800 women's colleges that cater to nearly 50% of girls enrolled in higher education. In a number of these colleges, however, enrolment is low, the standard of teaching is poor and they are financially not viable.

Enrolment of students has increased from 2 lakhs in 1947 to over 50 lakhs in 1996, of whom 18.65 lakhs are girls. Kerala, as can be expected, has the highest enrolment of women, 73.4%, and Bihar the lowest, 16.9%. Though the total number of girls enrolled in science, engineering, technology and architecture has undoubtedly increased in the last 50 years, the percentage has not changed significantly in the last decade. In medicine, of the total enrolment in 1950–51, only 6.6% were girls; it rose to 36.5% in 1993–94 but declined to 34.5% in 1995–96. The percentage of girls has declined, perhaps because of the capitation fees many colleges charge, and parents may be more ready to spend the money on boys. In 1995–

96, girls formed about 41.5% of arts faculty students, 35.5% in science faculties and 29.0% in commerce. The only professional courses open to women before independence were teaching, nursing, medicine and law. Admission to engineering and technical courses was possible only after 1948. Today, there are numerous vocational and professional courses available to girls such as mass communication, fashion technology, interior designing and architecture, business management, computer science, journalism, tourism, hotel management, etc.

Educated Women in the Labour Force

While the number of women who go to secondary schools and colleges has increased, and so has the number of middle class educated working women, still, very few of them are in the labour force. In 1993–94, according to the 50th Round of the National Sample Survey, of women in rural areas who were matriculates, 19.81% were in the labour force and only 14.31% of urban girls. As for women graduates, 47.85% rural and 35.60% urban women were employed. Thus, about 65% of women graduates in cities were not in the labour force. This small representation of educated women in the labour force is not surprising as women's place in India, as elsewhere in the world, has traditionally been in the home and there are still strong prejudices against women working. For middle and upper class/caste women these taboos have been particularly strong.

In India, as in other countries, certain jobs are regarded as suitable for women. Teaching is a popular profession, particularly at the school level, and women formed 29.47% of primary, 33.7% of middle, and 31.20% of higher secondary school teachers in 1991–92. Rural areas continue to face acute shortage of female teachers and at the primary stage, the proportion of women teachers is only 21% as against 56% in urban areas. In colleges and universities, the number of women teachers declines as we go up the hierarchy. According to a study done on Women in Higher Education Management by the Commonwealth Secretariat and UNESCO in 1993, in India, 7% of professors, 22% of associate professors, 38% of assistant professors, 56% of lecturers and 61% of instructors are women. Women are grossly under-represented in higher education management. Of the university-level institutions, only 6% have women vice-chancellors, 21% have women senior administrators and 10% have women heads of departments and principals of constituent colleges.

WOMEN AND DEVELOPMENT

It is now widely recognized that of the several areas for women's advance, education is one of the most important. Demographers have put forward strong cross-country evidence that increased schooling is positively associated with reduced fertility. In India, according to the Census of 1981, total fertility was 5.1 for women with no education, 4.5 for women with primary education, 3.1 for those with secondary education, and 2.1 for those with higher education. Recently published results of the 1992–93 National Family Health Survey for all the major states confirm the strong effects of literacy and primary education on fertility. While the determinants of differences in fertility rates are complex and not fully understood, one intervening factor is the increase in the age of marriage, which rises with the level of education. Declining fertility rates also change the amount and distribution of resources for education. Between 1965 and 1980, the share of the population of children below the age of 15 fell from 43% to 26% in the Republic of Korea and from 46% to 34% in Thailand. During the 1980s the growth rate of the population in the group 6–11 in Southeast Asia was very low. With a declining or slowly growing school age population, a country can spend more on each student and provide better quality education. There is also a strong relation between mothers' education and child mortality. Interestingly, it has been found that mothers' education has an even greater effect on the survival of daughters. Studies have shown that schooling improves a mother's child care skills, domestic management of ill health and efforts at preventive care, and increases immunization rates. Mothers' schooling also influences children's nutritional status. A study of two villages in West Bengal showed that children of literate mothers had a higher nutritional intake than children of illiterate mothers. While access to schools, enrolment and retention are important, the content is equally crucial. Education must improve women's skills so that they are not confined to low-paid and unskilled or semi-skilled jobs. The curriculum has also an important role to play in giving the girl child a positive self-image. Textbooks have to reflect these values and teachers also have to be made gender sensitive. Education by itself may not raise a woman's status within the family or society but it certainly helps in doing so.

Investment in women's education shows useful returns as it has a positive effect in improving health care, immunization, reducing infant and maternal mortality, lowering the birth rate, and enhancing readiness to send girls to schools. Among its economic effects are a greater readiness to mobilize credit and willingness to use banks and readiness to participate in and to establish co-operatives and small business enterprises. But a woman's education is also important because it enriches her personality and should give her greater self-confidence, economic independence and ability to take part in decision-making. In many instances, literate women have shown the capacity for leadership and a greater readiness to organize against injustice.

At the time of India's independence, India's population was 40 crore; today we have 48 crore illiterates, 63% of whom are women. While there has been a spectacular growth in the number of schools, colleges and universities and enrolment at all levels, most of the gains of this expansion have gone to the children of the upper and middle classes and more to boys than girls. Development cannot be based on education of an elite. The strength of a country's development effort ultimately depends not only upon the high level skills of the few, but also—indeed mainly—upon the educational competence of the many. No doubt there has been some social mobility and education has reached areas and groups that were outside its pale 50 years ago. More girls today go to school and college, but still 60% of Indian women are illiterate and 38.57% of those who join class I drop out before completing class V. As we have seen, poverty, irrelevance of the curriculum, poor facilities in schools, absenteeism and indifference of teachers all contribute to children leaving school even before they complete primary school. And as children drop out, the number of illiterates continues to grow. While numerous adult literacy programmes have been launched in the last decade, achievements have fallen far short of expectations. For the poor, literacy is often not the first priority. As some village women elected to the panchayats said: 'You ask us to send our children to school but literacy won't provide food.... We need food first, which only money can buy, then knowledge afterwards. Our children won't become judges or barristers. There are dozens of boys with higher education who are unemployed. Even if our boys go to high school, they will not get jobs and once educated, they do not want to live in villages or help their parents in farm work. Girls will get married. So what is the point in educating our children? It is better that they start earning for the family.'

People will learn to read and write effectively if during the learning process they can see the relevance of the skills they are learning to the tasks they have to perform. For instance, in Banda district of Uttar Pradesh the Mahila Samakhya collaborated with the Jal Niyam (the government agency responsible for the installation and maintenance of handpumps) to train some local people in pump maintenance and repair. Women took a leading part in this programme and, once trained, expressed a desire for more information and reading material on a range of topics. They may not have been motivated through a general primer using simple, child-oriented words but were eager to be able to read a handpump manual. When asked what each of them would like to read, a group of women in Jaipur, Rajasthan, chose several different items, but the majority of them expressed a desire to read cinema notices and they were taught successfully from these. It is important to find out what people want to learn and why and how it will benefit them. Without people's participation such programmes cannot succeed. Total literacy campaigns are promising approaches but it is not easy to ensure that something will remain when the initial enthusiasm has evaporated. The functional literacy approach backed by UNESCO has not proved too successful and, therefore, increasingly efforts are being devoted to promoting primary education.

Better quality education in the free primary and secondary schools holds the key to higher literacy and a higher quality of life. There has been a substantial gap between rhetoric and achievement.

In part it is a question of resources. In part, it is a consequence of the sheer size and growth of a population of which about three-quarters lives in rural areas, and a substantial number below the poverty line. Partly it is the result of bureaucratic controls and lack of commitment and political will to implement policies effectively. The complex social relationship between caste and gender also plays a role. Despite all brave words to the contrary, education has so far not fulfilled its commitment to the poor, especially women, and it has strenghened the hegemonic control of the elite. The future, said Nehru 50 years ago, was one of 'incessant striving' to end poverty, ignorance, disease and inequality. It is still.

REFERENCES

Adam's Reports on Indigenous Education in Bengal, reprinted in Di Bona, Joseph (ed.), *One Teacher One School*, Biblia Impex Pvt. Ltd., New Delhi, 1983.

'Alternative Avenues to Women's Empowerment and Education for Women's Equality', Report of the Second Dutch Mission to review the Mahila Samakhya Programme, Dept. of Education, Ministry of HRD, 1992.

Chanana, Karuna (ed.), *Socialisation, Education and Women*, NMM & L, Orient Longman, Statistics are cited from:

Census of India, 1991.

Development of Education in India, 1993–94, Dept. of Education, Ministry of HRD, New Delhi, 1994.

Dighe, Anita, 'Women and Literacy in India: A Study in a Re-settlement Colony of Delhi', Education for Development, Occasional Paper Series 1, No. 2, 1995.

Evaluation of Literacy Campaigns in India, Report of Expert Group, National Literacy Mission, Directorate of Adult Education, Ministry of HRD, Dept. of Education, New Delhi, 1994.

Human Development Report, UNDP, 1997.

India: Primary Education, Achievements and Challenges, World Bank Report, 1995.

Manpower Profile in India, Institute of Applied Manpower Reseach, New Delhi, Yearbook, 1997.

Ministry of Human Resource Development, Selected Educational Statistics, 1993–94.

National Policy on Education, 1986 (with modifications undertaken in 1992), Ministry of Human Resource Development, Dept. of Education, New Delhi, 1992.

Nayar, Usha, From Girl Child to Person, UNESCO, New Delhi, 1995.

Quinquennial Reports on the Progress of Education in India, Chapters on Female Education.

Rao, Nitya, 'Total Literacy Campaigns: A Field Report', *EPW*, 8 May 1993.

'Redefining Gender Relations, Redefining Politics, Nellore, Village Women against Arrack', *EPW*, 16–23 Jan., 1993.

The Report of the Committee on the Status of Women in India: Towards Equality, Govt. of India, Dept. of Social Welfare, Ministry of Education and Social Welfare, New Delhi, 1974.

Report of the National Committee on Women's Education, New Delhi, 1959.

Richey, J.A., Selections from Educational Records, Pt. II, 1840–59, Chapter II, 'The Beginnings of Female Education', Calcutta, 1922.

Sixth All India Educational Survey, Provisional Statistics, NCERT, 1995.

9

Mrinal Pande

Indian Women and the Electronic Media

Women in India have traditionally been peripheral to our media food-chain. They account for just a little less than 50% of India's vast population and half of the 300 million strong viewers of television, but the decision-making set-up in the media, as in the Parliament, did not, till about a decade ago, see them as an important group. Till a decade ago the dominant media was the print media. Here the low literacy rates of women (even now, two-thirds of India's women are illiterate) and their even lower buying power made them negligible as media consumers, and dispensable as workers and media managers. There were other reasons as well, such as the low visibility of women in society and in politics, low registration of the economically remunerative work done by them, and the usually high-risk, low-salaried nature of women's jobs. Coupled with the age-old biases against women's intellectual capacity, this generated a mind-set in commercial media circles that the average consumer of the media was a male and that women, if they did figure in it at all, were secondary, both as subjects for commentary and as arbiters of taste. This mind-set continued when the electronic media first began to expand.

Between 1982 and 1987 Doordarshan began to commission serials and programmes that would nudge the collective social conscience of Indian TV viewers and help them see women the way they really were, not as faceless mothers and workers or mere playthings. It was then that serials such as *Adhikar* (a 13 part serial on legal rights for women), *Aur Bhi Hain Rahein*—literally meaning there are other roads (an information package outlining career opportunities for women), *Udaan* (women making a breakthrough as cops) and *Kashmakash* (a serial on women's struggles) were screened. Largely untrained and hesitant feminists began to coach themselves to handle TV programming and several of them took to telecasting regularly even though the pay was poor and work was erratic.

It is noteworthy that although all these serials proved to be popular according to the ratings, the most popular programme was *Ramayana*, a commercially sponsored serial by a commercial film-maker on the mythological tale of Ram and Sita. The unstated attitude was, while *Ramayana* rakes in huge profits, let the politically correct serials keep the liberals happy. This could not and did not last. The sponsors were looking not for social messages but for viewership ratings, and so the socially relevant serials usually did not get a renewal of their contract. When they did get a renewal it was after a long battle and the producers were told politely that the government would not commission the serial and that they would have to look for commercial sponsors. One by one, these features and serials, though missed by the audiences, gradually disappeared because the sponsors, mostly the makers of chocolates, soaps and toothpaste, wanted loud entertainment consisting of spicy film extracts or else religious mythology. *Ramayana* went on to dominate the small screen for months and ran into several hundred episodes and was then followed by an equally crude small-screen version of the *Mahabharata*, which sent the cash registers ringing. The sponsors were now queuing up and asking for more of the same.

The sponsorship pattern of the mid-1980s retains its basic inner contradictions till today, in that here private capital must be used to finance government-created welfarism, and open titillation of consumers' base instincts must coexist with protests against a coarse consumerism that is destroying the cultural matrix and promoting greed and violence in society. The producers of most of the popular serials still remain Bombay-based with no previous experience other than that of producing advertisements or commercial cinema. The 'other' kind of serials on politically correct topics is produced only by idealistic young producers and activists with shoestring budgets and little marketing experience. That the quality and promotional powers of the one soon drive out the other has now become the recurring karmic pattern of the world of TV programming.

With the advent of the 1990s, however, some things have begun to change. Sounds and images from the audio-visual media now effectively penetrate the illiteracy barrier, while at the same time the daughters of the post-independence band of middle-class women from urban areas, who were deeply influenced by feminism, have joined the media (both the print and electronic) in large numbers. These young women, well-educated, articulate and aware of their rights, are also making vital decisions within urban households about the purchase of consumer durables and non-durables. And they make sure that the market takes serious note of their arrival. True, this class is limited, but when translated into numbers, even this percentage has yielded a sizeable group that has a fairly large sprinkling of senior media managers and artists in its midst.

The enhanced visibility and official clout of women, both in the print and in the visual media, may have generated its own backlash, but it has also made Indian women an unavoidably important component of Indian democracy and its markets. Inside media too, for the first time some women have begun to talk of the glass ceiling. They assert that when they acquire the skills and the seniority they should be given editorial and departmental control. Most of them were still pipped to the post by males who networked through the corridors of power. And when they joined the privately owned electronic media, partly as protest and partly as a natural mid-career switch, it was taken as a reaffirmation of their feminine disregard for propriety.

True, a country like India contains multitudes. When we go to the villages, we go back to the agrarian culture that wakes and sleeps with sunrise and sunset and marks out seasons by configurations in the sky. Here women can be seen but not heard and if they work, it is in the fields or within homes. But as we come closer to the cities, the villages too begin to show signs of change. Television antennae and satellite dishes become increasingly visible and the local culture and speech begin to reveal the unmistakable stamp of popular films and TV programmes. Then there are the metropolitan cities like Delhi, Bangalore, Bombay, Calcutta or Madras that have upper-crust pockets, seeped in the electronic revolution in the same way as their counterparts in the developed world. Computers have been around in India for over a decade. The internet revolution reached India some two years ago; and at the moment there are some 60,000 internet connections in the country, serving an estimated half a million consumers. But the enormous advantages of the internet and the new jobs that computers have created in India remain limited, largely, to urban males, since they require high levels of computing skills and constant creativity. Both are mostly denied to women, who remain sedimented in low-skill, low-paid jobs. If the electronic revolution has yielded any advantages to Indian women, the beneficiary has been the same limited group of upper class, urban women, who have in any case long been noticeable for being head and shoulders above the majority of their sisters, and also many brothers from the poorer sections.

Television was introduced in India in 1959 (with the help of a UNESCO grant) with the purchase of a 500 watt transmitter at a nominal price from Phillips, a multinational corporation. A pilot project set up to study its use was aimed at evaluating TV as 'a medium of education, rural uplift and community development.' Twice a week, hour-long programmes were telecast to an audience that gathered at specially created TV clubs or community centres in the capital city of Delhi. Two years later, aided by the Directorate of Education and the Ford Foundation, a weekly programme created for students of higher secondary schools began to be telecast. It was only in 1965 that regular daily telecasting began in Delhi. In 1975, when a Satellite Instructional Television Experiment (SITE) was launched, a politically cornered Prime Minister, Mrs Indira Gandhi, imposed the Emergency, which led to a ruthless censoring of all media. All India Radio and Doordarshan became blatant mouthpieces for the ruling party; and they have since not been able to de-stigmatize themselves totally in the public eye.

The next phase occurred in 1982, just before the 9th Asian Games were scheduled to be held in Delhi. At the behest of Rajiv Gandhi, son of the Prime Minister and a moving spirit behind the preparations for the games, the switch to colour TV was made. Political circles now began to debate liberalization of India's economy, and the ruling class began to doubt both Gandhian austerity and the Nehruvian brand of socialism. The import of TVs was put under the Open General Licence and licence requirement was waived for sets already imported. In July 1983, the cabinet okayed the plan to expand TV networks, adding 126 new transmitters for networking, through the Indian satellite system. TV now covered 70% of India's population. And this is where things began to change for women within the electronic media.

During the 1980s the government-controlled electronic media made several affirmative efforts, such as focussing the national attention on the girl child, family welfare and concern for pregnant and lactating mothers and mothers of school-going children. But programmes promoting this mind-set were still formulated firmly within the traditional model of integrating women into a given developmental framework. Most of these attempts, as a result, become what the film-maker Deepa Dhanraj calls the 'add women and stir' formula. They were doomed to fail for the same reasons that the Delhi-centric approach to the development strategies for the government had not succeeded. In 1986, when a panel (including this writer) interviewed the then Prime Minister Rajiv Gandhi for Doordarshan TV, his stock reply to women's concern about high mortality and low literacy rates among girls and women was that in his family they valued girls and that he did not subscribe to the patriarchal mind-set. As though what the women of the Gandhi family could expect and get, would be naturally replicated in the lives of millions of India's women living below the poverty line and haunted by endemic joblessness. By the end of the interview, it was clear that even this very suave and liberal young Prime Minister, who had ushered in liberalization and the latest in electronic media, still harboured the typical upper-middle crust Indian male's top-down assumption that Indian women are a uniform group with uniform needs, and that age-old differences of caste, class and social structures that operate and segregate one

networks in India. In spite of glib promotion and excellent technical quality, and in spite of being dubbed in Hindi, all these failed to attract audiences even a quarter as large as those commanded so effortlessly by serials based on song and dance sequences from Hindi films, musical game shows based on Hindi film songs, and Hindi, Telugu, Tamil and Bengali films.

This fact, ironically, helps women. English has for long segregated classes and genders in India more firmly than caste or colour. The percentage of Indian women who could read and write English has never been more than 1% of their total population. But since English speakers almost always come from an upper-crust, well-to-do urban class, their visibility and assertive loquaciousness has always been quite disproportionate to the actual size of this elite. TV has shattered the myth that English alone can get communicators a direct access to the average Indian mind. For years the highest-level government policy papers promoting women, feminist disclosures on women's issues, and economic analysis of women's actual contribution to the nation's economy have all chosen to use the English language as their vehicle. As a result, not only 99% of our women but also a substantial number of grassroots social workers and activists have had little or no dialogue with our top government policy-makers, feminists, economists and social scientists. Even the most eminent of India's economists and social scientists and anthropologists have been getting their data collected by (a largely unvetted army of) young researchers whose only qualifications are mobility within the geographic area being researched and a certain facility with the local languages.

Suddenly, what the pressures of academic research or five year plans or just plain common sense could not change for 50 years, commercial TV and its TRP (Television Rating Points) ratings have begun to challenge effectively. TRP ratings have revealed how home-based, near-illiterate women may also have an astute and shrewd perception of their rights as consumers of TV and may reject or force families to reject programmes that are outside of their own lives. Also, now given a chance, illiterate and semi-literate women workers such as those of SEWA (Self-Employed Women's Association, Ahmedabad) may even, with little training, be able to handle sophisticated cameras and video recorders and record the stories of their lives. The latter fact has still to find takers in the commercial world, but the psychographic profile of the average woman TV viewer has suddenly become a holy mantra to marketeers, who have at long last begun to look closely and with renewed respect at non–English speaking, non-assertive Indian women in lower middle class homes.

In visualizing the post-1990s mass communications environment, the marketeers have realized that they need, as never before, to give a local habitation, a gender and a name to the masses. Most Indians do not know English and would not care for technical sophistication beyond a point. Nearly 300 million men and women in the six northern states of Uttar Pradesh, Bihar, Madhya Pradesh, Rajasthan, Himachal Pradesh and Haryana want their programmes only in Hindi.

However, the West-created and largely West-perfected electronic media that is required to produce the saleable and commercially profitable TV programmes in Hindi (including the news bulletins) still uses an information technology largely locked up in English. Like the holy scribe or the fearsome brahmin, the ruling elite have once again encrypted vital information in an alien tongue. Information that, decoded, could empower millions of women. As the Indian press, television and radio congratulate themselves on their commitment to free speech, they have to remember that it is not always the ideas that create the market, but often vice versa. And in as much as market is functioning increasingly through webservers and websites, the webmaster may have quietly replaced the bureaurcat or the merchant, who were at least known devils.

Of course, there is something healthy about the fact that many such shibboleths from India's bureaucratically ridden and politically manipulated marketing past are being destroyed. If only for the sake of profit, our media barons are beginning to look where women and the Indian languages have stood for 50 years, forlorn and neglected. The results of the electronic revolution are also reaching the anglicized marketing gurus and advertising executives who have trained in Europe and the United States and had earlier looked at women and vernaculaurs as avoidable down-market entities. We are all now learning to see culture as something decentralized, flexible and very, very mobile. And this moment of historical vulnerability in the traditional Asian ethos, if tackled sensitively and with honesty, can help women achieve freedom.

Even a limited study of popular programmes on both the government-controlled Doordarshan and cable TV shows that the dominant image of the woman constructed as the norm has been urban, literate, middle class and westward-looking, The power of this image must not be understated. As urban societies change in India, and more and more joint families break up into nuclear ones, TV becomes a new and powerful teacher of cultural norms. Despite their individual and different motivations, the interests of the programmes, bureaucrats, advertisers and audiences can frequently coincide and converge to make a pro-woman bias inevitable. With the proliferation of TV sets in urban schemes and rural areas, middle class modes of social conduct, dietary patterns and consumerism may be scattering their seeds far and wide. But biases that are man-made can be unmade too. With a concerted effort the programmers as well as the law and order agencies and the general public can come together to counter, as never before, the rise in cases of rape and molestation of women, dowry practices and violent inner-city crime.

It is senseless now to plead a Luddite case for a life without TV and the electronic and print media. The point the electronic media has reached today also makes any debate on government control a meaningless proposition. Government in developing countries such as ours began the process of privatization in the 1980s and that process has gathered momentum in the 1990s. Privatization of airwaves may have been slow and drawn out, but it is a distinct possibility now. In a broad sense, privatization of the audio-visual media, the kind that the Supreme Court of India envisaged in a recent judgement when it declared airwaves 'public property', not to be monopolized by either the government or major publishing houses, meant that not only the government but also market forces must work towards meeting a society's needs for vital information and clean entertainment. Both markets and governments, however, are imperfect. To control TV programming completely through laws, so that 'socially relevant' programmes may be beamed into homes and all kinds of subversive capitalistic consumerism may automatically be filtered out, would require an autocratic and centrist State where all programmes are financed, supported or else jammed by government and powerful armies and generals. The experience of those who have tried to put the clock back shows that it is impossible to jam information today, except in dictatorships. We will be better off if we start by keeping in mind that in the coming times, private voluntary involvement, with leverage in the market-place, is the answer, not government-controlled programming.

Today, since the free market juggernaut is well on its way to privatization, it would do well to remember that the problems of poverty are located in the socio-economic system, problems such as the low and unequal wages doled out to women workers in the unorganized sector (which employs almost 90% of our women), or the politically motivated diversion of state resources to pay higher salaries to an ever-expanding group of government employees and doles and subsidies at the cost of the social sector, are basically born of sick political systems. Mere TV initiatives into 'socially relevant' programming can hardly be expected to bear fruit so long as the country is run by irresponsible and corrupt governments. The following facts, unpalatable as they may be, have to be kept in mind by all those who really wish to tackle the issue of a healthy and free media:

1. Social problems in India and similar countries that bedevil women are structural and not conjunctural, i.e. rooted in a particular time and set of circumstances. Interventions, when made here, have to have a teleological perspective.

2. The willingness of free market forces to share profits and resources with the less advantaged, the largest number of whom happen to be women, in any society, has been dubious at the best of times. There is no reason to hope that things will be different now. So, if women wish to be heard, they must become more alert and demanding as consumers, and more assertive and less eager to please as media executives.

3. Substitution of symbolic, emotive images on TV in the absence of substantive benefits (jobs, equal wages, health care, day-care) does not work. Therefore, if pro-woman, positive programming on TV has to have any lasting impact, it has to be matched and supported from the outside by assertive social activism and democratic tools at women's disposal such as the franchise and the

entry of women representatives into all media bodies and decision-making fora.

4. Ultimately, technology itself is neutral. The questions that spell the difference relate to who is using it and for whom. Indian women's problems are not the kind that can be solved by half an hour's TV serial-watching. Today, the decisions that affect the lives of all Indians are not taken by TV executives and producers alone, but by corporate executives and politicians embedded in major institutions of power where women are either non-existent or sedimented in the lower echelons. This has to change.

5. Isolated do-goodism is out. The personal ties between, say, an 'art film' maker and an NGO group or a particular village may be cute, but they cannot successfully overcome the impediments to mass social mobilisation. A few sensitive and 'feel-good' programmes on the saving the environment or tigers or the girl child are unlikely to make a permanent difference. We must, therefore, stop harping perennially on the heartstrings of an increasingly heartless system, and instead learn about the roots of problems and how to help others assert their rights locally, without being overbearing or petulant.

Today, the powerful forces of electronic communication individuate and globalize simultaneously. They isolate women by exalting their gender identity, while making them dependent, on mass markets. Both information and women are going to be free eventually, whether the societies and political systems like it or not. But freedom brings with it a new set of responsibilities. And the women and dealers and suppliers of information will also do well to remember that there is no such thing as free information.

10

TAPATI GUHA-THAKURTA

Women as Artists in Contemporary India*

'Suddenly,' to quote a recent article, '"women" are everywhere.'[1] As we mark the proliferation of 'women' and 'women's issues' across the spectrum of the nation's public life, we also confront their triumphant arrival on the contemporary Indian art scene. The prominence that has come to women's art in the past decades can be chronologically mapped along various axes. There is an obvious link with the growing power and confidence that the women's movement in India gained since the 1970s. The developments in art, one could argue, have kept pace with the rising centrality of women (as subject and object, agent and addressee) in a variety of fields ranging from academic research to public policy to social and cultural activism. In all this, there is an equally important connection to be drawn with the new wave of promotion, publicity and mega-sales that have flamboyantly transformed the profile of Indian art in the recent past. Money and media (national and international) today shower the kind of attention on artists and art events that was inconceivable even a decade ago, blowing these to proportions that are clearly

* This essay is dedicated to the memory of one of the greatest artists of our time, Meera Mukherjee, who died on 27 January 1998.

larger than life. The celebration of a new creed of contemporary women artists in India thus goes hand in hand with the unprecedented prestige and glamour that has come to surround the entity of 'modern Indian art'.

This essay takes up the current limelight and importance claimed by these female subjects of our contemporary art history. There is a particular play here on the term 'subject', with women actively navigating the divide between its dual connotations of theme and agency. For nowhere, as in the realm of the visual arts, has the transition of women from creations to creators been so pointed and pronounced. From being the most idealized and canonized image of Indian art, one that reigns supreme across the genres of temple sculpture and miniature painting, women have had to negotiate a new role in art history as artists and producers. The entrenched power of the artistic image made for both the difficulty and urgency of this negotiation. For, it is only by contesting the primacy and pervasiveness of the represented image that women could fight for a new subjectivity as artists, and effect the passage from motif to makers. The figuring of women as artists in modern India has involved, therefore, a reconfiguration of the very equation between women and art, a sharp shift from object to subject status.

The favoured theme of 'women in Indian art', once taken up by innumerable art books, is gradually giving way to the new theme of 'Indian women artists'. One of the first signals of this shift can be traced to the staging of an exhibition of contemporary women artists at the National Gallery of Modern Art in New Delhi in 1987. The fiftieth anniversary year established fresh landmarks: in January 1997, the release of a resplendently illustrated *Marg* publication on fifteen of the most renowned women artists of contemporary India,[2] and in April, as a complement to the book, a spectacular exhibition of a selection of works of these women artists, again at the National Gallery of Modern Art.[3] In scale and publicity, both the book and the show have been well in keeping with the high profile of the art scenario today, setting new standards in quality of production. Such occasions, with all the prestige they have brought to their subject, frame the main context of this essay.

I wish, however, to use this moment of success to scrutinize the ways in which the subject of 'women artists' offers itself for representation. The project of making women 'visible', whether in the past or in the present, in public or in private domains, has inevitably moved on slippery ground. Feminist studies have been increasingly sensitive to the problems and pitfalls of this agenda, arguing that there is no easy co-relation between empowerment and visibility, underlining, also, the need to question the very entity of 'women' that is being retrieved and relocated in different histories. What meanings do we attach, then, to this new, heightened 'visibility' of women artists in contemporary India? What are the longer, more troubled histories of frustration and endeavour that can be teased out of the present? What were the myths and the realities of gender disabilities that had to be overcome in the 'ladder of evolution' of women artists? Or, how have the crucial issues of gender difference figured in the positioning of women as artists in a professional milieu?

The problems can be posed at two levels. At one level, we find both artists and analysts grappling for ways of marking the specificity and separateness of 'women's art'. As many of the artists clearly resist such categorization (finding the slot of 'women artists' to be as much a trap as a bonus), we are forced to reconsider how far gender forms a prime criterion in the formation of their artistic dispensations. In what ways does the biological or gendered self reside within the artistic self? Which of the two components of the identity 'women-artists' is to be prioritized? Does the emphasis on the 'women' component detract from the integral importance of these women as 'artists'? These are the questions that have persistently dogged those who have been at the centre of the new initiatives of the book and the exhibition.

But there are also other dimensions to the problem, which do not figure within their concerns. These relate to the demarcation of peripheries vis-à-vis the mainstream, with the opening out to persons and practices that lie outside the centre. It becomes imperative, here, to question the terms on which women have secured for themselves a place on India's modern artistic map. The inclusion of a number of 'exceptional' women practitioners, beginning with Amrita Sher-Gil and covering the post-independence generations, has added considerably to the national canon of 'great artists'. Their selection has followed what seems to be the most natural art-historical criteria: those of excellence and talent. Yet, the invocation of merit can be rather insiduous, for it glosses over the many ways in which the arguments about 'excellence' operated in history as one of the chief means of the demotion and marginalization of women's artistic careers.[4] And it leaves unruffled the ideological premises of modern art history as a story of unique achievements and exceptional personas, where the notion of artistic genius tended to be implicitly male, where professional pre-eminence remained for long a male prerogative, and where women had to contend not only with their designated status as muse, model and art objects, but also with their devaluation as '*inevitably* and *naturally* artists of lesser talent'.[5]

The problems emerged most sharply in European art history, which has thrived on its powerfully canonized corpus of 'great masters' (old and modern) and on the categorical differentiation of 'feminine' sensibilities and skills in art since the 19th century. New gendered approaches in the field have had to wrest these 'feminine' spaces and stereotypes for 'feminist' rereadings. As they have searched out women artists in history, and recovered an impressive line-up of lost and suppressed figures from the Renaissance to the present century, feminist scholars have also interrogated the complex mechanism of their neglect and dismissal in society and art history.[6] Such processes and biases, we find, have a very different trajectory in the Indian context. In a setting where the very fashioning of the identity of 'artist' has a relatively short and a specifically modern/colonial history, the surfacing of women artists has an even newer time-frame, and the traditions they have stood within or against have been quite distinct from those of European art history. Nonetheless, here too, we need to question the modes whereby a canon of individual women 'greats' are inserted into modern and contemporary Indian art history. For, only in that process can we look behind the charmed circles at the more general trends and ordinary histories that have made up the world of women artists in modern India.

ESTABLISHING THE CANON: THE WOMEN WHO MATTER

Let us begin with the profiles and achievements of some of those select figures who have come to command a central place in the nation's modern art history. There can be no doubt that their positioning as 'exceptional artists' has redressed the historical imbalance of our male-dominated milieu of pedagogy, practice and public success. Through them, a major step has been taken towards what Germaine Greer called, 'repeopling the historical artscape'.[7]

This artscape in India, we find, constitutes a well-demarcated terrain, with its main lay-out of teaching centres, schools and trends. Its modern landscaping dates back to the 1930s and 40s, when the first waves of modernism broke in on the scenario of nationalist art and established its main personalities, genres and sites of activity. In the post-independence era, artists and groups steadily multiplied, claiming new spaces, bringing to eminence new institutions and places. Older centres such as Calcutta and Santiniketan, while they never ceased to produce star figures, gradually receded from the national mainstream. Other art schools, such as those of Bombay and Madras—the former for long a bastion of Academic salon art, the latter long confined to the demands of colonial craft education—were drawn into the grips of new Progressive movements that secured for these cities and their new assemblage of artists a distinct place on the art-map of independent India. The Delhi Polytechnic and College of Arts emerged on the cusp of independence as a new forum to reckon with, as did the Faculty of Fine Arts at the M.S. University of Baroda in the 1950s, the latter developing over the next three decades into the central breeding ground of the Indian artistic avant-garde. These years would mark a major shift in paradigm from the identity of the 'modern' to that of the 'contemporary' in Indian art: a shift that came to be enacted and institutionalized around a Delhi-Baroda-Bombay axis.[8] Admittedly, other groups and regions have periodically flashed in and out of the national spotlight, but, to do so, they have had to continuously contend with the hegemony of this established axis, or work their way through its shield and filter.

This may appear to many as a simplified and flattened view of the course of contemporary Indian art—an outsider's delineation of what surfaces as the most obvious centres of power, patronage and privilege. But it should suffice for our purpose. Our main concern, here, is not with the complexities and contests that have run through the world of modern Indian art—rather, it is with the positioning of women artists within this world. Has the featuring of a select body of women artists significantly reconstituted India's modern art-historical map, or has it served primarily to refurbish its dominant topography? The latter is probably more the case. Here the picture that is presented works largely as a point of strength for the artists concerned. It is a matter of great pride that those women artists hand-picked for the new volume and exhibition would figure in any sampling of the best of modern and contemporary Indian art. In each phase, these women have come to share the platform with male artists, and have often outshone them. Their artistic eligibility clearly transcends a 'gender quota', even where 'gender' has acted as the cathartic force in the birth of alternative identities. The argument has worked two ways: while these women artists are presented as some of the choicest figures of modern Indian art, they are also seen to reflect in a microcosm 'the developments in mainstream Indian art'.[9] Let us briefly cruise through this mainstream with these artists.

The Forerunner

Our story necessarily begins with Amrita Sher-Gil (1913–1941), the most celebrated exponent of a new modern Indian art in the 1930s. Here was an artist who, alone of all her sex, dominated the Indian art scene of her time and, in the course of the briefest of artistic careers (abruptly terminated by her death in 1941, at the age of 29), became an icon in her own lifetime and for all generations to follow.[10] Sher-Gil's has been one of the most resonant of our modern art legacies. The reasons lie partly in her background and career: a mixed Sikh-Hungarian parentage that made of her the most enigmatic blend of 'East and West' in our modern art history; a training at the Ecole des Beaux-Arts, Paris, which introduced her both to the strengths of Academic life studies and to the influence of post-Impressionists like Gaugin and Modigliani; her decision in 1934 to return and work in India, and consciously seek out new 'Indian' forms and subject matter for her paintings. We see the artist trying to evolve a special Indian facial type, physiognomy and body rhythm in a series of ethnic tableaux of 'Hill Men and Women', village girls, banana sellers or haldi-grinders. The project culminates in her famous trilogy of 1938 of 'The Bride's Toilet', 'Brahamacharis' and 'Villagers Going to the Market'

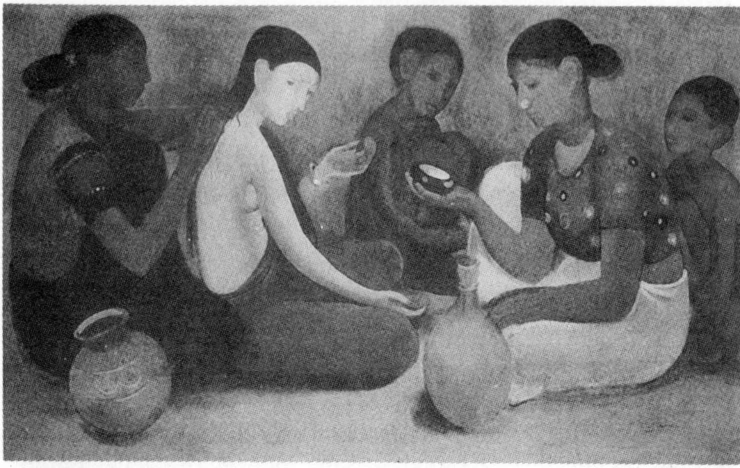

Amrita Sher-Gil, 'Bride's Toilet' (oil on canvas, 1937), Collection: National Gallery of Modern Art, New Delhi.

(Plate 1), painted under the immediate impact of her travels through western and southern India, where she was spellbound by the colours and landscapes, even more by the traditions of Ajanta and Kerala mural painting she encountered. Around the same time, she found herself equally fascinated by the pictorial potentials of north Indian miniature painting. Thereafter, we see her uncovering in oil painting various colouristic and compositional affinities with traditional Indian painting, taking us back to the inheritance of Ajanta and Pahari miniature painting through routes that were entirely different from the Bengal School.

The charisma of Amrita Sher-Gil also lies elsewhere. It rests in her assertion of a fiercely independent professional identity; in her articulation of pictorial choices and stances, where a vehement dismissal of the art of her Indian contemporaries (particularly those of the Bengal School) converged with the arrogant flaunting of an artistic ego; not least of all, it rests in her youthful and bohemian image, which her sudden death served to preserve and canonize. All along, it was her persona as much as her art which commanded the attention of writers and critics. Here, being a woman (daring, brilliant, beautiful, exotic even to her countrymen) singled her out all the more. Over time, it was her identity as a 'woman artist' which came to be foregrounded and reified—as hers became the most coveted legacy for the subsequent community of women who followed in her trail. The genealogical claim is clearly laid out by Nilima Sheikh, one of the many who trace their lineage from Sher-Gil:

> For a woman painting in India, Amrita Sher-Gil is inheritance. No perspective on our art is complete without reference to Sher-Gil. Her commitment to her self-image as an artist, as much as her brilliance and flair, has ensured for two or three generations of women artists since, *the right to be taken seriously*. (Emphases mine.)[11]

Sher-Gil, 'a celebrity almost from the time she started painting',[12] enacted this right in a way that marked her out in Indian art history. In her, we see the projection of a creative artistic self that is usurped from a male domain and freed of the strictures of gender. And we see her asserting this self with a precocity that, ironically, has no parallels even among the Indian male artists of that period. Such an artistic self-image prevailed in her as the surest sign of the 'modern'.

Yet, where in all this do we search out the specificities of her location as a woman in the field? Given her own low opinion about women painters, her stated view that 'they are as a general rule not passionate souls but sentimentalists',[13] it seems that one of Amrita's main cause was to rid her art of the stamp of the 'sentimental' and 'effeminate': markers that in India were associated less with women's art than with the 'Indian-style' paintings of the Bengal School. The potentials of an empowered feminine identity that later artists and scholars extracted from her work has opened up her career for mutliple meanings. It has made doubly significant her self-portraits, her nudes and her frontal engagement with the unclothed female form, and it has brought new attention to bear on her play with female sexuality in paintings like 'Woman on a Charpoy' (Plate 2). These readings, as they gained currency since the 1970s and 80s, rendered the artist a central phenomenon in the making of a new women's art of those decades. But, in many ways, Amrita Sher-Gil's legacy remained wrapped in the uniqueness of her power and position. That she emerged largely outside the pedagogic and professional frames of the art circuit in India meant that she could enter the scene on her own terms, and pitch her aspirations on quite a different plane. In a sense, hers is a success story that, in its brief span, rode above the disabilities and obstacles

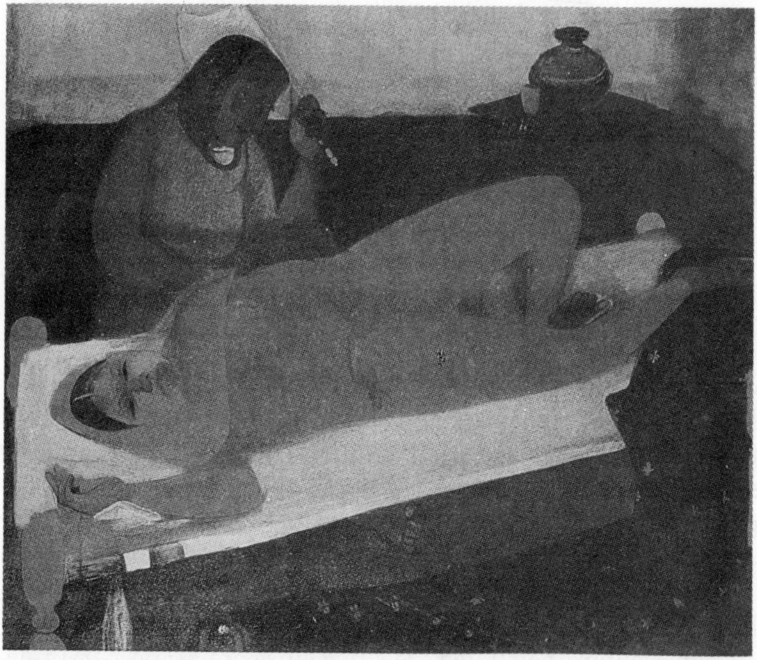

Amrita Sher-Gil, 'Woman on a Charpoy' (oil on canvas, 1940), Collection: National Gallery of Modern Art, New Delhi.

that confronted her gender. It is a mark of her exceptionality that few of the women artists of the same and succeeding years enjoyed the same limelight or leverage.

The First Generation

Leaving aside this foundational figure, the book and the exhibition introduce us to a cross-section of women artists of the next decades. These women, in their training and careers, stand within the more established institutional sites of modern art activity in India. On the one hand, they seem to chart a fairly conventional path of art education and art teaching jobs, with sometimes a stint of training in Paris, Munich or London, and with an accumulating list of group and solo exhibitions. On the other hand, they also lay out, through their individual trajectories, the changing directions of modern Indian art. While some, such as Devyani Krishna, Arpita Singh, Madhavi Parekh or Nilima Sheikh, are the spouses of equally prominent painters (Kanwal Krishna, Paramjit Singh, Manu Parekh

work as a key romanticized motif, engrossed in daily work or wrapped in dreamy introspection (Plate 3).

Meera Mukherjee, 'Thokal' (Woman at a loom) (bronze, c. 1992), Size not available. Photographed personally by the author from the artists' own home during her life-time.

In their choice of mediums, Devyani Krishna, Pilloo Pochkhanawala and Meera Mukherjee had each broken into what were till then essentially male domains of work. Each had involved herself with the complexities of the production process—while one delved into the intricacies of print techniques, the other two took on the physical challenge of large-scale sculpture and heavy wood and metal work. These artists also offer two main paradigms of visual form for their times: one non-representational and abstract, the other compulsively figurative. We find both these streams being carried in new directions by two succeeding artists. Let us juxtapose, here, Nasreen Mohamedi (1937–1990) with Arpita Singh (b. 1937).

With a Diploma in Design from St. Martin's School of Art, London, Nasreen Mohamedi located herself within a powerful lineage of abstract art in the West, stretching from the abstract expressionism of Kandinsky or Klee to the minimalist forms of Piet Mondrian, Agnes Martin or Frank Stella. Her own brand of meticulously ruled geometric drawings in pencil and ink can best be positioned at this intersection of late modernist and minimalist art in the West. The main aim of the artist, it is explained, was to disengage herself from the demands of representation, to deliberately defy and cancel 'the regime of the gaze, being sceptical of the appropriative/exploitative aspects of it'.[17] Pursuing this project to a subliminal extreme, Mohamedi's work has been linked with those of her contemporaries, Jeram Patel or J. Swaminathan, who in 1963 had formed the Group 1890, who were as passionately committed to the morphology of the 'negative image'. Yet, though based in Bombay and working for a while in the hub of art activity in Baroda, the artist's drawings increasingly fed only into themselves, steeped in the mysteries of their own formalism, belonging nowhere. Her intense isolation and abstractions went hand in hand, compounded by the anguish of physical afflictions that prematurely drained out her life.

To move from the work of Nasreen Mohamedi to that of Arpita Singh is to enter a diametrically opposite pictorial world: one that is bursting with stories and teeming with human figures, objects, flowers and foliage. In this artist (a Bengali grown up in Delhi, educated at the Delhi Polytechnic, and living here all her professional life), the forms and narrative structures of Indian folk painting find a lively new incarnation. Over the years, her oils and watercolours have evolved from densely patterned surfaces and decorative linear drawings to more condensed brevities of form and colour. Unlike Meera Mukherjee, Arpita Singh's dialogue with folk configurations have been more oblique, more encoded in the visual vocabulary of her own urban milieu. So, while her figures are worked out in a naive primitive style, her compositions have remained grounded in the artist's own setting of family traumas and street violence. Her series of paintings of the family of Ayesha Kidwai (a family that was for her 'a microcosm of contemporary India') are striking examples, as are a variety of other scenes where gun-toting figures, buzzing aeroplanes or hooting cars intrude into streets and homes, catapulting around a child bride or the artist's widowed mother, or shattering the afternoon intimacies of a middle-aged couple (Plate 4).

These effects are achieved often through a disarming use of decorative patterns: in this, we see her deliberately employing feminine art forms like *kantha* embroidery as a powerful new stylistic tool. Considered as 'one of the most contemporary of painters' in India, Arpita Singh is also marked out for her special output of 'feminine imagery', for innumerable paintings centred around figures of women, young and old, naked and draped, ranging from the innocent and vulnerable to the strong and stoical.[18] Whether this makes of her a 'women's artist', in particular, is up for debate. But it does open out a new dominant space of negotiation (of women appropriating the right to image themselves) that would be foregrounded in the works of all women artists of her and our times.

The Independence Generation

As we come to the generation born in the 1940s, we meet the bulk of the artists who make up the *Marg* book and the National Gallery of Modern Art exhibition. These are women whose careers have peaked over the 1970s and 80s, coinciding, on the one hand, with the growing primacy of the women's movement in India and, on the other hand, with the great boom in modern Indian art. Their works have not only found place in our posh hotel foyers and designer homes, but have also made their way into international exhibitions and collections. Their prominent place in the contemporary Indian art scene will hardly be borne out by the increasingly rushed profiles

I provide. My intention, here, is mainly to present an overview of the selected canon of artists and works, to take stock of the line-up as a whole and the modes of its configuration.

Predominant in this lot is a creed of painters, working with oils, tempera, gouache, acrylic and pastels, building on a variety of figurative and narrative traditions. There is, for example, Anjolie

Arpita Singh, 'Child Bride With a Swan' (watercolour, 1985),Chester Hermitz Collection.

Ela Menon (b. 1940), who moved from the J. J. School of Art to the Ecole des Beaux Arts on a French government scholarship in 1961–62, and in the course of her travels through Europe was enamoured by the iconic images of medieval Christian art. It is this aura that she has sought to bring to her repertoire of slender, elongated bodies and wistful, melancholy visages in richly coloured compositions, which she splintered with frames within frames, often using actual antique window panels on canvas (Plate 5). The effects

Anjolie Ela Menon, 'Mataji' (oil on masonite, 1982). Collection: National Gallery of Modern Art, New Delhi.

she has explored are those of memory and time, also those of viewing and being viewed, freezing her images with the gaze of the unseen voyeur.[19]

Nostalgia also permeates the themes and style of another painter of this generation, Madhavi Parekh (b. 1942). But, here, it revolves around a lost world of childhood and village life, taking us on a journey to the small Gujarat village where the artist grew up, and to its vibrant folk art motifs (Plate 6). In Parekh, we have the unusual case of an artist who emerges outside the route of formal

Madhvi Parekh, 'Sun' (oil on canvas, 1993), Private Collection.

institutional training, who is initiated into painting after marriage by her husband. It is tempting to link this fact to the naive, child-like quality of her paintings, to reify her as a spontaneous, unspoilt artist, who remains absorbed in the primeval fantasies of the sun, stars, trees, birds, animals and reptiles. Yet, for all her rural and nature-based images, what the artist offers us is a recognizably modernist version of folk art in large oils on canvas, constructing an adult surrogate of a child's world.[20]

With Nilima Sheikh (b. 1945), educated at Baroda, we return to a more consciously urbane sensibility and a pictorial language that looks back to a medley of Oriental forms: the narrative format of miniatures, the wispy figures and layered colours of the Bengal School, the exploration of landscape by the Santiniketan artists, the spatial rhythm of Far Eastern painting, or the weaves of textile designs. While preoccupied with natural elements of land, water, trees, wind and storm in most of her paintings, the artist comes into her own in a miniaturized series on the saga of a young girl, Champa, given in marriage, tortured by in-laws and destined to a violent death. It is a series that blends the grim and the playful, as it uses props and panels to segregate interiors and enact each episode as on a stage.

From Nilima Sheikh's delicate, translucent temperas, we jump to the large, boldly outlined, flatly coloured, single-figure compositions of Gogi Saroj Pal (b. 1945), who was trained in the Colleges of Art at Vanasthali (Rajasthan) and Lucknow. Her paintings are peopled by a disquieting pantheon of half-woman, half-animal figures, which she titles 'Shivapriya', 'Kamdhenu', or 'Hatyogini Shakti', playing on the women-beast analogy to raise her protagonists from a mute, submissive role to a virile sexual presence (Plate 7).

Alternatively, we can move within the more muted, monochromatic and ambivalent pictorial spaces opened up by the Bombay painter, Nalini Malani (b. 1946): spaces that are often blown large on gallery walls and theatre backdrops. Her images, in acrylic, pastels and mixed media, thrive on a dense opacity of meaning, embedded as they are in the references of Greek tragedy, modern European art history and contemporary dance and theatre.[21]

The cerebral overtones of Nalini Malani's paintings and installations can be contrasted, again, by the vividly pictorial, fresco-like quality of the vast oil paintings of the youngest of the artists to be featured in this selection, Arpana Caur (b. 1954), a largely self-taught painter. The themes she excavates in her meticulously designed compositions range from the trauma of war and violence to the alienations of city life, from ecological concerns to the manifold yearnings and anguish of women. As in the case of most of these artists, the female figure is lodged at the centre of the

Gogi Saroj Pal, 'Shivpriya' (gouache on paper, 1995) Private Collection.

whole corpus of Caur's paintings—a central motif of empathy, she is cast often within the artist's own milieu of strong Punjabi women, sometimes as a desexualized, monumental mother image, sometimes as one of the hapless 'Widows of Brindavan', or sometimes as a cowering nude in the hands of a male juggler[22] (Plate 8).

The one common strand that brings together the works of all these women painters is the privileging of the themes and images of women. The expressions speak of a multiplicity of approaches and concerns. In every case, however, they have worked towards dismantling the entrenched edifice of the voyeuristic, eroticized or spiritualized feminine form in Indian art, supplanting these with the issues of real-life struggles and pains, with counter-images of a heroic, nurturing female power, or with new explorations of women's desires and sexuality. Thus, the nude female figure, even as it recurrently appears in their work, is transformed from an object of male gaze to one of feminine empathies and bonding. In this predominant orientation, these women painters are joined by print-makers such as Anupam Sud (b. 1944), a product of the Delhi College of Art, where she now heads the department of graphics. In a series of bold black and white etchings, which she developed over the 1970s and 80s, we see large female figures, stripped stark naked, with their personas unmasked and all their defences down

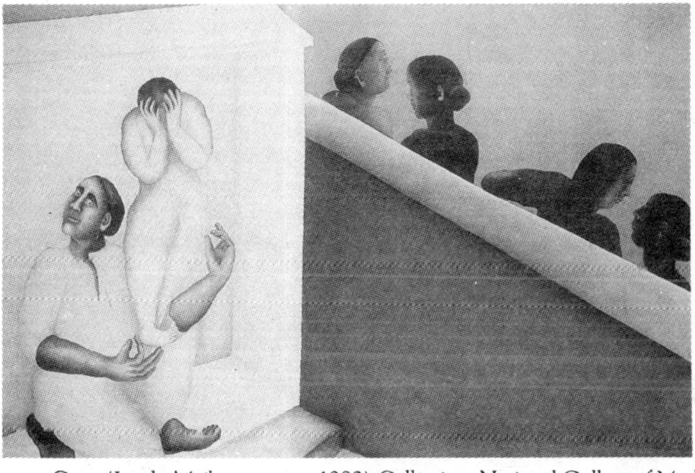

Arpana Caur, 'Juggler' (oil on canvas, 1982) Collection: National Gallery of Modern Art, New Delhi

(Plate 9). The act of unclothing becomes for her a way of uncovering the many exploitative practices in which her 'Pickup Girls' and 'Test-tube' mothers are ensconced.

Grounded in many of the same stances and concerns, the works of two sculptors of the generation, Latika Katt (b. 1948) and Navjot Altaf (b. 1949), stand here at an an interesting tangent. For, in them we see a continuing pull back to the abstractions of material and medium, and a return to the demands of figural representation. As Latika Katt turns from bronze and wood to a radically non-art

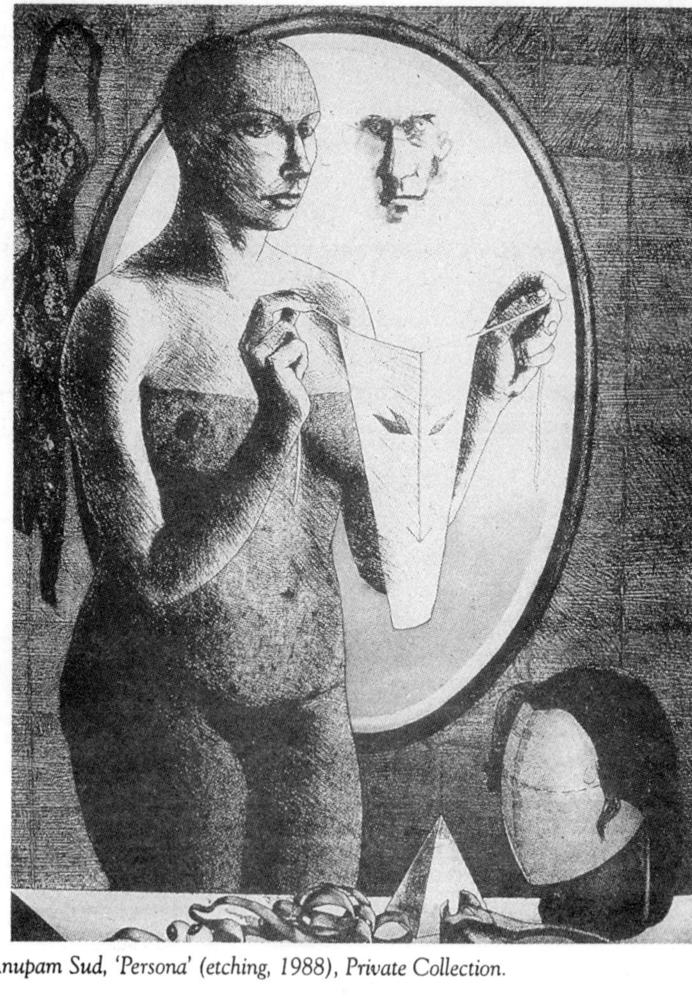

Anupam Sud, 'Persona' (etching, 1988), Private Collection.

medium such as cowdung, she also moves between geometric structures, primeval anthropomorphic shapes of heads, and the abstract symbolism of 'Sati stones'. Side by side, Altaf carries us through the spectacle of her many multi-media installations (where objects, boxes, snapshots and plaster-heads lie strewn across the floor, or giant metallic wires and tubes are sprawled across a gallery, in invocations of the riot-torn Bombay of 1994) to return us to the centrality of the human figure.[23] Drawing on the force of primitive folk imagery, particularly on the iconic potentials of painted wood sculpture, she builds up a set of heavy-limbed nude female figures, swollen in pregnancy, on writhing in the labours of childbirth (Plate 10). These figures now stand face to face with the compelling gallery of feminine forms that Indian women artists have evolved over the past decades, ranging from Meera Mukherjee's serene and toiling women to Gogi Saroj Pal's semi-mythical 'Icons of Womanhood' to Anupam Sud's dark, brooding naked figures. Working with a variety of genres such as painting, sculpture and installation art, artists like Navjot also mark out a new community of contemporary artists, who have felt the need to break out of the confines of any single medium to work with large spaces, more dramatic effects and closer artist-viewer interactions, just as they have felt the need to continuously reformulate the female image in art.

LOOKING BEYOND THE CANON

There can be no doubt, at the end of this long presentation of artistic profiles, that these women artists constitute the core of the Indian artistic avant-garde. From Amrita Sher-Gil to the latest painters, sculptors and print-makers, they have been at the forefront of new experiments with forms, media and techniques, delving both into the legacies of Western modernisms and post-modernisms, and into the rich reserves of India's historical and folk traditions. The modes in which these women artists have been presented—in the book, in the exhibition, and even in my overview—have powerfully buttressed this sense of a vanguard group. In establishing their claims to eminence, what are invariably singled out are the high points of their artistic careers and the corpus of their best and most mature works. Each artist is thus positioned within a ladder of success and achievement, their respective stories building up, in turn, a picture of the steady rise and progress of women artists in India. One can argue that this lies in the logic of art-historical studies, that it seeks out the best and marks out all that is different and new. But, in our context, it becomes pertinent to rethink the implications of such a screening of 'great artists' and their narratives

Navjot Altaf, 'Palani's Daughters' (painted wood, seven pieces 1995), National Gallery of Modern Art.

of progress. What are the other parallel histories that get suppressed and erased in this line of profiling? What are the tensions in personal lives and professional spheres that are glossed over? These questions would relate as much to the small group of women artists selected here as to the greater body of women who inhabited over these years the same world of training and work, albeit with far less prominence. In raising these queries, we may be able to grope towards some of the complexities that attended the making of 'women artists' in modern India.

One way of engaging with these issues would be to ask again (as it is often being asked), what is it that differentiates this selection of women artists from any concurrent listing of the best of male artists? Is there any ground for such a listing based on gender, except that 'women' now form the most fashionable platform for any discussion and activity? The answers, here, have remained elusive and ambivalent. Arpita Singh perhaps speaks for many when she says,

> To call me a woman painter does not have a special meaning. Whatever I do is as a woman because I am a woman.... I do not know what it is like to paint as a man. Therefore, it seems strange to even say that I am a woman painter. I would just like to *establish myself as a painter.* (emphasis mine)[24]

What she leaves unsaid is that, for many like her, establishing themselves as artists meant often an erasure of the marks of gender difference. Through the first decades of independent India, the fight was to make a place for themselves as artists and equals of men. The matter of gender is dissolved, here, into a biological fact: a natural component of their personal and artistic selves. With some of the younger artists, like Nalini Malani, Gogi Saroj Pal or Navjot Altaf, gender has come to provide a more conscious forum for searching out alternative terms of self-location in their artistic milieu, for the casting of ideological identities that could be termed 'feminist'. However, for Gayatri Sinha, the editor of the volume and curator of the exhibition, the 'feminine' and the 'feminist' have remained blurred, interdependent categories. In picking her subjects, she invokes gender more in the 'common reference points' of 'personal biographies, issues of birth and death, the treatment of familial life and motherhood, especially the vulnerability of the girl child, the discovery of the sexual self and its location in a social context.'[25]

Yet, it is precisely these strands of personal and social lives that have had to be brushed aside in narrating the artistic biographies of these women—in presenting stories that necessarily begin and end with their achievements in art. Our case is not to make a fetish out of gender struggle. It is only to argue that even for this clearly privileged and successful corpus of women artists, being women must have entailed a series of strains and tensions as they straddled the varied worlds of family and profession, and as they staked their claims to belong to the artistic fraternity. It is these undercurrents that link them to the more general circuit of their fellow women artists, and define (however tentatively) certain shared spaces of their lives and endeavours in art. The problems of gender become sharper once we look beyond the select circle of eminent artists to the larger numbers of women who remained on the margins or entirely outside the canon. In rounding off the essay, let me briefly touch on the contours of some of these other obscured or peripheral histories.

Clearly, women had been drawing and painting in modern India well before they marked out a professional identity for themselves as 'artists'. We stick here solely to the group of urban middle-class women: the emergent 'bhadramahilas' of Bengal and their counterparts in other parts of British India. For many of them, dabbling in the visual arts in the confines of their homes, under private tutors, was a part of their new genteel, modernized upbringing. They would have had as their models the many Victorian lady artists of England and colonial India. Few in the late 19th or early 20th century entered the institutional forums of the British art schools in Calcutta or Bombay, or the presitigious fine art societies' exhibitions: the occasional name of Parsi female students on the early rolls of the J.J. School of Art or of Bengali ladies among the entrants of the Calcutta Fine Arts Exhibition of 1879 underlined the exception rather than the rule.

It was the intervention of the nationalist art movement of Abanindranath Tagore and his school that drew in larger numbers of women to the new romanticized, spiritualized vocation of 'art'.

To a large extent, it was the privileging of traditional mythological/ literary themes and a special 'Indian style' that made room for women painters, as the idealized bearers of 'tradition'. It brought them into the informal art classes at the Jorasanko household or at the Indian Society of Oriental Art in Calcutta during the 1910s and 20s—even more into Nandalal Bose's Kala Bhavana at Santiniketan (which began in 1921), particularly to its new craft departments. But this inflow of women students, it seems, served mainly to inscribe a male-female hierarchy into the existing hierachies of the 'fine arts' over 'crafts', of greater over lesser talents. It took a figure like Amrita Sher-Gil to break out of this grid—to radically break free of the sentimentalities of 'Indian-style' painting, and to effect the transition from art as a private creative pursuit to art as a celebrated public profession. And it was the uniqueness of her artistic ago and presence that pushed into the shadows all other surrounding women artists: the few preceeding Bengal School artists like Sunayani Debi (sister of Abanindranath Tagore) or Pratima Debi (daughter-in-law of Rabindranath), or the number of women who formed the first batches at Santiniketan's Kala Bhavan. During Sher-Gil's time and well after her, the emergence of women artists into the national limelight was a great rarity.

The history of a more professional women's art in India has been largely coterminous with the history of independent India. It is mainly from the 1940s that female students became a visible presence in the metropolitan art schools like the J.J. School of Art, Bombay, or the Government College of Art, Calcutta, and all the more so, in the new art teaching centres like the Delhi College of Art (established in 1942) or the fine arts faculty at Baroda (begun in 1950). Their entry into art education involved, now, a more pointed attempt to break into a public sphere—to claim for themselves a new trained professional identity. Herein lay the main contests and tensions for a generation of women, whom we could today designate as the first of our 'moderns': 'moderns' both in the aesthetics they developed and the independent identities they sought.

We have the testimony, for instance, of two prominent Calcutta painters, Karuna Shaha (1921–1996) and Shanu Lahiri (b. 1928), who were among the first women to enter the Government Art

College, Calcutta (the former in 1939, the year it first turned co-educational, and the latter in 1947), who saw themselves as a new brave and rebellious generation of women in a male world. For Karuna Shaha, reared in the tumultuous atmosphere of the Quit India movement, the Second World War and the Bengal famine, already thrown into public political activity during her student days, the constant fight was to blend marital and motherly duties with her artistic ambitions. For Shanu Lahiri, a main challenge was to emerge from the shadows of her eminent writer and artist brothers (Kamal and Nirode Majumdar), to make a mark in her own right. For both, subsequent scholarships to study abroad (in Karuna Shaha's case, in Florence; in Shanu Lahiri's case, in Paris), which they took on despite marriage and motherhood, served best to establish their careers in art.

In Indian art practices of the time, we do not see the same hierarchy of genres that Western women artists of the 20th century had to contend with; there was no hard and fast categorization of 'feminine traits' and 'feminine genres' in art, relegating women to still lives, flower painting or sentimental domestic themes. Nonetheless, for these artists, a prime compulsion was to break the equation of women with the niceties of 'Indian-style' painting and assert a new boldness of image and technique. For some of that generation, like Devyani Krishna or Meera Mukherjee, it meant moving from painting to the new zones of print-making and sculpture. Karuna Shaha, through the 1960s and 70s, made portraiture, figure and life studies her forte, lifting these from the cast of Academic student work, specializing in studies of the female nude. We can identify in her volatile and forthright nude images, as in many of her later women-centred compositions, a distinct legacy for 'women's art'. We could also mark a different kind of legacy in Shanu Lahiri's repertoire of Picasso-esque female figures in enlarged oils, particularly, in her play with various narrative series since the 1960s, which take us from the myths of 'Ravana and Sita', the cadences of 'Ragas and Raginis' or the fabled world of 'Thakurmar Jhuli' into the current milieu of domestic violence and bride-burning. We can also trace in their artistic careers more overt lines of gender-based activity, as in their initiative in 1983 in founding the first working group of women artists in Calcutta. And in Shanu Lahiri, we also see, over the last two decades, a mounting commitment to a new arena of public art in the city.

That artists like Karuna Shaha or Shanu Lahiri remained outside the national limelight has much to do with the way new centres and enclaves came to be carved out in the post-independence modern art scene. These were years when the locus of avant-garde art activity clearly shifted away from sites like Calcutta or Santiniketan to converge around Bombay, Baroda and Delhi. And the cases of these artists would have their parallels in several other women artists in other cities, asserting in different ways their own professional and artistic spaces, yet edged out for the most part from what came to be the national mainstream. The low profile of Calcutta artists or the absence of any from Madras in the current selection of our 'women greats', whatever its justifications on grounds of merit, underwrites a certain politics of exclusion. It points to the hegemony of a particular camp of critics and artists, and the increasingly entrenched power of certain centres (prime among them, Baroda) in defining the routes of renown and recognition. In many ways, in focussing on the present group of women artists (those featured in the *Marg* volume), we have reinforced the dominant frame of our contemporary national art history. That names like Karuna Shaha or Shanu Lahiri, like hosts of others in other cities, are now available only to 'provincial' histories of modernism bears out the strength and durability of the 'national' canon.

In figuring women as artists in modern and contemporary India, we must underline the need for a more elastic and permeable canon: one that would be more inclusive and accommodative. The argument is not a simple one of greater numbers (that the selection of fifteen be expanded to thirty) or of national coverage (that the selection be representative of all parts of India); nor does it pick a quarrel with the aesthetic criteria of selection, aware that a choice of a different set of women artists would be no less partial or partisan. The point would be mainly to open up the history of women in art beyond the exclusive circles of these reigning figures—to probe what prevents many from belonging to the national core, or to map the more ordinary trends and life stories that the very eminence and success of some have sidelined.

As they stand in the premises of the book and the exhibition, our women artists exude the same rarified, in-house ambience that envelops the charmed world of contemporary Indian art. Their dialogues are largely with each other, and with their male counterparts in the same artistic zones. Let us turn their faces, instead, towards the larger community of women who have struggled over time to find a foothold in the same professional arena: women who may have shared the same creative aspirations, but who encountered, in different forms in different phases, the cutting edge of the exclusive field. Let us also situate them vis-à-vis the vast numbers of women who today flock to various art schools all over the country (easily outnumbering male students), few of whom ever graduate to the identity of 'artist' in our terms. To talk of women artists, as we have done, is to have worked with a firmly constituted and packaged entity of women as 'artists'. These other scenarios take us into a more chequered and unfulfilled history of women trying to become artists in modern India: one that also needs to be documented.

NOTES

1. Tharu, Susie and Tejaswini Niranjana, 'Problems for a Contemporary Theory of Gender', *Social Scientist*, 22 (3–4), 1994.
2. Sinha, Gayatri (ed.), *Expressions and Evocations: Contemporary Women Artists of India*, Marg Publications, Mumbai, 1997. This essay can be seen as an extended review written around this landmark book: it has drawn heavily on the articles about the selected fifteen artists and on the illustrations of their work. All the plates except plate 3, are reproduced from this book and the Exhibition catalogue, *The Self and the world* National Gallery of modern Art, New Delhi, 1997.
3. The exhibition was curated by Gayatri Sinha and jointly presented by the National Gallery of Modern Art and Gallery Espace, New Delhi, 5–30 April 1997. It has been documented through *The Self and the World: An Exhibition of Indian Women Artists*, Gallery Espace, New Delhi, 1997.
4. On the exploration of this theme in Western art history, see, for example, Linda Nochlin's classic essay, 'Why Have There Been No Great Women Artists?' in E. Baker and T. Hess (ed.), *Art and Sexual Politics*, New York, 1971, 1973; and the essays in Rozsika Parker and

Griselda Pollock, *Old Mistresses: Women, Art and Ideology*, Routledge, Kegan Paul, London, 1981.

5. Parker, Rozsika and Griselda Pollock, 'Critical Stereotypes: The 'Essential Feminine' or How Essential Is Femininity' in *Old Mistresses*, pp. 44–45.
6. A pioneering work in this line was an exhibition mounted at the Los Angeles Country Museum in December 1976, titled 'Women Painters, 1550–1950', and the accompanying catalogue by Linda Nochlin and Anne Sutherland Harris, of the same title. These were followed by a number of books unearthing the lost history of European women artists over four or five centuries, including K. Petersen and J.J. Wilson, *Women Artists: Recognition and Reappraisal from the Middle Ages to the Twentieth Century*, London, 1978; and Germaine Greer's famous *The Obstacle Race, The Fortunes of Women Painters and Their Work*, Picador, London, 1979.
7. Greer, *The Obstacle Race*, p. 10.
8. This history is best theorized and encapsulated by Geeta Kapur in her article, 'When Was Modernism in Indian Art', *Journal of Arts and Ideas*, Nos 27–28, March 1995.
9. Gayatri Sinha's introduction, *The Self and the World*, p. 7.
10. Of all the artists here, Amrita Sher-Gil alone has occasioned a substantial body of art-critical and biographical writing, which began from her own time. A useful compendium of the artist's own writings and letters, along with essays by Geeta Kapur, Vivan Sundaram, K.G. Subramanyam and Gulamohammad Sheikh, is the *Marg* issue, *Amrita Sher-Gil*, XXV (2), 1972.
11. Nilima Sheikh, 'On Amrita Sher-Gil: Claiming a Radiant Legacy', in Gayatri Sinha (ed.), *Expressions and Evocations*, p. 19.
12. Sinha, *Expressions and Evocations*, p. 22.
13. Letter from Amrita Sher-Gil to Karl Khandalavala, dated January 1, 1937, quoted by Nilima Sheikh, p. 27.
14. Malik, Keshav, 'Devyani Krishna: The Fire of God', in *Expressions and Evocations*.
15. Contractor, Anahite 'Pilloo Pochakhanawala: Disharmony and Inner Mechanics', in *Expressions and Evocations*.
16. Guha-Thakurta, Tapati, 'Meera Mukherjee: Recasting the Folk Form', in *Expressions and Evocations*. The art of Meera Mukherjee, along with that of Arpita Singh and Madhavi Parekh, has featured

prominently in a recent book by Geeti Sen, *Image and Imagination*, Mapin, Ahmedabad, 1996.

17. Kapur, Geeta, 'Nasreen Mohamedi: Dimensions out of Solitude', in *Expressions and Evocations*, p. 61.
18. Dalmia, Yashodhara, 'Arpita Singh: Of Mother Goddesses and Women', in *Expressions and Evocations*.
19. Chawla, Rupika, 'Anjolie Ela Menon: Images and Techniques', in *Expressions and Evocations*.
20. Ray, Praṇabrajan, 'Madhavi Parekh: Child's World, Mother's Fantasy', in *Expressions and Evocations*.
21. In the 1990s, Nalini Malani's works have dramatically shifted from gallery walls to stage installations, to function closely in tandem with theatre and dance choreographies, featuring often live performances of Alakananda Samarth on the Bombay stage. Kamala Kapoor, 'Nalini Malani: Memory Stress and Recall', in *Expressions and Evocations*.
22. Sinha, Gayatri, 'Arpana Caur: Confronting Womanhood', in *Expressions and Evocations*.
23. Sambrani, Chaitanya, 'Navjot: Of Response and Responsibility', in *Expressions and Evocations*.
24. Interview with Yashodhara Dalmia, quoted in *Expressions and Evocations*, p. 72.
25. Sinha, Gayatri, *The Self and the World*, p. 11.

11

Nabaneeta
Dev Sen

Sisters in Sorrow
Contemporary Indian Women's Re-telling of the Rama Tale

In the women's folk tradition in India, never mind where you are, which century you belong to or what language you speak, you are all sisters in sorrow.

Though the singers may live in different parts of the subcontinent, wear different clothes, cook very different food and vote for totally different political parties, when they sing the story of Rama, they are astonishingly close to one another. In their feelings, their perceptions, their expressions, their choices of events and their responses they echo each other. So much so that it took me a good deal of careful screening and categorizing of the songs to keep their identities clearly separated in my mind.

For some time I had been working with women's Ramayana in Bengali. On reading my paper on Chandrabati, published in 1991, A.K. Ramanujan suggested that I look into Telugu women's folk songs. He felt that a lot of Chandrabati's perceptions were shared by them. It was 1993 when I came across Narayan Rao's work on the Telugu women's Ramayana, and taking references from him, went to Andhra Pradesh to collect new material. Since there was a wealth of Ramayana material in the Telugu women's work songs, it occurred to me to look at the Marathi peasant women's work songs, which have been collected for four decades by anthropologists. Unfortunately, I could not lay my hands on any translated material either in Telugu or in Marathi. I had to depend on translators, and to ensure the accuracy of translation, I had to get each song translated by two persons.

All these songs opened up a rich world of women's Ramayanas. While weeding or sowing in the field or husking or grinding in the courtyard, women all across the country sing these songs. While working with Bengali, Telugu and Marathi, I thought of looking into the Maithili folk songs, as Mithila was Sita's hometown, and Maithili is one of her names (the daughter of Mithila). These are more ritual songs rather than work songs connected with different moments of a women's life, and here, again, Sita is the name of the woman who attains puberty, gets married, gets pregnant, is exiled and gives birth.

Although the collection of folk songs I was working with categorically mentioned that there were no women's Ramayanas in Maithili, there were 47 songs dealing with different episodes from the epic. This is natural with women's retellings of the Ramayana. They pick and choose the episodes and are not interested in the heroic epic cycle, which has no relevance to their lives. A woman's retelling is usually the pick of the epic. If it is fragmentary, it is because their life is fragmentary. For them, it is the whole story. It reflects a woman's world in its entirety. So, these are the four languages of my present interest. Bengali in the East, Marathi in the West, Telugu in the South and Maithili in the northern Hindi belt. The material was collected between 1950 and 1997, mostly in the last 25 years.

The favourite episodes of the women singers seem to come mostly from the Balakanda and the Uttarkanda, the two so-called spurious books, excluded by strictly classical Ramayana scholars. The Balakanda deals with the birth and marriage of Sita and what happened before Rama's coronation plans were made. And the Uttarkanda tells us what happened after the war, of Rama and Sita's return to Ayodhya, of the establishment of Ram Rajya, Sita's abandonment by Rama, her life in exile, the birth of children in the forest, their fight with their father and the ultimate rejection of Rama by Sita. Molla, we have seen, just touches upon and leaves the Uttarkanda, so does Kampan, in the proper Bhakti style. So that there is no question of criticizing Rama's later actions. Uttarkanda is not a flattering book for Rama: he beheads a Shudra ascetic to bring a Brahmin's son to life and banishes his pregnant wife to quench some nasty gossip. And the great warrior is defeated by two little boys in a straight combat, in the forest.

The topics that interest men do not seem to interest women. They leave out the details of war, Rama's glory, the details of Brahminical rituals etc. The women seem to sing mostly of abandonment and injustice, and of romance, weddings, pregnancy and childbirth. Naturally, the songs centre around Sita, rather than Rama..The areas where usually Rama shines brilliantly, those of moral strength like father-worship, and of physical prowess, like demon killing, do not seem to interest the women at all. One area of Rama's moral judgement does bother them though—his wife-testing and wife-abandoning. Incidentally, the man who seems to appear most in the songs is Lakshmana, the brother-in-law and forest companion of Sita (the other slave of Rama). He appears to be the only man the rural women of India and Bangladesh care for, and the only one with whom Sita can communicate.

The six major themes in these songs are (1) Sita's birth, (2) her wedding (with a touch of pre-marital romance), (3) her abduction, (4) pregnancy, (5) abandonment, and (6) childbirth. These major themes can be broken down into ten sub-themes, which I am going to illustrate with songs from different languages. Next, we shall see what purpose these songs serve in the day-to-day lives of the women. The overall tone of the songs, however, seems to be one of loneliness and their subject is injustice. These Rama Sita songs that I have worked with are sung mostly by peasant women; their interests spring from their class and express their work a day concerns.

The rural women in India and Bangladesh have shared the same historical experience and the same socio-economic situations, and their responses to an elitist patriarchal text naturally show a great deal of commonality. Their values are not very different from each other's but they are very different from those of their ruling males—which are the concerns of an epic. Hence, the Ramayana sung by the mainstream bards has little in common with those women's songs.

The topics that we are going to look into are derived from the ten major themes:

1. Sita, the foundling: the girl child as the essential orphan.
2. The worry of parents about getting their daughter married.
3. Child marriage and its concerns.
4. The giving-away songs.
5. The in-laws and domestic abuse of the brides.
6. The golden deer. Blaming the victim. 'She asked for it.'
7. Woman's desperate need to bear a son to keep her place in patriarchal society and the value of male life.
8. Pregnancy—the cravings, the desire to be spoilt a bit.
9. Childbirth under dire conditions.
10. Abandonment—facing rejection and dispossession of one's social identity.

These themes, obviously, have no religious significance, nor concern men very much. These are songs that deal with the most difficult or dangerous areas of a woman's life, the intense moments of insecurity or physical risk. They do not complain about hard work or poverty, all the songs complain about neglect and denial of their rights. The songs show us that a woman has no social identity of her own, her husband lends her his identity and defines her by it.

The Sita songs are the songs through which we can hear the voice of the silent majority, whereas the epics sing the glory of the powerful few. Let us see how these songs deal with the topics we have just pointed out.

Each language seems to have its own special touch while dealing with Sita's travails. For example, Marathi seems to be the only one of these four languages that has the detailed accounts of Sita's sufferings at the hands of the in-laws and the useless husband who plays into their hands. And songs depicting Janaka's desperation to find a husband for Sita recurs the most in Maithili. The support Sita receives from all the women of the household when she is being sent off to the forest is to be found only in Telugu songs. The Bengali songs contain probably the most harsh words about Rama, although practically every woman worth her song in the other languages criticizes him too. In Bengali he is not only portrayed as jealous and suspicious, but is also termed 'stone-hearted' and a 'sinner'. Chandrabati calls Rama a deranged wimp and to make the picture clearer describes him in such a way that he appears to be closer to a dragon than a king. She also holds him responsible for the fall of Ayodhya. Which ironically did come true 400 years later with the destruction of the Babri Masjid by Rama fanatics. Across the country, village women have an incredible identification with Sita, and though they have affection for Rama the child, or Rama the lover, they do see him as a tyrant and an unjust husband. Never mind that Rama is a god and is presently on a comeback trail to save the world, in these women's folk songs he will always be a less than perfect man, and a far cry from a hero.

Orphan

Now let's look at some songs. We begin with the theme of Sita as the essential orphan. In a Marathi song, Sita, in forest exile, talks to the birds and trees because she has no one to talk to: Sita says, 'What kind of woman am I? I was given away to Rama when I was five years old. What sort of mother's love have I got?... Dear plum tree, dear babul tree, Sita is telling you the story of her life. Please listen... I was found at the tip of a plough. How can I have parents? I was found in a box, in the open field.' The eagerness of a woman to communicate.

This feeling of being utterly alone and unloved is echoed in other languages. I quote from Chandrabati's Bengali poem, where Sita tells Lakshman:

> I have no father, no mother
> I was found at the tip of a plough
> I don't know who my parents are
> Or who my brother is
> Like moss in a stream
> I float from shore to shore...

In a contemporary Marathi work song, Sita echoes her 400-year-old Bengali self:

I have no father, no mother
I have lived my life in forests, eating wild fruits
I have no sister, no brother
My soul has become an exile
Living in the wilderness

And in a Munda tribal song from Chhotanagpur (very close to Mithila), we hear Sita's sigh again:

On the grassy uplands, the ploughman found me
they took me to the King's palace
... I grew up like an edible fruit
Though Janaka gave me in marriage to Rama
I didn't forget my sufferings...
Never was I happy...

Why is it that all these women choose to sing of Sita as an orphan, rather than a princess? The commonest epithet for Sita in Bengali (also found in Maithili) is '*janam-dukhini*'. It is because of the fundamental insecurity underlining their lives: all of these songs see the universal woman as an essential orphan, as a being without an identity, an ever-alienated self in exile.

Finding a Groom

Even though these women empathize with Sita as an orphan, at the same time they show great sympathy for Sita's foster parents, who had the responsibility of finding a suitable match for their girl child—which to this day is seen as a terrible burden all over India.

Here's one about looking for a groom. 'Princess Sita is scrubbing the floor. Her sari slips off her shoulders and her mother the queen tells the father—Up, up, king Janaka: what are you doing here? Go, get a groom for Sita. She is ready for a husband. So Janaka gets up, puts on a clean dhoti, ties his pagdi on his head and takes his peasant's staff in his hand and sets out toward Mungher and Magadha' (No. 508). Clearly, the father here does not rule a Kingdom, but tills the land.

In another song, the young princess Sita is cleaning the courtyard. She comes across a hefty bow and lifts it with her left hand while sweeping with her right. Janaka faints on seeing this, as he had never been able to move it himself. Then he bursts out into loud laments—'ab Sita rahali Kumari, yo!' (Now Sita will remain unmarried, woe!). Since a woman needs a husband stronger than she is and Sita has such extraordinary power, would she ever meet her match? Sita's suitor must be able to string that bow! A *swayambar sabha* is called, and suitors arrive from all over. The same story appears in Maithili, Bengali and Telugu, with variations. In Maithili, Sita plays an active part in the process, which is not found elsewhere. For example, when one after another suitor fails to string the bow, Sita's parents are in a panic—'*ab Sita rahala Kumari, dhanusha na tootala he!*' (Now Sita will remain a spinster, the bow remains unbroken!). But a broken-hearted Sita climbs to the rooftop and shouts—'Oh, mother, is there no one strong enough in this world who can string the bow and keep my father's vow?' ('*Unchi jharokhe chadi Siya Chahundishi chitvathi he/Mai he, nai koi duniyame bir Pita-Pran rakhata he?*') A naturally bad-tempered Lakshman is most annoyed when he hears it—'Why is she so desperate? Rama will come in his own sweet time and string the bow.' Well, Sita didn't want to take a chance.

One song begins without any preliminaries: Sita herself goes to her father and says—'*Sunu Baba araji hamari yo, kumari katek din rakhalva? Iho na uchit vyavahar yo!*' (Listen father, I have something to tell you. How much longer do you plan to keep me unmarried? This is not right!). Thank god Lakshman didn't hear this conversation. Janaka of course reacted promptly and got the astrologers over.

In almost all these songs Ravana comes as a suitor, and falls on his face unable to lift the bow. Sita cannot help laughing, and a humiliated Ravana takes an oath to get Sita by force some day. The women take great pleasure in describing how the ten-headed demon failed miserably, in Telugu, in Marathi, in Bengali, in Maithili it is the same. As opposed to Ravana, there is Rama, a teenager, tall, dark and handsome. Sita is worried, this lean and hungry-looking sadhu will never be able to lift the bow. She even expresses her anger toward her father for taking such a harsh vow. But the tender boy does it, he breaks the bow.

The Significance of Sita's Picking Up the Bow of Shiva

We can think of two possible explanations for the bow episodes. It appears only in the women's and the tribals' stories, never in the classical Ramayana. It could mean that even if Sita possesses equal strength, her gender role does not allow her to use a bow. She can lift it and wipe the floor, but cannot string it to protect herself.

However, in one Telugu peasant women's song, Sita asks for Rama's bow and arrow to go and get the golden deer herself when Rama does not agree to pursue an illusory figure. Thereupon Rama promptly leaves for the kill.

Another significance could perhaps be that it is not physical prowess but the strength of inner purity, and maybe chastity too, that allows her to lift the bow, when a demon with ten heads and twenty arms falls flat on his face. It is not physical power but inner strength that lifts the bow of Shiva. This is where Sita and Rama are made for each other, the perfect match. This ideal match breaks down—through the relentless demand in our society to prove a woman's chastity in public. Rama becomes complicit in the unholy and oppressive demand, and he loses Sita. If Rama had to pick up the bow of Sita at the end of the Ramayana—rather than at the beginning, when he was untainted— would our women singers allow him to pick it up?

Child Bride

Next comes the theme of child bride, getting her ready for the wedding, getting her ready for the in-laws. In these songs we can hear the heart of the Indian woman, the lament for a very young girl, not yet ready to start an adult life, being sent away in marriage. Take this Telugu song: 'The tiny girl is only as tall as seven jasmine flowers/ She can stand neither the heat nor the rain/... Such a lovely child is being given away in marriage, to Rama.'

Then this Bengali song, from Bangladesh: 'Little by little pour the water, let's dry her hair with a towel, or Sita might catch a cold.' (*'alpa alpa dhailo re jal/sitar hoibo sardijar/gameha diya tuilo kesher jal go'*) Sita's aunts are bathing her—the basic paradox of child marriage is seen here. A child who is not yet physically capable of taking care of herself is being forced to take up the social responsibility of wifehood.

Giving Away

In the giving away songs the anxiety of the parents comes out sharply. In one Telugu story Janaka takes Dasaratha, Rama's father, to the wedding hall and shows a small child, Sita, sleeping in a huge wedding bed. 'Look, how helpless she looks in that flower-bed, she is still an innocent child.' Clearly, there is a fear of marital rape here and an appeal is made to good sense.

In another Telugu song, Sita's mother Bhudevi has a woman-to-woman talk with Rama's mother—'From today Sitamma is truly your daughter/She knows nothing/... teach her to boil milk/ to make ghee from butter/... she has not yet been taught the household chores.'... And here is the advice she gives Sita when she leaves, making it clear that the time has come for the girl to act like a woman :

Don't visit your neighbours after sunset
Don't go to the washerman in the evenings
Never leave your hair open in the street
Don't laugh showing all your teeth
Don't look around when you are in a crowd
Keep your eyes downcast in public
Never step upon the rice husks
Strewn on the kitchen floor.

And most important of all—'Never offer flowers to any man other than your husband.' The song has its place in Andhra weddings even now, since the mother's advice is still the same. It reads more like an etiquette book for rural housewives than the wedding song for a future queen.

Sasurbas

But in spite of all the lessons taught the child bride has a tough time at her in-laws. In Marathi, the *sasurbas* songs of Sita give a clear picture of the torture of the bride by her mother-in-law. *Sasurbas* is an important category of Marathi women's songs. They tell us the story of a girl whose fateline was crooked. I quote: 'Brahma was in a hurry/Drawing the line of fate/on Sita's forehead/The line became crooked'...

Here's a taste of Sita's *sasurbas*:

Ram gave Sita his love
On a tiny tamarind leaf
Kaikeyi poured poison in Rama's ears
So he chews his paan alone
All by himself
While Kaikeyi waits behind the door
Like a scorpion.

Tamarind leaves are minute, Rama clearly didn't have much to offer Sita. 'Chewing his paan alone' means Sita doesn't enjoy Rama's company even when he is relaxing—his mother doesn't allow it.

The description gets pretty graphic from time to time:

Sita was tortured by one and all
They fed her only bitter neem leaves for twelve years
They didn't let her wear kumkum for twelve years
Her hair is all tangled up
For twelve years they didn't let her wash it.

A clear domestic picture of abuse, both physical and mental. She is not allowed to eat, nor to groom herself, she is not allowed sexual pleasure either.

Sita has been in exile
Right inside her bedroom
Rama didn't share her bed
For twelve years
She was locked up behind seven doors
Rama is absorbed in his own business
Poor Sita's youth is wasted away.

She was deprived of her husband's company, and not allowed to step out and make friends. While her husband is busy with his work, she leads a life of total imprisonment.

oil every day, and just before the chariot leaves she turns back and checks once more—'Are my Rama's fresh clothes kept in his bathroom?' Before we get too exasperated with Sita's obsession with her wifely duties, let's take a look at the end of the longish song. The singer turns around and tells us:

> Sita is going to the forest
> She is pouring her heart only to you and me (saying)
> 'Rama has no compassion
> I am five months pregnant.'
> Sita is leaving home
> She is sharing her sorrow with you and me, (saying)
> 'No one felt any pity for me here
> I am carrying a little baby in my belly'

The Golden Deer: The Value of Male life

There are many variations of the story of the golden deer and the abduction of Sita. In some she wants the beautiful animal as a pet to keep her company in the desolate forest (Bengali). In Marathi, Sita wants a golden blouse made of the gold deer's skin. In a tribal song, Sita wants to cook venison for a change, after long years of fruit and roots. In a Telugu song, Sita has been caring for a small plant that a deer comes and chews up every day. She wants the deer caught and the plant saved. Whatever the reason, Sita wanted her husband to chase the golden deer and sent her brother-in-law after her husband, although he had been specifically requested by Rama not to leave Sita alone. So she breaks the female code of behaviour more than once: once at the *swayambar sabha*, when she had laughed at Ravana, a strict no-no for a woman; a second time by forcing her brother-in-law to disobey his elder brother; and again, when she crosses the magic circle, the boundary line drawn by Lakshman on the ground (not to be found in Valmiki, like the vow of Ravana).

In most songs, Sita steps out in order to give alms to the monk-mendicant, because it is sinful to refuse a sadhu his alms. In Bengali it is just a single line, in Telugu and Marathi it involves crossing three or seven protective circles. In this Telugu song that women sing while sowing seeds, Sita asks Lakshman what will happen if she steps out of the magic circles. 'You will be abducted,' he says. When Ravana comes in the guise of a sadhu and asks her to step out, she puts the same question to him. Ravana says: 'If you cross one circle you get one son, if you cross two you get two sons, if you cross three.... ' Sita takes no chances and greedily crosses all the seven circles. Because she wants sons. But she also knows of the abduction. So? What do we make of it?

In India, producing a son is an essential duty of the wife. Failing that, women suffer tremendous physical and mental abuse and, most often, abandonment. The social and familial persecution also leads to frequent suicides. The rate of female infanticide after birth and now even before, with the help of amniocentesis, is alarmingly high. It is not surprising, then, that Sita took the risk.

An alternative reasoning is found in a Bengali women's song. Ravana blackmails Sita into crossing the Lakshmanrekha, he threatens to kill himself at Sita's door if she did not come forward and hand him some food and water. Sita is afraid of 'Purush-hatya maha pap'—the great scene of taking a male life. So she steps across the line to save a male life at the risk of her own.

In both cases the value of male life, be it a son, seven sons, or a begging sadhu—is considered greater than Sita's own life, by Sita herself. Women provide many reasons for Sita's transgression but the general consensus is against her. Because Sita broke the codes of behaviour, she was punished. This is what I call the 'she deserved it' mentality that surfaces in society when a woman is molested.

It is a lone struggle for the woman. Even the nearest ones choose to remain outside her painful experience, as expressed so well in this Marathi song:

> How did they do it?
> It melts our blood into tears...
> Who is fighting so bravely in the forest?
> Who is all alone?
> Rama is reading about Sita's exile
> In a book...

The alienation of Rama's reality from Sita's is very clear here. Rama is totally detached from Sita's suffering. He reads about it in a book.

He is not part of the book, but outside it when women sing the Ramayana.

Childbirth in Exile

The exile songs are probably the ones that touch the very core of a woman's heart, as the Marathi and Telugu songs seem to indicate. In Maithili, exile is mentioned as a part of the birthing songs. Take this one:

> Sita leaves the palace, opening the golden gates
> Sita walks to her forest exile
> Girls, exile is written for Sita.
> Sita goes one mile, she goes two miles, girls.
> In the third mile the pain arises
> Now life wishes to be born, girls,
> Call the midwife, quick!
> The tree came out of the forest
> So, you are my friend, my wellwisher?
> You take my golden bangle then
> And cut the cord of the baby...
> Alas! if only Rama would understand!

This song brings out the loneliness of a pregnant woman thrown out of her secured home who has no one to help her in a moment of distress.

The loneliness of a woman giving birth alone in the jungle haunts women's folk Ramayanas. Let's take another example, this one from Marathi:

> Where is the smoke coming from, in the dense forest?
> In the dense forest, Sitabai has given birth.
> Water is being boiled
>
> Sitabai has given birth.
> Where will Sitabai find a bed?
> Dark beauty Sitabai
> You better make a bed of rocks
> And sleep on it.
> Sitabai has given birth
> Where will Sita find nourishment?
> There is no one to cook her a meal

Sita is in exile, there is no cradle for her babies
Sita made a bed of flowers
And placed her twins in it
Sitabai has given birth
The hills and the forests are rejoicing
She has no one else to call her own.
Sita says, 'I have lived a life of rejection.'
All her life she has been neglected by Rama,
Yes, all her life.

The wretched condition in which women in rural India give birth to their babies, the insecurities, the lack of help, lack of comfort, lack of healthy environment, all come out in Sita's birthing songs. The infant mortality rate, and the death rate of mothers at childbirth in India is still quite alarming. Anaemia is common among mothers and babies. Post-partum care is very poor.

For twelve years she has been alone in the forest
Sita is hunting for roots
She must eat something
She has given birth.
For five days Sitabai has had nothing to eat.

No one to brew a tonic, no one to cook special confinement food for her.

Rama has given me this gift of exile
Like a sudden gust of wind...

Sita tells the trees and the birds and then she asks the crucial question about the kingdom of Rama (Ramrajya):

Where is my Rama reigning now?
Rama, how could you do this to me?'

The blackberry bush seems to have an answer for Sita's question. In another Marathi song:

Sita is nine months pregnant and in forest exile
Because Sita is a woman
She had to face such rejection, such neglect
And so much pain
Because Sita is a woman...
Rama, just because some wild people talked
You have sent virtuous Sita into the forest!

The sympathies of the wilderness are with Sita, the child of nature. In Bengali too, the exile songs are heart-rending, but not necessarily softly worded. Bengali women freely use very harsh words, including expletives in Sanskrit, for Rama, Example:

'*Panchamasher garbha Sitar Chhilo Rajdhame/Pashands hoiya Ram Sita dilo vane!*' (Five months pregnant, Sita was in the royal palace, a heartless Rama sent her off to the forest!). In another song, we find 'princess Sita' going off to exile like a 'golden idol immersed before its time': '*Kichhu kichhu jayre Sita, pichhu pichhu chay/Tathaapi papishthi Ramer/Puri dekha jayre puri dekha jay!*' (Sita takes a few steps and looks back a few times/But oh! the palace of that sinner Rama still rises high). To call someone who is commonly known as Karunasindhu or the ocean of kindness, 'ruthless' (*pashanda*) takes a great deal of accumulated anger. But to brand the Patika pavan, one who redeems sinners, as a sinner (*papishthi*) himself, goes that unbelievable step further.

IDENTITY

In Marathi songs too, Sita looks back at every step as she leaves home. She keeps stopping Lakshman for things she has left behind. Wait! her blouse is on Rama's bed. And oh, her saree is there too. Then her box of sindoor. Finally, she says: 'I have forgotten my face on Rama's bed.' Presumably the 'face' is her mirror. And most certainly it is her identity that she has left behind. For in Indian society even today, it is believed that the wife's identity is derived from her husband. And when he throws her out, she does have reason for existential crisis.

That a woman's identity is defined by her husband is also clear in a Telugu song, where Sita walks into Rama's bedroom and finds a lovely girl. She is shocked and hurt and complains to Rama till he comes up and embraces her. Sita sees the pretty girl in Rama's embrace now, and recognizes herself in the mirror. She is a woman without an identity till Rama affixes it for her. To send her to exile, away from her husband, is to deprive her of that borrowed identity. What remains is the foundling. From the *Mahabharata* to *Moby Dick*, exile has always been a symbol of disempowerment—of dispossession of rights, of exclusion from society.

The forest for Sita—or the desert for Sarah—serve the same purpose. Wilderness is the opposite of society, exile is the annihilation of all social relations. For Sarah, as for Sita, it shows the fragility of women's status. In epics, exile and abandonment are not exactly the same thing. There can be heroism and dignity in exile—it can be a male experience. Rama himself is sent to exile, but there is no question of course of his being abandoned. For Sita, as for Sarah, exile equals abandonment. Not just being dispossessed, but being rejected and driven out of home forever. There is nothing heroic in being abandoned, it can only be shameful. Abandonment happens to women, to those in power, to those who are weak. Deserted wives are a common concept but how often do we hear of a deserted husband? A man's identity belongs to himself, but a woman's identity is lent to her by a man—with abandonment that identity is snatched away from her.

Sita's exile
Let us share it among ourselves.
Sita's exile
How many times will it happen
Sita's exile
Is happening every moment, everywhere
When leaving for the forest
Sita distributed it amongst us all bit by bit.

In this Marathi song, women see Sita as a symbol of the suffering that is inextricably linked with womanhood. Sita, for them, is the universal woman, by singing about her the women sketch out the stark reality of their lives.

Sita, then, offers a voice to the silenced women of the subcontinent. Through her, women express fears and sorrows, their hopes and wishes. Sita is just any other hard-working woman, ill-treated by in-laws, neglected by her husband, with nobody to fall back on, punished for no fault of hers. But till the end, Sita remains a good housewife. Take this Telugu song, where the war is over, Ravana is dead, Sita has just been rescued and is being gently led to Rama. She points to a stone lying half-buried in the ground and says shyly to Hanuman: 'What a lovely grinding stone that will make! I would like to take it back to Ayodhya.' So Hanuman starts digging. But then Jambuban finds out and stops Operation Grindstone, saying it is below the dignity of a queen. So, a corrected Sita hangs her head in shame. It's a song where women laugh at themselves.

Whether it's a comic greed for domestic appliances or the fear and agony of giving birth alone and unattended, the women's songs reveal genuine concerns. Take their fascination for Sita's childbirth in exile, for example. Even today 67% of women in India give birth by themselves, without the help of a doctor or nurse. The maternal mortality rate is 570 per 100,000 live births. And 88% of pregnant women have anaemia. Is it surprising then that these village women sing about the lack of nourishment, the pain and fear of a lonely childbirth? Sita is their voice, for they, like Sita, have been programmed not to rebel.

In her study of Indian society, Sally Sutherland had found that 90% of Indian men and women regard Sita as their ideal woman, and not Draupadi of the *Mahabharata*. One can understand why. Sita has lent dignity, even glamour, to suffering. When there is no escape from suffering, one prefers to accept it with grace. Sita helps them do just that. She is a victim who suffers in grandeur, without being vengeful. Usually, in epics, preys turn into predators and vice versa. And when a woman turns from prey to predator, out of anger or vengeance, she doesn't win. Even if she does on the surface, her victory leads to total disaster. Those who remained victims, like Andromache or Helen, pose no threat. Draupadi, a victim who turns aggressive and urges her five husbands to avenge her humiliation, wins the battle of nerves but loses her five sons. An angry Dido killed herself in Aeneid, leaving her dream city of Carthage incomplete. Nothing happens however, to the hero Aeneas, who abandoned her. He fulfils his mission to start his own dynasty and build his own city. The anger of Amata is looked upon as madness, and derided. In *Nibelungenlied* part I, Kriemhild is a victim. But in part II, a vengeful Kriemhild is portrayed as a near demon and her whole family is wiped out, like Draupadi's. Sita remains a victim, and her sons live to become heroes.

Draupadi is too dramatic to be a role model for the weak and the exploited. Women cannot identify with Draupadi, who has five husbands and Lord Krishna for a personal friend. With her unconventional life and thirst for vengeance, she inspires awe. Sita is a figure closer to home, the girl next door, a person they know too well, a woman whose pain they can share. She is not part of the elite, and she never rebels. She symbolizes sacrifice, a woman's greatest virtue according to patriarchal traditions. She laments but does not challenge Rama in the songs. Other women speak for her just as they expect others to speak up for them. So even in Chandrabati's poem, where Rama is severely criticized, Sita remains a docile wife while Chandrabati the narrator lashes her whip under her own name. Sita has infinite forbearance and is thus a winner even when she loses. This is what makes her a role model for Indian women. For in spite of the sweeping changes across the subcontinent in the last decades, for the silent majority of Indian women justice remains a dream, equality an absurdity and suffering at the hands of a patriarchal society an everyday reality.

12

VINA MAZUMDAR &
INDU AGNIHOTRI

The Women's Movement in India. Emergence of a New Perspective*

UNCHANGING ISSUES IN A CHANGED GLOBAL CONTEXT

The twentieth century promoted the cause of gender equality by internationalizing women's and other oppressed people's struggles for justice. These struggles had earlier mostly remained confined by locale, limited focus and nature of issues, and their relative weakness against the structures and ideologies that oppressed them. The same century, however, also strengthened the powers of oppression and exploitation by globalizing their arena of operation, creating new instruments for hegemony and weakening the balancing mechanisms and ideologies that sought to place limits on their rapacity. In the first half of the century, ideologies and movements based on the values of freedom, self-determination, equality, democracy and justice—social, economic and political—found international expression through the

*An earlier but more detailed version of this paper was published in *EPW*, XXX(29), July 22, 1995.

movements against imperialism and for national liberation and social transformation in different parts of the world. Women's struggles against their own subordination were intertwined with many of these, in varying degrees.[1] The revolutionary changes that followed each of the world wars created some fora and structures that promoted debates and limited acknowledgement of women's rights.[2]

The defeat of fascism and the forced retreat of imperialism on the international plane around mid-century set the stage, so to say, for the social advance of which gender relations was a key component, along with the other broad objectives of human rights, self-determination and the end of exploitative and iniquitous social orders. Many of these still remain on the agenda, including those of several international conferences, and in the broader terrain of historical conflicts. But the women's movement at this point of history cannot help taking note of the changed context in which these movements are now being fought, and of the shifts affecting the ideologies.[3]

The current phase of the women's movement faces the opening up of those very issues that were considered to have been resolved through protracted struggles over decades. This is increasingly clear from (1) the blow to the hopes of a new international economic order based on more egalitarian relations between nations[4] and (2) the various combinations of xenophobic-fundamentalist upsurges overcoming one country after another in the South and the North, the 'developing' and the 'developed', the 'free-market industralised' and the legatees of the 'centrally planned' (i.e. erstwhile socialist) segments of the world economy. The context in which the international struggle for advance of women's rights is being waged has been transformed. Moreover, it is actively promoting debates that twist the very premises or values on which the movement has been based.

For example, women's rights to literacy, education, employment, and participation in decision-making and the political process, demanded for long as basic human rights essential for an equitable social order, national or international, are now frequently being justified as necessary for fertility reduction or population stabilization. Such arguments, which give primacy to women's reproductive role, tend to undermine the fundamental rationale for gender equality through an instrumentalist approach.

A similar intrusion is the replacement of 'equity' by an 'efficiency' argument in justifying women's access to new skills and knowledge, required for adaptation to the new technology-based globalized economy. Such arguments are constantly propagated by statements that are fast acquiring the power of religious beliefs—that 'there is no alternative'.

The last quarter of the 20th century, which coincides with the beginning and spread of an economic 'recession',[5] clearly shows that movements for self-determination, and the search for an alternative political identity based on birth, race, ethnicity, religion, culture or language, can also be waged using the language of 'historic justice' and 'democracy', within the framework of a world view that opposes even basic democratic values, leave alone the urge for a more radical transformation. It is not surprising that subordination of women, in which women's reproductive role is seen as the only natural historical one, forms an essential component of this world view, with a harking back to 'tradition' and 'culture' forming a necessary appendage and justification.

The history of the international women's movement has, from the start, been intertwined with these socio-political developments. Any gaps that may exist form the subject of numerous studies by young women, whose scholarship has opened up several new dimensions of old as well as forgotten struggles by our sisters over the centuries. The tendency of organizations or individuals who believe in gender equality to be aligned with movements for social change within their respective countries is today a well-established historical fact. But the realization that is creeping in, even among those who have shied away from it earlier, is that sisterhood cannot be based on just biological premises. It has to be based on an ideological commitment to certain basic human values and notions derived from struggles for social advance of oppressed sections through history.[6]

The need to reiterate this stems from the fact that the struggle for hegemony over social movements is today not separate from the struggle for control over the instruments of equality evolved through this long period of human history. Even terms thrown up by the women's movement, like empowerment, choice, reproductive freedom and spiritual autonomy, are being appropriated, misinterpreted, and distorted by forces inimical to the goals of the women's movement.

Through the criss-cross of ideologies and movements, however, the 20th century gave birth to several institutions that provided the international support and the institutional fora required for creative interaction between differing perspectives and peoples. It also provided the environment for development of international scholarship that demystified the links between economy, power structures, cultural practices and gender relations. However, today the clash between contending ideologies and forces threatens these very institutions and the environment and instruments they promoted (international covenants, standards, values). The critical question for all of us then is how to ensure the continued existence of fora that provide the space for interaction between ideologies and peoples from different backgrounds and also mount pressure for intervention in favour of more equitable gender relations—at the level of international realpolitik, as well as ground-level processes.

The link between this awesome global reality and the grassroots is provided by both official and non-official agencies that stand, theoretically at least, for change, within and between countries. The capacity of our networks, institutions and movements to withstand the forces of reaction, hegemonism and unaccountable power, the strategies and coalitions that we work out collectively as well as the issues we focus on will determine the manner in which the changing global situation affects the 'women down there'. And she could be all or any one of us.

> Globalisation, therefore, presents a political challenge. The various modes of globalisation are tantamount to a universalisation of power, now being concentrated into the hands of new multinational actors. These transcend the sovereign nation-state and supplant the spirit of internationalism developed in earlier decades. The new structures and protagonists of world power are relatively anonymous; they lack accountability and often operate without controls—given the absence world-wide of effective, accountable regimes of regulation and supervision. Deregulation has been the pivot of economic globalisation and

has radically reduced the power of individual governments. This is best exemplified by the unsettling effects of international currency speculation on national economic policies. Governments, less able than before to choose policies in the national interest, must be able to react effectively to new international economic perceptions. In an effort to strengthen controls over public spending, many governments are compelled to reverse gains made by the welfare state by tightening their own social policy and its benefits.[7]

THE INDIAN MOVEMENT—BACKGROUND, CONTEXT AND AN APPROACH

In India too, the period of colonial rule and the freedom struggle marked the beginnings of a political awakening among women. The differing streams within the anti-imperialist anti-feudal struggle posited different, even contentious images of identities for women.[8] But they all shared a concern for women and so a consensus emerged at the time of the making of the new India, which postulated freedom, justice, dignity and equality for women as a stated goal within the Constitution.

In the post-independence period, women drawn from various social groups came forward to explore avenues for socio-economic mobility, creative self-expression, or a search for new identities, as well as political mobilization in the new-found democratic set-up. What they came up against were the limitations of a third world ex-colonial state. This posed a dilemma at several levels, regarding the stance to be adopted vis-à-vis the State. The stated welfarist goals of the Nehruvian era provided legitimacy to some of these efforts, and co-option of some leaders and activists in the movement.[9] Others, handicapped either by their ignorance of their new rights, or by the burdens of values carefully promoted by a long-standing patriarchal social hierarchy (or a combination of the two), were unable to negotiate the vast gap between the stated goals and the emerging reality. The women's movement became fragmented, and the women's question faded from the public arena. This is not to imply that no struggles were waged during this period: we only wish to state that they could not form the basis of spurring agitations that could catch the public imagination cutting across sectional demands and organizations.

A recent seminar at Baroda[10] addressed the unwritten history of the first two decades after independence from a woman's perspective—with both personal testimonies of women who had participated, suffered and been transformed through these struggles, and critical analyses of the Nehruvian paradigm of national development or the 'nation-building project' by several analysts of different generations, including 'insiders' as well as 'outsiders' of that process. The outcome of the seminar will certainly enable us to reassess and rewrite the record of women's agency, and the 'politics' of representing the woman question during those decades and thereafter.

The resurgence of the movement in contemporary India was both a response and a reaction to the deepening crisis within our society and the State. These crises are not totally endogenous. There are factors influencing them from outside India also—some historical, some contemporary. The women's movement also has developed interaction with both internal and external forces as well as ideas and movements at different levels that need analysis.

This paper cannot undertake the exercise of spelling these out. We seek to trace only some of the dominant features reflected in the shifts in priorities and strategies as well as the techniques and alliances built up by the women's movement over the last twenty years. This may help assess the extent to which it has developed a momentum as well as foci and an ideology of its own. These could be regarded as an index of its maturity, as different from its original character as reactive politics.

Broadly, it is during the period between the 1970s and the 1990s that Indian society, the State and the women's movement experienced shifts in internal dynamics. Shifts in foci and awareness of problems that impinged on women's lives, the social construction of gender relations and the location of women from different classes in their attempts to resolve the problems of the national economy and polity occurred during a period of dissolving certainties that characterized local, national or global systems.

On the one side, there are contradictory trends in the transformation of Indian society, e.g.:

1. A fast-growing infrastructure designed to promote educational, economic, scientific and technological growth, coupled with growing inequality, poverty, unemployment and mounting numbers of a marginalized, illiterate population (of which women and children constitute nearly three-quarters).

2. An expanding communication network that provides outlets for consumerist life-styles that represent 'growth' but threaten the nation's natural resources and the social environment, as well as for the voices of dissent and protest at local, national and even international levels.

3. A steadily rising crime graph within which crimes of violence against women—domestic, social and political—co-exist with innumerable examples of heroic struggles by women and men of different classes and backgrounds to find innovative and constructive solutions to the many maladies that characterize society.

If one were to single out one major characteristic of Indian society during these decades, it would be to describe it as the end of the age of complacency, apathy and acceptance of the existing social order. This upsurge from below has both harsh and benevolent faces, but it would be ahistorical not to recognize in it the outcome of nearly half a century of the world's largest experiment in democracy.

These contradictions within society are reflected in the State's structures. The 1970s began with deepening crises of legitimacy and efficiency of the Indian government (despite the towering personality of Indira Gandhi), leading to the declaration of national emergency. The decade ended with an extraordinary reassertion of democracy with the people's rejection of an authoritarian regime. People's movements of many kinds exploded all over the country, demanding drastic changes in the functioning of government, the planning process and development strategies. The women's movement was one of these burgeoning efforts at reassertion of the claims of ordinary citizens to participate as equals in the political and development process.

While most of the movements still retained some faith in the capacity of Indian democratic institutions to pull the nation out of these crises, there were some sections that adopted a hostile stance.

The 1980s saw the growth and spread of the politics of identity and the increasing use of violence for political ends.[11] It is difficult not to relate the increasing use of destructive weapons by the State and its enemies as well as between competing socio-economic groups for political power with the global spread of the armaments industry, and relate its need for new markets. The crises of confidence, leadership and efficiency of the governmental system, heightened by the failure of its attempts to restructure the international economic and political order, manifested itself in growing dependence on external assistance, risking India's economic sovereignty.

The 1990s have so far mainly recorded the inevitable outcome of these crises. The global collapse of a balance of power coincided with the virtual collapse of the capacity of India's national government to resolve its threatened bankruptcy, leading to a policy of subservience to the World Bank, the International Monetary Fund and other external agencies, which dictate drastic changes in national economic policies, most of them in total violation of the principles prescribed in the Constitution. The period has also been characterized by an upsurge of politically conservative and economically reactionary forces, which in the Indian context work not so much for the status quo as for fundamentalism/revivalism, as opposed to the radical demands and upsurges coming from below.

Among the latter is also the women's movement. The changing character of and contradictions within the government structure can very easily be analysed by its shifting attitude towards the women's movement. A major question facing all governments in office has been how to respond to the movement and its demand to place women's questions on the political agenda. The government's response has been teetering between conservative and radical forces.

The movement too has experienced major transformations through this period. The 1970s, viewed by many as a period of re-awakening, saw the gradual spread of the women's movement— in response sometimes to immediately local situations, sometimes to the ideological inspirations coming from the international women's movement, and sometimes to the growing national crises. These diversities manifested themselves in many ideological cleavages and the fragmented, regionally uneven growth of the movement.

The 1980s may be viewed as a period of organization building, attempts at alliances and coalitions, and defining the movement's identity, purposes and strategies for both internal and external relations. Issues that had not featured in the debates of the pre or post-independence decades erupted into the movement's efforts to define its nature and purpose. The preoccupation with economic independence and social equality of individual women and establishing an independent position for the movement in international fora had to make room for responses to communalism and anti-women implications of all fundamentalist/revivalist policies. Criticism of State policies and development strategies that had failed to bring about gender equality continued side by side with attempts to find a base for the movement in issues being articulated by poor women at the grassroots in both urban and rural areas, and a gradual absorption of the latter's issues, aspirations and capacities into the movement's range of concerns.[12]

While the 1990s have introduced an element of urgency and confusion with the rapidly changing political and economic scenario, the movement has not so far shown any sign of flagging. Perhaps the reason lies in its having found solid roots among the large masses of women at the grassroots, and having been able to see its own role as much broader and enduring than finding immediate solutions to a single definition of 'women's issues'.

True to its pre-independence legacy, the movement stayed firmly rooted to democratic rights. Any alliances or coalitions that were to be worked out had first to be negotiated on the terms of a firm commitment in upholding democratic rights. Thus, the issues on which women first articulated their visible opposition covered a vast terrain—ranging from those that were gender-specific to those that impinged on citizen's rights, class formations, values and the direction of social transformation and development in general.

By the mid-1970s, the devaluation of life had become an everyday experience for women. This point was driven home by the report of the Committee on the Status of Women in India.[13] The committee's findings made it clear that the disenchantment of women with the post-independence 'development' scenario was not a stance dictated by exogenous political considerations. Demographic indicators such as the accelerated decline in the sex ratio, increasing gender gaps in life expectancy, mortality and economic participation, or the rising migration rate were disturbing enough. But the utter failure of State policy to live up to its constitutional mandates in any field of national development was found to have in fact contributed to, even accelerated these trends. The committee noted clear linkages between existing and growing social and economic disparities and women's status in education, the economy, society and the polity.

The committee's report, while drawing attention to the wide diversities in 'culturally' prescribed gender roles in India's plural society, raised serious doubts about the 'development' or 'modernization' models that not only ignored the real differences that revolved round caste, class and ethnic history, but exaggerated the influence of religion, culture and 'social attitudes' on gender role prescriptions. Finding these biases to be stronger among the educated intelligentsia, extending even to women's organisations, political parties, trade unions, media, the bureaucracy and academia, the committee questioned the role of the educational system in contributing to this continued 'invisibility of women' in areas or sectors where they were largely involved, and pleaded for a renewed concern that would reflect real life issues and aspirations of the majority of women—diverse as these were.

The women's movement in the late 1970s, added growing violence as a major issue.[14] The movement, in its interaction with the State and other levels of society leaned heavily on the legal, educational and political processes to redirect the process of change towards empowerment—for equality and participation. Approaches and priorities, however, varied, sometimes to the point of contradiction.

Some of the issues that affected the committee so deeply characterized the new wave of the women's movement.[15] This is not to claim that the movement was unleashed by the committee's report. No movement can be inspired by a document. Its foundations have to lie deep in social crisis. In this case, the large majority of women who brought their angers, energies and aspirations to influence the contours, thrusts and direction of the movement could not even read, and had never heard of the Committee on the Status of Women in India. At the most, one can say that the report contributed to a more sympathetic climate of opinion among a section of the intelligentsia, including the bureaucracy and the media, and provided the educated women activists with some processed information that they learned to use with great skill, in their mobilizing and pressure politics—vis-à-vis the State, the educational system and the legal system. It also laid the foundation of the women's studies movement through indigenous sponsorship.

Problems of Perception and Analysis

Like most movements, the women's movement is neither homogeneous nor monolithic in nature but a multi-level, multi-class process, manifested through a growing number of organizations with widely divergent ideologies and operative strategies, but overlapping objectives and connections. Such a complex phenomenon is bound to pose serious problems in perception and analysis, which could ultimately affect the treatment and selection of factual data.

The movement was neither born nor did it develop on a *tabula rasa*. It was a political movement, despite the initial hesitation of many of its participants to acknowledge it as such. As a political movement it was influenced again and again by shifts in the political scenario of the nation and the world outside. One could argue about the degrees of such influences, and question whether they brought about any drastic alteration in goals, perspectives, choice of strategies, or the language of discourse, but to regard the women's movement as totally autonomous and detached from the various other forces of change convulsing the country and the global politico-economic order would be ahistorical.

Thirdly, there is the elusive entity of change. One could list many substantive changes in laws, organizations and other structures, resource allocations, and opening of opportunities supposedly favourable to women during this period.[16] But if many of them have remained unenforced or ineffective in changing social perceptions about women or their roles and entitlements, then defining them as gains may be exaggerated. If, however, one can find clear evidence of a change in patterns of social behaviour and perception, even in the demands or in the discourse of the women's movement, such patterns can surely be examined as indicators of change. However, changes may be transient and ephemeral in their duration and influence. The women's movement has gathered considerable experience of such transient changes dependent on external factors, which are often themselves vulnerable.

On the other hand, changes that are transformational—at the individual, group, community or institutional levels—seldom receive much acknowledgement or acclaim, though they may produce more long-term effects. For example, are the movement's decentralized structure and multiple arenas of interaction—with the State, education and health systems, local communities and political groups—and simultaneous adoption of protest politics, advocacy and demonstrative co-operation with the groups, systems or institutions a point of strength or weakness? Is the movement's excessive preoccupation with the State's development policies and legislation 'welfarist' in its objectives, rather than 'feminist' or 'radical'? Does the extension of the issue of violence against women from the domestic to the social and political arenas indicate a backsliding on the part of the movement or an advance? Should the women's movement get involved with the environment, population, child rights, globalization and marketization, international debt and other controversial issues affecting the nation as a whole, or retain its autonomy and concentrated focus?[17] Or come out with a *cri de coeur*—'We have the movement but they (the others?) have the women!'

Such debates have taken place within the movement as well as among its supporters and critics inside and outside the country, and they have influenced the directions of its growth. Issues of economic welfare for millions of India's poor working women represented issues of survival, equitable recognition and acknowledgement (as contributors to the family and the national economy) of their entitlement first, to a share of their own produce and of development resources, and second, to a voice in the shaping and choice of policies that affected their lives. It was also a beginning, of a process of redefining what were women's issues in the Indian context, especially in the politics of development.[18]

A shift in the focus of attention to the issues of the majority, initiated by the report of the Committee on the Status of Women and the ICSSR's follow-up research programme, forced the nascent movement to ask some pertinent questions and to demand different answers. Both the processes were carried on through the next two decades by women's studies scholars and the reawakened women's movement. The pressure from the hitherto unheard and invisible majority became increasingly clear. The Women's Studies Programme of the ICSSR was in fact designed to counter the politics of the Emergency by bringing the real life issues of the 'invisible' majority before the public, the policy-makers and the women's movement. Every member of its advisory committee was a known critic of the Emergency.[19] The document produced by this committee in August 1977[20] was aimed to provoke government action and to arouse public opinion.

The demand for women in positions of power and influence was increasing from women in the west. In India, several women had stepped with ease into high offices since independence. Since 1966, the country had been ruled by a woman acknowledged as one of the most powerful rulers in the world. Though a demand for increased representation of women came with the new movement, by the late 1980s, the movement's critique of the National Perspective Plan for Women[21] emphasized reservation up to one-third in only grassroots bodies for local self-government—to throw up 'new leadership from below'—and rejected reservation in state assemblies and Parliament.[22]

The growing focus on violence against women also raised problems. Are rape, dowry deaths, wife-beating and sati only issues involving the female body? Even the initial protest in 1979 from four legal academics on the Supreme Court's judgement on the Mathura case[23] made it very clear that at stake were two constitutional promises: (1) levelling of socio-economic power inequalities by a State founded on principles radically different from the 'inherited social system' and (2) the judiciary's role as guardians of that promise.[24]

Dowry deaths to the Indian women's movement were much more than an attack on women's right to life. They indicated increasing dysfunctionality of the institutions that Indian women value greatly—their natal and matrimonial families. In the 1920s and 30s the women's movement had protested against dowry as a humiliating indignity against their persons. In the 1970s to 1990s, dowry has come to provide a rationale for murder of adults, infants and female foetuses involving collusion between families, law enforcement agencies, medical and other professionals, and certain identifiable policies of the State, such as population control. It was a 'social menace' and an instrument manipulated by growing economic forces and hidden external influences.[25] Today, activists report that it is increasingly becoming a quiet source of resource mobilization for petty business and economic enterprise.[26]

The roots of the revival of sati have been examined in depth by many scholars and activists.[27] Its location in a period of rising communal intolerance and identity politics—and the consequent paralysis of government—gives it a crucial connection with Indian politics. Isolating it from that context weakens its significance, to the women's movement and the Indian political system as a whole.

Such complex interconnections between different sets of issues help to explain the movement's need for multiple arenas of action, and periodic shifts in foci, priorities and agenda. The earlier phase of the current women's movement is characterized by the politics of protest, blending often and fairly easily with the politics of demands and recommendations, occasionally including some messages for the movement itself. Even when some of the groups involved adopted as their basic ideology that the State and its subsystems are oppressive and exploitative and could not be expected to meet the people's demands, the demands were, nevertheless, articulated. Since they also insisted on autonomy of the women's movement from any other political groups or movements, there has been a tendency among many analysts and participants to emphasize the dichotomy between the 'autonomous' and the 'aligned' wings of the movement.[28]

There have been other efforts at such sharp and exclusive categorization—the 'autonomous' section being regarded as more 'feminist' while others preferred the umbrella term 'women's movement'. Yet another classifying effort referred to degrees of centralization or hierarchy that characterized different organizations, or were reflected in the formality or informality within organizations. Within the women's studies movement, the recurring debate was over 'academics' versus 'activists'.

This preoccupation with classification began from the late 1970s and still continues today. Such classifications sometimes fail to highlight or appreciate the sources of inspiration and dynamics of the movement, the compulsions of the issues that the groups espouse, the changing socio-political scenario, and the responses that emanate from it to the women's movement. Movement politics, especially as developed in India, tends to contain elements that defy simplification. Ideological differences exist, but within a continuum, and they tend to get blurred when choices have to be made on immediate priorities. The sharpness of articulation also differs according to the audiences being addressed. The upsurge of poor women's organizations in urban and rural areas, a hallmark of the movement during the last few decades, demonstrates extraordinary unity in perspectives, priorities and preferences given the fact that the choices are stark and the issue is one of survival. Often there is agreement on the formulation of demands or short-term tactics while differences in perspective remain in view of long-term visions and the choice of options based on ideological frames.

One could also argue that overemphasis of the differences leads to excessive preoccupation with the highly articulate sections of the leadership of different groups, who tend to reflect the ideological divisions and fragmented characteristic of the organized sections of the Indian women's movement. In contrast, the overall impact of the grassroots upsurge has only partly been assessed. Increasing interaction with and understanding of the former's personalities, perspectives and social milieu has made many of us conscious of the transformation in our own perspectives. Some of us have even questioned the excessive importance attached to established feminist principles, such as the public-private dichotomy, or the sexual division of labour as the source or cause of women's subordination. Similarly, the concept of empowerment, frequently used in the debates, made some of us question who is empowering whom.

A current attempt is to clarify the concepts of equality and empowerment from different perspectives. Is equality a personal attribute, leading to confusion over identity with men? Or is it a normative social value, rooted in human rights and the concept of justice? Is it a static concept that causes discomfort to participants in the movement, or is it a mobilizing force that provides articulation to internalized angers, aspirations and socio-political urges of women who were forced to accept oppression because any alternative was outside their reach—physically or mentally? Such questions assume critical importance in the changed global and national context and the emerging issues facing the movement within and outside national boundaries.

NOTES

1. Jayawardena, Kumari, *Feminism and Nationalism in the Third World in the 19th and Early 20th Centuries*, ISS, 1982; Phadnis, Urmila and Indira Malani (eds), *Women of the World: Illusion and Reality*, Vikas, New Delhi, 1978; Mazumdar, Vina and Leela Kasturi (eds), *Women and Indian Nationalism*, Vikas, New Delhi, 1994.
2. Among them are the Women's International League for Peace, Women's International Democratic Federation, International Labour Office, UN Commission on the Status of Women, UN Commission on Human Rights and Centre for Social Development and Humanitarian Affairs.
3. For a general discussion on this see Hobsbawm, E.J., *The Age of Extremes*, Viking, 1995.
4. Mair, Lucille, *The International Women's Decade: A Balance Sheet*, CWDS, New Delhi, 1985.
5. The replacement of 'depression', very much in vogue through the 19th and the first half of the 20th century by the far weaker term 'recession' in recent years marks a clear example of the 'politics of language' used by the theologians of the free market.
6. Agnihotri, Indu, and Vina Mazumdar, 'Changing Terms of Political Discourse, Women's Movement in India, 1970s–90s', *EPW* XXX (29), 22 July 1995.
7. 'Caring for the Future: Making the Next Decades Provide Life Worth Living'. Report of the Independent Commission on Population and Quality of Life, Oxford University Press, 1996, p. 47.

8. Sangari, Kumkum and Sudesh Vaid (eds), *Recasting Women: Essays in Colonial History*, Kali, 1989.

9. 'Towards Equality: Report of the Committee on the Status of Women in India', Government of India, 1975, chapter 7.

10. The First Two Decades after Independence: Women's Perspectives, organized jointly by Indian Association for Women's Studies, Centre for Women's Development Studies and the Centre for Women's Studies, M.S. University of Baroda, August 1997.

11. See Das, Vina (ed.), *Mirrors of Violence: Communities, Riots and Survivors in South Asia*, Oxford University Press, New Delhi 1990.

12. See 'Perspectives from the Women's Movement, Report of a National Debate', Government of India, Dept. of Women and Child Development, 1st draft, NPP, 1988 (mimeo).

13. 'Towards Equality', chapters 2–8.

14. 'Towards Beijing: A Perspective from the Indian Women's Movement', AIDWA et al., New Delhi, 1995.

15. Tharu, Susie and K. Lalita, *Women Writing in India, From 600 B.C. to the Present*, Oxford University Press, New Delhi 1993.

16. See Government of India, Women in India, 1985, and 1995, National Perspective Plan for Women, 1988, Statistical Digest (Dept. of Women and Child Development) 1977, and First Report to CEDAW, Implementation Committee.

17. See 'Defining Women's Politics', Note for theme workshop, Women and Politics, National Conference on Women's Movement, Calicut, 1990, unpublished.

18. Sharma, Kumud, 'Women and Development: Gender Concerns', CWDS, Occasional Paper No. 2.

19. Mazumdar, Vina, Keynote address at inauguration of the Women's Studies Centre, Calcutta University, March 1989, unpublished.

20. 'Critical Issues on the Status of Women: Employment, Health, Education Priorities for Action', ICSSR, 1979.

21. 'Perspectives from the Women's Movement, Report of a National Debate', 1988.

22. For more comprehensive discussions on this issue, see *Seminar*, September 1997.

23. An Open Letter to the Chief Justice of India by Upendra Baxi, Vasudha Dhagamwar, Raghunath Kelkar and Lotika Sarkar, Supreme Court Journal, 16 September 1979 (1979) 4 SCC.

24. Ibid.
25. The literature on dowry and dowry violence is vast. We would, however, like to emphasize (1) the Report of the Joint Parliamentary Committee, 1981; (2) Report on Dowry Deaths and Law Reform: Amending the Hindu Marriage Act, 1995, Indian Law Commission; (3) Palriwala, R., Women Are Not for Burning: The Anti-Dowry Movement in Delhi, paper presented at symposium 99, Anthropological Perspectives on Collective Actions, An Assessment of the Decade, Mijas, Spain, 1985.
26. As reported by volunteers in the AIDWA's Legal Aid Cell, New Delhi.
27. For debate on 'voluntary' sati see 'Institutions, Beliefs, Ideologies: Widow Immolation in Contemporary Rajasthan', Vaid, S. and K. Sangari, *EPW,* Vol. 26, No 17, 27 April 1991, pp. ws 2–18.
28. Katzenstein, Mary Fainsod, 'Getting Women's Issues onto the Public Agenda: Body Politics in India', *Samya Shakti*, A Journal of Women's Studies, VI,(1991–92), pp. 1–16.

Index